THE TRIUMPHS
AND TRIALS OF
Lotta Crabtree

THE TRIUMPHS AND TRIALS OF

Lotta Crabtree

by David Dempsey
with Raymond P. Baldwin

WILLIAM MORROW & COMPANY, INC.

NEW YORK 1968

This book is for Joan Baldwin

Illustrations

following page 120

Contents

viii   *Contents*

THE TRIUMPHS
AND TRIALS OF
Lotta Crabtree

PROLOGUE

The Fountain

AT THE intersection of Geary, Market, and Kearny Streets in downtown San Francisco stands Lotta's Fountain, a shaft of fluted cast iron that rises some thirty feet in the air. Erected in 1875 as a $10,000 watering spot for horses and men, it is worth a million dollars in sentiment today, having survived the San Francisco earthquake, the subsequent fires, and all attempts by public officials to move it to a less conspicuous location where it would cease to impede the passage of the automobile. By and large, the fountain is one of the homeliest monuments anywhere, but sentiment reigns and it continues its vigil, reminding those who drink from its water bubblers—even the curious and the sight-seer—that San Francisco produced at least one famous actress: Lotta Mignon Crabtree.

The fountain later acquired a tablet to the opera singer Madame Luisa Tetrazzini, whose name has been immortalized as a method of preparing chicken. She sang in front of the fountain on Christmas Eve in 1910. Some critics have suggested that it would have been more fitting for Lotta to be memorialized by the tablet and Tetrazzini by the fountain, but San Franciscans disagree. Tetrazzini had the greater voice, but Lotta was the greater institution. Besides, she commissioned the fountain herself, at the age of twenty-seven, when she was already one of the most highly paid actresses in the country.

Lotta Crabtree was a professional actress for thirty-seven years, yet she was only forty-five when she retired. For twenty-five of these years her name was a household word, her popularity as a comedienne unmatched, her earnings unsurpassed in the theater. Lotta began her career as a child of eight, entertaining the

3

miners in the gold fields of California. Walter Leman, an actor
whose path crossed Lotta's during the gold-rush days, broke into
rhapsody at the very recollection of her. "How thou didst squirm
and do a 'walk-around' and do all with an impunity and vim
that defied all opposition and criticism," he wrote in *Memories
of an Old Actor,* a book which, except for the passages on Lotta,
is written in ordinary prose. "For thou was bright and merry,
and everybody loved to see thee, laugh at thy capers, enjoy thy
fun, and toss into thy lap the coins and nuggets of the land of
gold."

During the height of her fame, in the 1870s and 1880s, she was
still playing children's parts and, indeed, continued to do so
until the end of her career. When Macauley's Theater went up
in Louisville, Kentucky, in the summer of 1873—"the finest theater in the West" it was called locally—one of the five huge
portraits adorning the walls was that of Lotta Crabtree. (Along
with Joe Jefferson, she represented comedy. Charlotte Cushman,
Edwin Booth, and Rachel Macauley typified tragedy, while manager Macauley reserved for himself the central arch over the
stage, where his portrait was upheld by two cupids.) He was
paying tribute to success; for the next several years, Lotta would
pack the theater, which, because it stood between two churches,
had gone up over the protests of the city's bluenoses. Louisville
society, on the other hand, not notably puritanical, occupied the
upholstered folding chairs of the orchestra, watched, admiringly,
when the footlights changed from red to white to blue as the gas
man operated the new valve mechanism, and gradually got used
to the Swiss landscape, with its lakes and mountains, painted on
the act curtain. Few plays that arrived in Louisville were set in
Switzerland; certainly not Lotta's.

Leading citizens vied to entertain her. Once, she and Mary
Ann, her mother, were honored at a breakfast. Lotta's play at
the time was *Musette,* in which she took the part of a gypsy. At
what must have been great cost, scenes from the play were repro-
duced in flowers on the dining table. Not all of her admirers

could afford such homage, and in any case her fans filled the pit as well as the more expensive seats of the parquet. At DeBar's Opera House, in St. Louis, the Boot and Peanut Brigade elected Lotta the "Pet of the Pit" and let it go at that. In Nashville, the newsboys celebrated her arrival with a giant torchlight parade. Arriving in New Orleans one year, she was presented with a new banjo and made an honorary member of the Lotta Baseball Club. Such were rewards of theatrical fame in the nineteenth century.

In 1871, when her fame was soaring, Lotta was only twenty-four years old. She had already been touring for seven years, and, counting her earliest appearances in California, had been acting for sixteen. One of her assets was sheer beauty, not an impressive feminine beauty—Lotta was too petite, too lively for this—but an impish and infectious radiance that teased audiences with its faint suggestion of impropriety. Improper, however, she was not; her mother saw to that. But charming she was. Her brown eyes, sparkling and roguish, were set in a broad brow; the lips were expressive, the chin dimpled, and a prominent jaw indicated strength of character. Lotta stood five feet two inches tall, when she stood at all, which was not often. More likely, on stage, she would be perched on the edge of a table, hanging from a yardarm, or doing a "breakdown" (a vigorous dance then popular). Her hair was light red, and she sprinkled it with cayenne pepper in order to catch the reflection of the footlights. Photographs show it parted in the middle, with bangs loosely curled and ringlets tumbling down the back of her neck. Sometimes she wore a straw hat with a short, canted brim; in her more demure moments, a hair ribbon. She dressed plainly, wearing a choker collar and pendant or a figured scarf. Like almost all dancers, she prided herself on an exceedingly erect posture. Her figure was "as flat as an ironing board," a member of her company was to recall later. Always she gave the impression of a young girl, never a woman, but of a girl who delighted in flouting convention. It came as a surprise to those who saw her off stage for the first time

to discover that she smoked thinly rolled black cigars. And somehow, this enhanced her appeal.

As her fame grew, the gifts rained down in increasing volume,
and by the time of her triumphal return to Lucky Baldwin's
Academy of Music in 1879, Lotta was the most lavishly rewarded
actress in San Francisco. The newspapers described this occasion,
not inaccurately, as a "bumper." Lotta came away with a solid
gold wreath, which wasn't particularly useful, and a hefty packet
of gold eagles, which was. Admirers who were not in this high-
flying class had their own way of swearing fealty: they bought
hundreds of tickets and tore them up. With knowledge of this,
the box office sold many seats several times over, thus increasing
Lotta's share of the take, which, on benefit nights, was fifty per
cent or "half clear."

Just ten years before, David Belasco, while still in his teens,
had organized an amateur theatrical group called "The Fire-Fly
Social and Dramatic Club," in honor of the Inimitable Lotta.
Like Lotta, Belasco had been brought to California as a child,
and he was smitten with her from the first time he saw her
perform. One of Lotta's resounding successes in 1869 was a play
that had been written for her the previous year called *Firefly*
(an adaptation of Ouida's *Under Two Flags*) in which she
played a rebellious hoyden, danced on parapets in very short
skirts, fraternized with Legionnaires, wore a plumed helmet,
packed a keg of brandy on her shoulders, flung herself into a
volley of hostile bullets, and, as the *Spirit of the Times* commented, in general "made the Fire Fly." (The journal *Figaro*
called the play a "Lightning Bug," to which the *Spirit* added,
"Lightning Humbug.") Actually, the play was written to develop
Lotta's talents as a soloist on the snare drum, and the effect of all
this on young Belasco and his friends was electrifying. Taking
the name of "Fire-Flies," they not only provided strenuous support from the gallery, but went around the city putting on plays
of their own. Belasco was to persist in his infatuation until he
became an actor in Lotta's San Francisco company some years
later.

Lotta was one of the first actresses to inaugurate the "combination system," that is, to travel with her own cast rather than rely on the local stock companies to furnish supporting players. With her mother, Mary Ann, and for a time her father, John Ashworth Crabtree, she traveled the length and breadth of the country packing theaters wherever she went. With her first triumphs in San Francisco, at the age of twelve, she began to support her parents and two younger brothers, and she would do this for the remainder of her life.

Her father was happy to have it this way. He enjoyed the good life, and the confraternity of the saloon. Even when in his cups, which was often enough, he gave an impression of considerable dignity. A fairly tall man, he made himself taller with a beaver hat and enhanced his standing as a man of leisure with a black frock coat. In the West, he had sported a pistol under this coat, and for a time after Lotta began her tours of the East and Middle West, he continued this practice. The Crabtrees traveled with accumulated receipts from Lotta's performances, which, since the money was frequently taken in cash, could add up to several thousand dollars as the tour went on. Moreover, Mary Ann insisted on getting Lotta's share each night, after the box office closed, rather than wait until the end of the week. She had a mortal fear of theater fires, which were common during the gas-footlight era, and for all she knew, the box office might not even *be* there at the end of the week.

In the California mining camps, the take had often been in the form of gold nuggets and silver dollars, tossed onto the stage by the "Argonauts of '49" and scraped off the floor by Mary Ann. Paper currency was rare, checks almost unknown. Thus, early in the game, Lotta's mother had adopted the custom of carrying a good-sized leather grip in which to pack the winnings. They were heavy, and the bag rattled like a kit full of plumber's tools as Mary Ann dragged it from town to town. Later, the valise and its successors bulged with other things—paper money, correspondence, contracts with managers—but until the very end of Lotta's career the old lady traveled with a supply of silver dollars and gold eagles, possibly to give ballast to lighter components of the bag, but more likely out of sentiment. Mary Ann never really went off the gold standard. In the hotel suite which she and Lotta shared while on tour, Mary Ann would sit for half an hour at a time, staring out a window and dropping coins into her lap while Lotta napped in the adjoining bedroom. The clink was reassuring.

Like her daughter, Mary Ann was small of stature. To the casual observer, it might appear that she owned but a single dress, a black taffeta made in one piece, princess style, for she seldom wore anything else. Her hair was curly, the color of spun silver—"like new dimes," an actress in Lotta's company recalled. As Lotta's fame grew, and with it the receipts from her performances, Mary Ann's black bag was supplemented by a larger container; later, she would accept checks from managers, but in the 1870s she was still stuffing the overflow into a steamer trunk. It was for this reason that Lotta's father carried a pistol, but it should be noted that Mary Ann carried the key. In fact, the only known attempt to rifle the trunk was made by Crabtree himself. He succeeded in prying it open in Cincinnati.

Obviously, something had to be done. The money was getting too cumbersome to carry around, and Mary Ann, conservative by nature, yet with an odd, speculative turn of mind, hit upon the idea of simply leaving large blocks of it behind as the family moved from city to city. This was done by investing in local real estate and municipal bonds. She would tramp the streets in San Francisco, Kansas City, and Boston trying to anticipate the direction of the city's growth, then buying up vacant land. It was risky, but the risk was hedged by the purchase of bonds. Few towns on the Crabtree intinerary were too small to qualify: Fort Wayne, Indiana; Council Bluffs, Iowa; Charleston, West Virginia; Waco, Texas, and a dozen other places borrowed a share of Lotta's earnings while they applauded her talents.

In general, Lotta laid the foundation for the Crabtree fortune with her acting; Mary Ann made it grow with her investments, and Lotta's two brothers, George and John Ashworth Crabtree, Jr., along with her father, did their best to spend it. Even so, there was enough left at Lotta's death to make it well worth fighting for. At the height of her career, Lotta earned upwards of $80,000 a year, and her box office receipts, as she never tired of pointing out, frequently exceeded Edwin Booth's. In terms of today's money, her income was easily equivalent to $200,000 annually; and, of course, it was tax free.

Lotta herself seldom carried money on her person, and what little she might have was doled out by Mary Ann. This was not mere stinginess. Until Lotta retired, her mother expected to take care of everything; still, it could be awkward for Lotta if she saw something she wanted to buy. Once, at the age of forty, she borrowed a dollar from her business manager, Eddie Dunn, and then lost it. Like a child confessing a minor dereliction, she told her mother, who promptly sought out the business manager and reprimanded him. "Mr. Dunn, Miss Lotta told me that you gave her a dollar the other day, a dollar which she promptly lost. Never again give her more than ten cents *at one time.* She has no knowledge of money, nor has need for it." The astonished Mr. Dunn complied.

Essentially, Lotta was indifferent to money as a means of personal gratification; she saw it as an instrument of good rather than the root of evil, and in spite of her mother's thrifty temperament persuaded her to scatter sizable amounts among the poor. Newsboys enjoyed a special standing in her scheme of charity. There were no child labor laws then, and many of them were self-supporting, in a marginal sense; they slept in doorways, lived on the streets, and, what is more, spent a good deal of their free time in the pits of theaters. Today, they would be watching television in a settlement house, but in the last century, before organized charity began to take a serious interest in them, they cheered live heroes and booed what they hopefully thought were dead villains. And Lotta was one of the heroes.

In this sense, she enjoyed a special relationship with the pit.

Many of her roles were boys' parts, frequently gamins, orphans, or abandoned waifs. (This genre reached its height—or depth—in a play, *Pawn Ticket 210,* written for her by David Belasco and Clay Greene, in which the infant heroine is "pawned" by her mother and raised by the owner of the shop.) While the stalls were entertained by Lotta's foolishness, the pit—to use a modern expression—"identified" with her. Besides, the "b'hoys" appreciated a woman who smoked cigars. In Cincinnati, it was not uncommon for the police to form a double file from stage door to curb so that Lotta could get safely into her carriage without being mobbed by her young admirers.

The question has been raised by theater historians, was Lotta really an actress? Constance Rourke, in her book *Troupers of the Gold Coast,* sums her up as "one of those personalities which belong to the theater but not to the drama, which will overpass any proper vehicle with lawless force. She broke the traditions of the stage; she broke traditions as to the place of women in life as well as in the theater." At her death in 1924, in her seventy-seventh year, *The New York Times* called her "the immortal child," and to a generation for whom her name was the embodiment of mischief, this was what held them in thrall. "My dear Lotta," Ellen Terry had said to her years before, "when I see you it makes me more sorry than ever that I am compelled to spend so much of my time tearing around in tragedy. Weeping and tearing my hair certainly makes me look old, and if I had my way I should never act anything but comedy, which has served to keep you young for so many years."

"Actress" she might not have been; comedienne she certainly was. Francis Wilson, the late-nineteenth-century actor, once declared, ". . . it is my belief that Lotta touched comic heights attained by few other comediennes. Others satisfied and delighted; Lotta did this also, but swept you up into a whirl of enthusiasm." "Miss Lotta's methods are peculiar to herself," a reviewer wrote in 1885. "They may be described briefly as

anatomical. . . . No one can wink like Lotta. No woman can
perform so wide a variety of contortions with her features . . . no
one can wriggle more effectively. No one can kick higher or
oftener."

But there was more to it than a statement such as this pre-
sumes. In Lotta's time, it was not uncommon for an actress to
find a particularly felicitous role and to hang on to it for the
remainder of her acting life. Lotta kept alive not one, but half a
dozen major roles for the better part of two decades, in addition
to scores of others which served a mere five or ten years. As if to
make up for their shorter life spans, as many as six comedy parts
—male and female—would be packed into the same play, with
Lotta doing them all. "She originated the school of performance
with which for years she has favored the public, and when she
retires, the school will be dismissed," a Boston critic predicted
near the end of her career.

But while school kept, attendance seldom flagged. For millions
of Americans, Lotta was youth incarnate—mischievous but good
at heart, the kind of heroine that lodged comfortably in their
own hearts as they grew older and Lotta didn't. The theater had
never seen anyone quite like her, and when she did retire, in
1892, the school was, indeed, dismissed.

So far as anyone knew, Lotta never married. At a time when
some actresses changed husbands almost as often as they changed
roles, she remained mysteriously single. Mysterious? Not if one
gives credit to Mary Ann for all the occasions when she reportedly intervened to head off romance. "She was guarded like an
odalisque in a harem," Helen Bates, one of her supporting players, wrote later. There is a theory that Lotta married would no
longer have been acceptable to the public as a child actress; put
less cynically, it meant that her career came first. And when
Lotta left the stage, it was too late for romance.

But by this time she had a fortune to husband rather than a
man, and she made the most of it. Lotta took up where Mary
Ann left off. The woman of forty who was not to be trusted with

a dollar became, at seventy-five, the second largest individual taxpayer in Boston. She had acquired race horses and hotels; theaters, office buildings, city lots, jewelry. "My beautiful fortune," she called her wealth, as though it were something to be caressed. And it existed but for one purpose: to be given away.

Lotta was not simply playing Lady Bountiful in her works of charity. Her own early life had skirted real poverty, and she had roughed it too many years not to sympathize with misfortune. Her compassion was genuine, not only for people but for animals, who had always held a special niche in her affections. The fountain, which would succor both horses and mankind, was the great symbolic act of Lotta's life. The brilliant, vivacious young performer of twenty-seven who had donated it in gratitude to San Francisco and the elderly, even eccentric, spinster who died in Boston forty-nine years later had never stopped being the same person. And the fountain had never stopped flowing. Lotta had no dependent heirs. Her will left $4,000,000 in perpetual trust to charity.

Book One

THE BLANKENBERG CASE

1

⊙⊙⊙⊙

Lotta Testate

THE OLD Suffolk County Courthouse in Boston, a large, rectangular building of brick and limestone, fronts on Pemberton Square near the gilded dome of the Massachusetts State House on Beacon Hill. In contrast to the Bulfinch elegance that characterizes the capitol, it is a plain structure whose exterior appearance belies its importance as a hall of justice. Inside, terra cotta floors, oak paneling, and three tiers of balconies overlooking a central well, impart a feeling of unexpected grandeur.

On the second floor, at the end of the southwest corridor, is the Probate Court for Suffolk County. The room's only windows— tall and narrow—look out on a street running north from Pemberton Square. Here, on the raw, wintry afternoon of December 11, 1924, a will disposing of almost $4,000,000 was being offered for probate. As might be expected with so much money at stake, more than a few lawyers were in attendance.

One of these was William A. Morse, Esquire, counsel for the proponents of the will of Lotta M. Crabtree. When the hearing opened at two o'clock, he rose from his chair—somewhat unsteadily, to be sure—and approached William M. Prest, the presiding judge. Prest had just returned from lunch, donned his black robes, and taken his place on the bench. Short and baldheaded, he presided with a sternly disciplined New England bearing not always associated with the Suffolk County courts. Morse on the other hand, a man of sixty-one at the time, was large and lumbering; moreover, on this particular afternoon, he was—well, Morse had been drinking. Six months before, his wife had died; he had never fully recovered from this personal tragedy, and alcohol had come to be a solace. The other attorneys in the room, who still held Morse in esteem, tried not to notice his condition. Judge Prest was not yet aware of it.

"If your Honor, please," Morse began haltingly, "the Lotta Crabtree will is returnable on this day, December 11. Probably your Honor has read the will."

"No, I haven't," Judge Prest replied.

"Well, I will tell your Honor the substance of it, that it is an estate of four millions and we have given two millions to the veterans and we have given hundreds and hundreds of thousands to every public charitable trust except the five cousins. Now, my wife has just died and I am terribly upset—"

THE COURT: Perhaps you would rather not—

MORSE: Oh, I want to state the claim . . . I have been her attorney and her friend for years and years and years, but I was very careful when I drew this will—I drew every word of it—and I said to Miss Lotta, I said, "Now, there is a great trust of $2,000,-000 and you ought to have a good man on it," and she said, "What do you think of General Edwards?" and as a matter of fact I have been in control of Miss Lotta's property for a great many years and she has always been so honorable and so high-minded and so clear . . .

THE COURT: There are a number of motions to strike appearances from the record. . . .

At this, Morse flushed angrily. In layman's language, Judge Prest was saying that others beside those designated in Lotta Crabtree's will wanted to be cut in on the bounty. Morse, of course, knew this; attorneys for some of the claimants were in court. Who were they to meddle? Who among them had known Lotta, as he had, during the long twilight of her life? Except for a scattering of elderly theater buffs and keepers of scrapbooks, Lotta was largely forgotten.

Of course, many famous actresses had made money, but unlike most of them, Lotta had hung onto it. Morse was determined to see that it got to the intended beneficiaries. Except for small annuities to five first cousins, these were charities—and some rather strange ones at that. No less than $300,000 was earmarked for a Lotta Dumb Animal Fund, and part of this was to be used for the erection of "drinking fountains for men, horses, birds and dogs" all over the country. Two million was to go into a trust for needy veterans of World War I. Dumb animals and doughboys were Lotta's obsession, an observer remarked at the time.

"Now this ought to go right off," Morse lectured Judge Prest. "It is all wrong to object, and we have got all these hospitals and all these soldiers, and I tell you, Judge Prest, on my word of honor, when it comes up that there isn't a thing in it that is anything but Lotta . . ."

Judge Prest was having difficulty maintaining his patience. "You understand that this hearing is to be put down simply to strike certain appearances from the record," he said to Morse. "There is not going to be a hearing on the merits of the will. Suppose we say the 28th of January. Does anyone object?"

But Morse was not to be pacified. "Your Honor has already ruled that they must go ahead; and, your Honor, they should go ahead; it is blasphemy . . ."

"Upon whom is the burden of going ahead?" interjected an attorney named Withington. "I represent some cousins once removed: if there are first cousins, they have no standing."

"You are cousins, second cousins," Morse retorted excitably. "There are five first cousins and she has remembered every one of them in her will. . . . I am surprised that such great lawyers would come in and try to get a standing. They are all tracking round, these great lawyers—just give them a rebuke from the bench."

THE COURT: Let counsel finish their statements.

MR. WITHINGTON: I understand that there are other people who claim to be interested, one who claims to be a niece of Miss Crabtree.

MR. MORSE: Do you expect that Lotta didn't know what she was doing?

Exasperated at last, Judge Prest turned to the garrulous Mr.

Morse. "Won't you keep quiet a moment?" he all but shouted.

Chastened momentarily, Morse fell silent. In the interval, a Boston attorney named James Hoy stood up at the counsel's table and addressed the bench. "We represent Carlotta Cockburn, Carlotta Crabtree Cockburn, whom we understand to be a daughter of Jack and Annie Leopold Crabtree and that Jack was the only brother that Lotta had, so it would look as though she were a niece if we can establish—"

"Jack died ten years ago," Morse cut in irritably and inaccurately, for Jack had died only four years before. Hoy was wrong, too. Lotta had another brother, George, who died in 1891, leaving no survivors.

MR. HOY:—our rights, because the daughter would share his rights.

THE COURT: You will have to show that your client is an heir at law in order to be entitled to come in and be heard in opposition to the will.

"May I speak, your Honor?" Morse interjected again.

Advisedly, Judge Prest turned to the counsel's table. "Are there any other attorneys who want to be heard?"

There was one who had waited patiently for just such an invitation. "Do I understand at that time," asked Mr. William J. Kurth, explaining that he represented another set of alleged cousins, "that we have a right to contest the right of somebody who says they are a niece? In other words, will it be a sort of free-for-all?"

Morse's worst fears had been realized. Court procedure left Judge Prest no option. "Naturally the door is open," he replied blandly.

Thwarted by the court, which was legally bound to hear evidence from all possible claimants, Morse began the tedious business of filing motions to strike out the appearance of each of them on the ground that they were not next of kin. As Judge Prest had declared, "The door is open." Indeed it was. During the next few months, 101 men and women would step forward, all of whom claimed some relationship to Lotta Crabtree. Of these, thirty-six were Crabtrees or had a "Crabtree" in their name. Others were Liveseys, which was Lotta's mother's name. They came from as far away as Balboa, Canal Zone, and Quebec. There were Mitchells and Bartletts and Bancrofts, Campbells and Biddles and Bells, most of whom could prove a Crabtree somewhere in their lineage. The motives varied. "Am without occupation or means," replied one woman when asked to state her occupation. "Hope to obtain enough out of Lotta's estate to buy myself a small automobile and a farm," stated Mr. Edward Crabtree, a forty-four-year-old cotton farmer of Tyler, Missouri. All told, these frantic dashes to the end of the rainbow gave employment—for the most part briefly—to thirty-four different Boston law firms.

Not all the claimants had dishonest motives. Many simply thought they might be related to Lotta, and one way to find out was to put their foot in the door and see what happened. It was Morse's task to slam the door shut, but it soon became apparent that he was in no condition to carry on the protracted legal wrangling necessary to such a course of action. Morse was a sick man.

On the evening of January 20, 1925, his chauffeur drove him to the home of Judge Frederick Hathaway Chase. Judge Chase, as he continued to be called after his retirement from the Superior Court bench a few years earlier, lived in nearby Concord. He was a slim man of medium height, with sparse gray hair, a prominent nose, close-cropped mustache, and courtly manners; and although he was not a native Bostonian (he had been born in Concord), he was indubitably a proper one. At this time, he was in his middle fifties and a partner of Frank H. Stewart in a three-man law office that had recently acquired a young Harvard graduate, Raymond P. Baldwin. Morse had chosen Chase's firm with reason: the Judge was used to litigating big money. "The case is a lawyer's dream," Morse told Chase, regretfully admitting that he was too ill to carry on.

Of all the claimants, only one at the moment appeared to be a serious threat. This was Mrs. Carlotta Cockburn, of California, who contended—not without an impressive array of evidence—that she was Lotta Crabtree's niece. It would be her tactic, Morse knew, to attempt to have the will set aside by proving that Lotta had been incompetent when she drew it. Once this had been done, she would be the closest living heir; and considering Lotta's eccentricities in her old age, the chance that a jury would find her incompetent was a dangerous possibility.

Morse's apprehension about taking on the burden of defending the will was well founded. Four days later, he was dead. As it turned out, he was spared an even more formidable assault on Lotta's will than Mrs. Cockburn's. Scarcely a month after his death, a last-minute claim was filed by Mrs. Ida May Blankenberg, of Tulsa, Oklahoma. Ida May, whose maiden name had been Crabtree, insisted that she was Lotta's legitimate daughter, even though, on the record at least, Lotta had never married. But if Mrs. Blankenberg could prove that Lotta was her mother, she could strive to have the will set aside, and, if successful, would be entitled to the entire estate.

Thus, in the summer of 1925, began the first of two bizarre trials that for the next two years intermittently occupied the Probate Court, and incidentally entertained the Boston public, with performances that displayed cupidity, perjury, comic relief, fantasy, and, not least, some refreshing honesty. More than a hundred witnesses would be brought in from all parts of the country; a score of Burns and Pinkerton agents would find employment investigating both witnesses and principals; and actors would be summoned out of retirement to play a last role in court. With a fortune at stake, the firm of Stewart & Chase left no possible line of defense unexplored. Not the least of their efforts was a reconstruction of Lotta's career on the stage, a trail that led from the mining camps of California during the gold rush decade to the elegant theaters of Boston and New York. As Morse had predicted, the case was a lawyer's dream.

2

The General Comes to Call

LOTTA DIED on September 25, 1924, almost seventy-seven years old, her fortune intact. Death came in Boston's Hotel Brewster, on lower Boylston Street, which Lotta owned, and where she had lived the last sixteen years of her life, but it did not come quickly or easily. "I feel like a tired race horse," she had told her doctor, some time before. Except for a small circle of friends—the excitable William Morse, who, in Lotta's declining years, had carried her in his arms from the Brewster to his car, like a child to be taken for an airing; the affable General Edwards; Miss Emma Donovan, for fifteen years her secretary-companion; Mrs. Maria Bryant, a Boston acquaintance of long standing—except for these she led a life which, if not that of a traditional recluse, suggested at least the crotchets and eccentricities of old age. An unfinished sandwich, eaten at the Georgian Cafeteria, would be carried back in a paper bag to Lotta's room; the food at the Brewster was "too expensive" for regular dining.

Before infirmity confined her to her room, Lotta could be seen standing on the curb of a downtown Boston street in summer, fitting straw hats on the unshaded heads of passing horses. Dr. David Judd, who had treated her some years before her final illness, recalled that she had wanted him to take charge of a home for dogs. Such things as these had provoked attorney Morse to his outbursts in the Probate Court; why invite a challenge of Lotta's competence when there were problems enough with her ordinary eccentricities? Morse had no doubt that, should the will ever be contested before a jury, an able lawyer might well persuade some doctor to testify, in response to a hypothetical question, that Lotta was not of sound mind. It might not be true, but juries were notoriously free with other people's money.

Lotta bought the Brewster in 1909, four years after Mary Ann's death. The manager at the time was a Mr. Walsh, who had never met Lotta, and whose business dealings were conducted through Lotta's brother, Jack. Jack Crabtree had moved into the hotel, rent free, with his wife, Annie Harris (not Annie Leopold, the mother of Carlotta Cockburn), soon after the purchase. One evening, several months after this, a heavily veiled woman arrived and asked to be shown to Jack's room. Since Walsh knew that Jack's wife was away, he not so politely refused. The visitor upbraided him. "I suppose you think you can make a success of this hotel by running it on Sunday School principles," she declared sharply. The manager remained firm, and only after some harsh words was he persuaded to send for Jack and bring him down to the lobby. At his appearance, the veil came off.

"This is my sister, Miss Lotta," Jack said, introducing her to Walsh. It was a dramatic entrance, Walsh recalled, describing the incident to attorneys for the estate many years later. "That was the first time I met Lotta. She was trying to see how really strict I was."

Lotta moved into the hotel soon afterward, and until the end of her life she called it home. Sunday School principles prevailed. "She was pure and upright, but the Brewster was run-down," a friend said of it once. Even so, Lotta was fussy about the hotel, and the employees were continually having to roll up the big lobby carpet whenever it rained, and to unroll it when the rain stopped. Lotta was temperamental in her old age, and managers were hired and fired almost yearly. For a while, Jack managed the Brewster, but Jack was a man of intemperate habits, and the Brewster's bar was at that time the longest in Boston. Lotta adopted the practice of stalking into the bar after it closed at night and, with a ruler, measuring the contents of the open whisky bottles. In the morning, she stalked in again and measured them to see if Jack had been drinking.

Lotta began drawing her will soon after she took over the
Brewster. "She was a quarter of a century composing it," Minnie
Maddern Fiske, the leading Ibsen interpreter in the United
States and a friend of Lotta's, wrote to Mr. Fiske not long after
Lotta's death. "She talked about it for days at a time." Mrs. Fiske
exaggerated; Lotta started on the will fifteen years before her
death, but only during the last twelve did she buckle down to the
job in earnest.

In a succession of documents, she shuffled her benefactions like
a playwright working out the plot of a nineteenth-century melodrama, making sure that good triumphed over evil. Yet, in
Lotta's mind, what was "good" in 1909 did not always survive to
the day of reckoning. A $600,000 Lotta Memorial Home for
Theatrical People and a $1,500,000 Stage Fund for needy actors
—included in an early will—dwindled in the intervening years
to a $100,000 Lotta Theatrical Fund to help "deserving members
of the theatrical profession . . . and for the education of young
women" who aspired to the stage. Her contemporaries, many of
whom read about the bequest in the parlor of a theatrical home
for the indigent, could hardly help but notice that an equal sum
of money had been earmarked for "aiding discharged convicts"
and that three times as much had been set aside for the care of
horses and dogs.

This latter concern took curious forms. At Morse's urging, an
early bequest to do away with blinders on horses had given way
to the $300,000 Lotta Dumb Animal Fund. The actress's compas-
sion for animals was not to be taken lightly; in 1921, while
staying in Brockton, Massachusetts, the urge to make another will
seized Lotta, and she visited the law office of an attorney
named Fletcher. It was on this occasion that her first bequest, a
comparatively modest $100,000, was set up for servicemen who
needed help. At one point during the consultation Miss Lotta
noticed two stuffed owls and a deer head affixed to the wall in
front of her. "Are you a hunter?" she inquired of Mr. Fletcher.

Supposing the question to have been motivated out of admiration, he stated that indeed he was. Shocked, Lotta departed forthwith. She never went back to the Fletcher office again.

It must have been a cause of satisfaction to leave so much money to those who had never asked for it—indeed, who couldn't have known they were going to get anything. One of Miss Donovan's chores was to fend off the mendicants who beseeched Lotta for help; perhaps Mrs. Fiske, strictly speaking, did not belong to this group, but she had fallen on hard times in her later years, and Lotta sent a few hundred dollars now and then to help her out. Minnie Maddern had known her since she, Minnie, as a child, had hung around backstage at New Orleans' Charles Street Theater, which her father managed, and where Lotta had appeared in an early escapade called *Captain Charlotte.* The older actress became Minnie's idol, and the girl imitated her shamelessly when she went on the stage herself. "All you need is a black cigar," said Aunt Emma Maddern, "and you'd look like Lotta Crabtree." Her debut at seventeen, in Augustin Daly's *Fogg's Ferry,* was played in the Lotta manner. The two became friends and remained so long after Mrs. Fiske changed her style of acting and became the greater actress. She described Lotta as "the cloistered, mysterious little nun of the theater," but in the end Lotta stole the scene. Mrs. Fiske wrote her husband:

Do you remember the day that the little imp stole from me my afternoon reception at Harvard? She must have been seventy then, but she was still a girl in spirit and roguish beauty. The boys had no eyes for any of the girls present—no eyes for me, the guest of honor. Not at all. They formed a dense circle around Lotta.

Of the old friends who were left, Mrs. Fiske was one of the few to merit an occasional gift of money, although it was not for lack of trying that others failed. Back in 1886, Mrs. Charles A. Doremus had written a slight play for Lotta called *Larks,* one of the actress's less successful vehicles. By 1918, the Kentucky-born dramatist, who was also a granddaughter of President Harrison, no longer wrote plays for a living, but she had not given up the idea of making money on Lotta. Letters arrived at the Brewster begging for help. Mrs. Doremus was "utterly without means"; her house in New York was about to be foreclosed. The appeal must have struck Lotta as false (rightly so: Mrs. Doremus lived comfortably in a New York hotel long after Lotta died), and in any case she was not easily fooled. "I have talked to your good mother," wrote Mrs. Doremus, "over the 'Ouija Board,' which of course you know about and it is *simply marvelous,* and she said to tell you that she would be *glad* to have you help me, and to write to you." The rappings went on, the letters kept coming, but Lotta stood fast. Assuming that the cadging playwright *had* been in communication with the spirit of Mary Ann Crabtree, it would mark one of the few times that Lotta disregarded her mother's wishes. "If you don't know the 'Ouija Board,' you would be astounded at what you would get," Mrs. Doremus insisted up to the last. When the will was opened, Mrs. Doremus got nothing.

The final will, in addition to annuities of $1,000 each to five first cousins, contained provisions for eight major bequests. One of these, a fund of $100,000, was set up in memory of Mary Ann, the income to be disbursed to the poor of Boston, in the form of food, clothing, coal, and—appropriately—"small amounts of money" at Christmas time. A fund of fifty thousand dollars went to provide free beds for the indigent sick in local hospitals; the income from $25,000 would pay the expenses of four pupils at a time in the New England Conservatory of Music. Dumb animals ($300,000), needy actors ($100,000), and discharged convicts ($100,000) brought the total to $675,000. And Lotta hadn't really gone to work yet.

The remaining portion of the estate included provision for a Lotta Agricultural Fund, to be administered by Lotta's trustees and lent by them without interest, to graduates of the Massachusetts Agricultural College who needed money to set themselves up in farming. At the time of Lotta's death, the Fund amounted to about one and a quarter million dollars, and characteristically, in setting up the Trust Lotta added the hope that borrowers would perforce be kind to their animals.

There was still a sum of almost $2,000,000 awaiting final disposition. Until 1919, this money—about half of Lotta's fortune—had been shuffled around, in successive wills, from expensive dog pounds to million-dollar theatrical homes, and then shuffled back again as Lotta withdrew further and further from the life of the stage. It was as though the money were really consigned to a sort of limbo, awaiting some final inspiration.

It was at this juncture that Lotta received a call one day from a man she had never met—General Clarence R. Edwards, a Bostonian and a professional soldier who had commanded the 26th (Yankee) Division in Europe. A West Point graduate of 1883, Edwards had organized the 26th Division in August, 1917, sailed to France the following month, and remained overseas until after the war. Meanwhile, a Yankee Division Club had been opened on Commonwealth Avenue, and to help furnish it, Lotta sent over rugs, a basket of tea things, and some cutlery from the Brewster. Soon after he returned from France, the General came to pay his respects to the donor.

This was to be a fateful meeting. A man of fifty-nine at the time, Edwards was a tall, big-chested man of soldierly posture, with gray hair and a stubby gray mustache. He had an outgoing manner, an eye for the girls, and a certain affable charm. As a boy, he had saved his allowance to buy front-row seats when Lotta played at the Park Theater in Boston. He was not long in reminding her of this, since the Brewster was around the corner from the Park and adjoined it at the rear. "I want to see if my recollections do justice to the most beautiful ankle in the world," he declared. It had been a long time since anyone had made such a daring bid for her affections. Lotta was then in her seventies, but she jumped laughing onto the divan, gathered up her skirts, and exposed a small slippered foot, an ankle, and a generous length of calf.

Although there is no evidence that the General ever again saw "the most beautiful ankle in the world," the two were to remain friends until Lotta died. Among other things, they discovered a mutual interest in horses. Edwards's father had been president of the American Harness Racing Association, and the General himself knew his way around the race tracks. For five years, Lotta had owned a stable of trotters, and like so many things in her life that she touched, they had once made her a great deal of money.

Thus, on his visits, the General talked horses, and he talked theater. He remembered well the plays at the old Park, and they gave him another clue to Lotta's character: her weakness for military roles. "She liked nothing better than to appear in uniform with bands playing and soldiers marching across the stage," he was to remark later. In his own way, the General took advantage of this; at the end, he talked soldiers, impressing upon Lotta the plight of the wounded doughboy who had come home from France to find himself the forgotten hero. At some point, Lotta discussed with him her will, disclosing that she had set aside $100,000 for the rehabilitation of just these returning soldiers. "Only one hundred thousand?" the General said in some astonishment. Such a sum would hardly serve as a beginning. . . . Discussions followed. Then Lotta went to see Morse. When the General's charms had done their work, a $2,000,000 trust for veterans of World War I stood waiting to help them.

Lotta's will was never again changed. Undue influence? Morse, who had great respect for General Edwards, and who had drawn the will himself, would have defended the Trust unremittingly. "It ought to go right off," he had pleaded with the court. That it didn't undoubtedly hastened his death.

3

In Terrorem

MORSE'S STRATEGY in drawing the will had been aimed at protecting the estate not only against the depredations of outsiders, but equally against the named beneficiaries who might try to upset it for their own advantage. Lotta had left an annuity of $1,000 to each of five first cousins; to minimize the danger that these next of kin might bring a contest, Morse had introduced an *in terrorem* clause, which meant that anyone who attempted to break the will would automatically lose his annuity. Whether for this reason or not, the cousins were agreeably cooperative. All of them indicated that they would take the $1,000 a year, even though the division of money might seem inequitable. Miss Sophia Livesey, for instance—the daughter of Mary Ann's brother—barely scrimped by on the income of a fourth-class postmistress in Belvedere, California; whereas her sister, Mrs. Annie Fretwell, widow of a banker, was independently well off and lived in Mexico City. Three English cousins—Mrs. Mary Shuttleworth, John Henry Crabtree, and Sarah A. Crabtree—were of modest means but rather hopeful expectations, and an additional £4 a week for the remainder of their lives represented comparative affluence.

But there was a sixth cousin, Louis A. Livesey, of Shelburne, Vermont, who had gone unremembered in the will, and whose exclusion was one of the mysteries inherited by Stewart & Chase when they took over. Lotta's mother had reared him after the death of his parents, and Lotta knew him well. Why, in taking care of five cousins, had Lotta ignored Louis? Yet Livesey not only had made no claim on Lotta's estate, but had astonished everyone by engaging a Boston lawyer to file a waiver of interest in its probate—a positive step in renouncing any theoretical claim he might have. His position was unique, to say the least. However, when it was discovered that the waiver was not under seal, had been filed without any consideration having been paid, and might, therefore, be repudiated in case Livesey should change his mind, the position was also seen to be dangerous. In that case, he would be entitled to attack the will not only on the basis that it was improperly executed, but also on the more vulnerable grounds that Lotta had not been of sound mind when she signed it, or that she had done so as the result of undue influence.

Getting Louis Livesey to sign an agreement under seal became, therefore, one of the first orders of business, and on April 10, 1925, Raymond Baldwin began his first of two trips to Vermont. He took the night train to Burlington, which is not the most attractive city in the world—at least not around the railroad yards. The carbon smell of the trains pervaded the dining room at seven in the morning and seemed to have soaked into the iridescent edges of the ham, into the bubbles in the whites of the eggs, and into the butter mopped onto the soggy toast. But by eight o'clock, the garage had a car ready, and soon the city smells were washed away by the cool, fresh morning air as Baldwin drove into the open country.

Livesey lived on a farm well up in the hills overlooking Lake Champlain. The house was of old pink brick. The courtyard was neat, and the flagstones stretching along the east wall were well swept. Grass growing long over the stone path to the front door showed that the entrance used was in back.

A woman of middle age came to the door and introduced herself as Mrs. Livesey. She was of medium height, with gray hair, which would have reached to her waist, done into a bun at the back of her head. She was slim, with intelligent brown eyes, and might have been a schoolmistress. There was something of an urban air about her. Her husband was in the barn, she explained, but she invited Baldwin in, and introduced him to her aunt, short, chubby Minna Read, who owned the farm. Then she went to fetch her husband, leaving Baldwin with the obviously somewhat senile Miss Read, who very politely played a little-girl piece on the piano over and over again until Mrs. Livesey returned and took Baldwin outside to her husband.

Livesey looked uncannily like the photographs of his aunt, Lotta's mother. Although he was in his late sixties, he seemed no more than forty-five, a short, slim, well-knit man with black hair and deep-set eyes. He was neatly clad in faded overalls and blue cotton shirt, and his shoes and fingernails were clean. His features were worthy of fine sculpture, but no bust could ever do justice to his eyes: black, piercing, young, alive—yet the eyes of a fanatic.

Mrs. Livesey left them, and they sat on a wooden bench which stood along the sun-warmed brick of the east wall of the house. Livesey answered Baldwin's introductory questions pleasantly, and volunteered the information that Mrs. Livesey, whom he had met and married in New York, had been the daughter of the owner of the old Hoffman House in lower Manhattan, but they had not been able to manage the cost of living in New York and had come to Vermont a few years back to live with Aunt Minna.

"But when I got to the real purpose of my visit," Baldwin recalls, "which was to induce him to make his waiver of contest of the will legally binding by accepting from the estate an annuity like the other cousins, he froze."

"Lotta had her own good reasons for not leaving me anything," Livesey said. "I don't want a cent of her money. I retained Harrison Barrett of Boston as my attorney to consent to the allowance of the will. He had me sign a waiver. It's on file in the Probate Court. I won't sue, and I won't take a single dollar for not suing. I don't want to discuss it further." Livesey rose. Baldwin rose. They returned to the kitchen.

There was a gleam in Miss Read's eye. Hastily, Baldwin said to Mrs. Livesey, "I saw chicken coops on the hill. Do you keep hens? If so, please come and tell me how you take care of them. We raise our own eggs, and I'd like to get some pointers." Mrs. Livesey was a quick study, and they were outside in no time.

"Listen, Mrs. Livesey," Baldwin said when they were out of earshot of the house, "no offense, but you aren't too well off. Miss Lotta must have thought your husband had died. It would be perfectly legitimate for us to agree that, in consideration for his agreement not to contest her will, he receive the same annuity as the other first cousins. But he won't talk about it."

"Louis is very determined," she said. "He won't contest, and he won't take a cent." Why this should be so remained as much a mystery to Baldwin as why Lotta had left him out of her will in the first place.

"Let's look at the hens," Baldwin suggested. And they did.

"Work on him, will you?" he pleaded, as they again neared the house.

"I will," she promised. "I wouldn't want him to try to break the will, but it does seem fair that he get the same as the others."

There was one other matter to be taken up with Livesey. Since he had been intimately acquainted with the Crabtrees, his testimony might be needed in the trial. Before leaving, Baldwin drew him aside for another talk. It involved the delicate question of Jack Crabtree's escapades as a very young man.

According to Mrs. Carlotta Cockburn, the woman who alleged herself to be Lotta's niece, her mother, Annie Leopold, had met Jack Crabtree in 1880, in Tombstone, Arizona, and although there was no evidence that they had married, the following year Carlotta was born to them. Shortly afterward, Jack deserted her mother, who thereupon left Tombstone with a gambler named Raab. Carlotta was adopted by Ed Bullock, Jack's partner in a livery stable, sent to Hannibal, Missouri, to live with Bullock's sister for a number of years, and then brought back to Tucson and placed in a Catholic orphanage. Although she had used

Bullock as her maiden name, she had always understood her real name to be Crabtree, which she promptly restored upon learning of Lotta's death.

It was known that Jack Crabtree had spent some time in Tombstone—ostensibly for his health—but the attorneys for the Estate hoped to discover that he had gone there too late to have fathered Carlotta. Baldwin wanted to see if Livesey could shed some light on the matter.

Livesey could, and did.

Jack, he explained, had been spending a good deal of money, foolishly, for the most part, and Ma Crabtree had taken advantage of his spirit of adventure by offering to send him west. He was run-down, and there was suspicion of tuberculosis. What he needed was a healthy life out of doors, as well as a chance to set himself up in business. A couple of years earlier the first big silver strikes had been made in Tombstone, Arizona. The town was booming and opportunities abounded. With her character-istic eye for any venture that promised big returns, Mary Ann arranged to finance a trip to Tombstone; possibly she recalled the wild, gold-rush days in California, when eggs were selling for $6 a dozen and the miners had tossed golden nuggets at Lotta's feet. Being uncertain of the accommodations in the new settle-ment, she bought Jack a complete camping outfit, including a tent and a folding bed with mattress.

As a town of opportunity, Tombstone was everything that was claimed for it. As a convalescent spa, however, it was hardly what Mary Ann could have had in mind. At that time, it was probably the wildest, most uninhibited, and freest-drinking town in the United States. This was the period of the Crystal Palace and the Oriental gambling halls, where Bat Masterson dealt faro; of the bawdy Bird Cage Theater; of the three Earp brothers who, with the notorious Doc Holliday, killed Billy Clayton and the two McLaury boys in a historic sequence of gunplay that has since been re-enacted numerous times on television.

Livesey remembered Jack's departure for Tombstone very

well; he had accompanied him to the railroad terminal in Jersey City to see him off. Yes, it *had* been in 1880—there was no disputing it.

And had Jack really camped out in Tombstone? Baldwin wanted to know.

Livesey smiled for the first time that afternoon. As a matter of fact, Jack hadn't. It was with obvious pleasure that Livesey recalled the ferry trip to Jersey City forty-five years before. Halfway across the Hudson, he explained, Jack tossed the entire camping outfit into the water, tent, mattress, cooking gear, everything, declaring as he did so—somewhat profanely into the bargain— that he was not going to lug all that stuff out west.

Baldwin left for home soon after. From the standpoint of the defense, it had not been a very encouraging trip.

4

The Search for Evidence

IN THE MEANTIME, Mrs. Cockburn had placed an advertisement in the agony columns of twenty West Coast newspapers:

Will Annie Crabtree, my mother, who lived in Tombstone, Arizona, during the years 1879-80-81-82-83 and later in Phoenix, communicate with me? I need my mother's help now more than I ever did. Carlotta Crabtree Cockburn, address Room 61, 68 Post Street, San Francisco.

Obviously, Mrs. Cockburn intended to press her claim with a vengeance. Yet, in spite of Louis Livesey's information—it was, after all, based solely on memory—Frederick Chase of Stewart & Chase was not convinced that Jack Crabtree had necessarily arrived in Tombstone in time to have fathered Carlotta. The baby had been born in March, 1881; Jack had left for Arizona in the late spring of 1880. However, there was some reason to think that his arrival might have been too late to coincide with Mrs. Cockburn's claim of paternity.

To substantiate this possibility, Baldwin went to the Hotel Brewster to dig through Lotta's files, for Jack had lived with his mother and sister both before and after his sojourn out west.

The Brewster still stands, a dingy hotel later called the Paramount which, early in 1966, was gutted by fire when an explosion in the basement ripped through the bar killing seven patrons. It was a depressing place even in Lotta's last days, its stone front, black with smoke and city dirt, blending grimly into the general air of desuetude that had overtaken lower Boylston Street. When Baldwin arrived, Emma Donovan, Lotta's secretary and companion, was waiting in the actress's apartment.

"I don't know what you'll think," she said. "I've tried to find some things about Ashworth [the name by which Jack was known in his family], but her memento room is very disorganized. She would never let me put it in order."

Miss Donovan led the way out into the corridor and to a locked door at the back of the hotel, opened it, and groped for the bare electric bulb. When, next, she raised a tattered shade on a dirty window looking out onto a ventilating shaft, the effect was one of chaos. Letters, photographs, theater programs, clippings, costumes, and bric-a-brac were piled high; play scripts, covered with dust, lay stacked in a corner. There were gold-plated horseshoes from Lotta's racing days—the actress had found it difficult to throw anything away. The very air seemed to be preserved from another time. It was said that Lotta had sometimes slept in the memento room, and no wonder: a lifetime of triumphs was immured here. Baldwin poked and prospected through this mass of memorabilia for clues to Jack Crabtree's western interlude without success; it was apparent that everything would have to be removed to the attorney's office and sorted out. When this was finally done, the amount of material was so great that an extra room had to be rented to store it.

By this time General Edwards, one of the three special administrators appointed by the court to represent the Estate, had begun running down his own leads in the case. Counterintelligence had not been the General's military specialty, but his genial brassiness made up for lack of experience. ("He was incapable of ten minutes of sustained thought," Baldwin remarked of him later, "but largely due to his charming wife he did have contacts which he was always cheerfully ready to use.") A wartime friend, Colonel T. F. Murphy, was appointed aide-de-camp at the General's self-styled command post, and a minor ally discovered in the person of the Reverend Endicott Peabody, Head-

master of the Groton School, whose first pastorate had been an
Episcopal mission school in Tombstone during the silver-rush
days of that frontier settlement. Chase knew Dr. Peabody, at
whose suggestion Colonel William Breckenridge, a deputy sheriff
in Tombstone during the 1880s (later U. S. Marshal for Arizona), was drafted out of retirement in California to comb the
West for possible witnesses. Because he did not consider it necessary to shoot a man when arresting him, Colonel Breckenridge
never achieved the fame of his contemporary, Wyatt Earp. Nevertheless, he had known almost everyone in Tombstone, and
might be of considerable value to the case.

To this impressive nucleus of former military men, the vast
investigatory apparatus of both the Burns and Pinkerton detective agencies was added; their operatives were dispatched to Arizona and points west. By early February Colonel Murphy was
settled into Tucson's Santa Rita Hotel, making his own recon-
naissance of the Tombstone area. An inspection of the plat books
and tax records revealed that young Jack Crabtree had been a
resident of the town in 1880-81 and that his mother was the
owner of record of a half interest in a livery stable business
managed by him and Ed Bullock. There was no evidence that
Mary Ann had ever been in Tombstone; but, from all indica-
tions, she had set him up in business.

One person in particular was of signal importance to the case:
Dr. Nathan Gibberson, who had moved to Tombstone in the late
1870s, fresh from medical school in Pennsylvania. According to
Carlotta Cockburn, this young frontier doctor had been the man
who delivered her. Locating his whereabouts was one of Colonel
Murphy's immediate aims, since his testimony would be vital in
proving, or disproving, Mrs. Cockburn's claim. On the morning
of Sunday, February 8, 1925, accompanied by Judge George
Darnell, a Tucson attorney whom Judge Chase had retained as
Arizona counsel, Murphy set out for Tombstone. Although the
town's reputation survived vividly, most of its inhabitants had
scattered, some to vanish into respectability; from a population

of twenty-five thousand in 1880, Tombstone had shrunk to a ghostly collection of three hundred persons. Among those who had long since departed was Dr. Gibberson—in fact, he had left in a hurry, taking with him the wife of a local judge. Colonel Murphy wired Boston: "Dr. Gibberson was known and run out of Tombstone in about '84. Wright, Hoy [Mrs. Cockburn's Tucson and Boston attorneys] allied with questionable element in this country. Suggest you cause every delay possible as they plan to hurry things."

Murphy made this plea with good reason. James M. Hoy, a stocky, six-foot Irishman, had lined up a shrewd Tucson attorney named James Wright. Hoy had come to Arizona, and he and Wright had also hit the trail in search of witnesses. The race was on.

Murphy and Darnell had already left Tombstone for Pearce; there were also stops at Bisbee, Lowell, and Douglas. Forty-nine persons were interviewed on this swing through the mining country, and although sometimes Murphy and Darnell got to them first, at other times Hoy and Wright beat them to it; the outcome was a dead heat. As Colonel Murphy complained in one of his numerous reports, nobody who had been anybody in Tombstone during its salad days wanted to talk.

. . . the women will not tell what they really knew of life in Tombstone in '80 and '81, because such statements immediately tax them with having associated with a class of people they wish to forget, and the men who might testify as to the real facts are just as reluctant in naming the women now living. . . .

Despite this reluctance, the trip yielded two important breaks. The elusive Dr. Gibberson was understood to be living in San Francisco, and the name of Mrs. Kate Taylor was mentioned as a probable witness to the affairs of Jack Crabtree. Her Tombstone career had embraced five names if not necessarily four husbands (in addition to Kate Taylor, she had also been Samantha Hale [her maiden name], Samantha Taylor, Kate Logie, and a Mrs.

Fallon) and at one time she was said to have danced in the Bird Cage Theater. Later she became a hotel proprietor, and it was in this latter role that she had starred in the life of the city. The few old-timers who would talk (presumably their reputations were beyond damage) recalled that the lobby of Kate Taylor's San Jose House served as a convenient meeting place where the demimonde could mix with respectable society—such as it was in Tombstone—and, when necessary, emulate it. One of the hotel's liveliest roomers between 1879 and 1881 was Ulysses S. Grant, Jr.

By piecing together random tags of rumor and fact, Colonel Murphy learned that Mrs. Taylor had left Tombstone for Los Angeles. But a preliminary search was futile and he turned the matter over to the Pinkerton agency. Meanwhile, Colonel Breckenridge was flushing out the illustrious Wyatt Earp. Earp was then in his late seventies, but his memory of Annie Leopold Crabtree was altogether intact; unhappily, it corroborated Mrs. Cockburn's story. "Bullock and Crabtree came there [Tombstone] in the spring of 1880," he told Colonel Breckenridge, "and built a corral on Allen Street, between Fourth and Fifth Streets, next to where the Grand Hotel was built. They built a small office and fixed up a three-seated carriage for a sleeping place, and I believe the baby was born in that carriage. It was a common rumor at the time that a child was born there. I knew both Crabtree and his wife and knew that a baby was born to them but don't know whether it was a boy or a girl. . . . I saw Mrs. Crabtree several times at the San Jose rooming house kept by Mrs. Taylor. She knows all about Mrs. Crabtree."

Judge Chase was not overjoyed when he heard this. Still, the evidence was largely hearsay—"common rumor," as Earp had put it—and might well be stricken as testimony. Wyatt had told them that Annie Leopold had had a loose reputation, and Carlotta could well have been fathered by someone other than Jack Crabtree. If the defense could prove that Jack was not in Tombstone seven to nine months before the child's birth, the proof would be conclusive.

Since Dr. Gibberson might shed some light on the matter, it became imperative to locate him. Colonel Murphy, proceeding to San Francisco, tracked his quarry through a visit to the local medical society; the doctor maintained a practice in the city and (as Murphy discovered later) was still living with the woman he had purloined from a Tombstone judge forty-odd years before. She must have wondered whether the escapade had been worth it, for the Gibbersons lived in three rooms adjoining the doctor's office. It was a slum neighborhood inhabited largely by Italians and Negroes.

The aging doctor did not seem at all surprised by this visit from a stranger. As Murphy soon discovered, the other side had gotten to him first. Gibberson listened patiently in his examination room as the Colonel asked him to recollect the incidents of his Tombstone practice. No little of his time, it appeared, had been spent plugging up bullet holes, but such mundane matters as childbirth were not beyond recall. He had, so he claimed, delivered Carlotta Crabtree Cockburn.

In Boston, Judge Chase, anxiously awaiting some message from Colonel Murphy, was doing his best to delay the hearing. At last, a telegram came—"The doctor has evidently agreed to a story and intends to tell it."

But then something happened that made delay of the Cockburn hearing no longer a paramount tactic: On March 18, 1925, Florian Arey, a Boston lawyer, filed an appearance for Mrs. Ida M. Blankenberg, of Tulsa, Oklahoma, who claimed to be Lotta's own daughter. If her claim could be substantiated, she—as nearer of kin than a niece—would take precedence over Mrs. Cockburn; and Ida May went to the head of the line.

As proof, Ida May offered a handwritten entry—possibly done by Lotta herself—in the flyleaf of what purported to be a family Bible.

Ida Manning Crabtree [sic] was born October 18, 1878. In England, at Crabtree Chateau, Lancashire. Ida Manning was daughter of George Manning and Lotta Crabtree Manning (An Actress) who married in Lancashire, England, December 25, 1877. George Manning, Father of Ida Manning disappeared suddenly March 13, 1878. Could never be found again. Ida was born in lap of Luxury but the Mother in great sorrow brought her to home of John E. and Ann Jane Crabtree at Crabtree Ford in Illinois. Wedding certificate and birth papers all in keeping of her mother with complete family history. Dr. Broadbent of England was at birth of Ida. F. W. Charles Wolverton and wife witnesses at marriage of Lotta.

Mrs. Blankenberg herself was described, in an International News Service dispatch from Tulsa four days after she had filed her claim, as "titian-haired, of medium height, plump, and middle-aged. She has the appearance of a successful American businesswoman. A stamp of the foot, head thrown back, and a forward push of the chin accompany the words: 'It's my fortune and I intend to get it.' "

Lotta's own whereabouts between 1877 and 1879, rather than brother Jack's, now became of first importance. Relics from the memento room assumed a value that not even their owner could have foreseen, and a trained assistant was hired to sort all the old playbills, clippings, posters, letters, and family documents.

Pinkerton detectives, fanning out through the country, retraced the itinerary of Lotta's touring company during the years 1878-81, hoping to prove that the actress had been on the road during the year she was alleged to be in England and that brother Jack had been with her, at least in 1880. Hotel records were studied and retired desk clerks interviewed from Montreal to St. Louis, but without much success. Few hotel registers had survived the forty-seven-year gap, and those that could be disinterred from storerooms weren't much help; Lotta's company was usually "signed in" as a group by the business manager.

The major Pinkerton effort was directed at uncovering the background of Ida May Blankenberg in Crabtree Ford, Rock Island County, Illinois. At this task, they were careful to assume the proper Hawkshaw attitude: when Operative J.M.M. arrived in Rock Island from Chicago, on March 30, 1925, he interviewed the local librarian, as he noted later, "under a pretext," and was promptly rewarded with five different books on Rock Island. One of these, the *Historical Encyclopedia of Illinois and History of Rock Island County,* produced the following data:

During the past several decades the real estate business in Rock Island County, Ill., has grown to astounding proportions; fortunes have been made during the phenomenal growth of this section of the state; and the development of this line of business here has brought forth some of the keenest, most farsighted men of the day, but it has remained for a woman, Mrs. Ida M. Blankenberg of Rock Island to become the largest real estate dealer in the county. In these days when the rights of women are being so justly and steadfastly advocated by our leading men and women and opposed by others, Mrs. Blankenberg is an interesting example of what can be accomplished by a woman in the business world and her success should be a strong argument in favor of those who do not believe that woman's sphere is in the home.

Her parents were pictured as country people who, on the paternal side, were descended from aristocracy, her grandmother being "a daughter of Lord Lewisgile" in England and her father "a plantation owner in Virginia" who had moved to Illinois following the Civil War. Although Ida May was "one of the leading land dealers in the county," she nevertheless found time "to devote to anything of educational or social character" and was an excellent housewife, "as will be attested to by those who visit her comfortable home, drawn there by the genial, social and pleasant nature of understanding." A few rhinestones were scattered among the gems (her husband, Gustav, did not enjoy a listing of his own in the *Encyclopedia*), but they seemed to shine from the glitter of Ida May's own brilliance. It was an inspiring success story, and well it might be, since, as Operative J.M.M. discovered when he returned to Chicago and called on the publisher, the biographies had been written by the subjects themselves, who paid a modest fee for the privilege of telling their story.

Mrs. Blankenberg had since left Rock Island for Tulsa, where

she first read of Lotta's death in the *Tulsa World*. Soon thereafter she appeared at the law office of Woodson Norvell, a local
attorney who had represented her in connection with some oil
leases. Norvell was surprised to hear, on this particular visit, that
his client claimed to be an heir-at-law of Lotta Crabtree. He
wasn't even sure that he had ever heard of such a person, but
$4,000,000 was a lot of money, and he obligingly sent for a copy
of the will. After studying it, he advised Ida May that if she
intended to lay claim to the riches, she would have to establish
some tangible proof of relationship to the deceased. An alleged
niece had already filed an appearance, but of course if Mrs.
Blankenberg were Lotta's daughter, she would take precedence.

During the next few months, Mrs. Blankenberg did nothing
more about staking her claim. Then, early in March of the following year, she returned to Illinois, where she had always supposed she had been born, and where she most certainly had been
reared, to clear up once and for all the mystery of her relationship to Lotta; or, as she explained to Judge Chase later, "to find
out who I was." As she was to maintain in court, this relationship
to Lotta was the great secret in a family that in other respects
had no privacy at all; at one time John E. and Ann Jane Crabtree and five of seven children lived in a two-room cabin on the
banks of the Mississippi. Although the Crabtrees later progressed
to a farmhouse and twenty acres of land, the farm yielded a
niggardly living; nevertheless, Ida May had attended high school
across the river in Muscatine, Iowa, instead of having to "work
out" as had been the case with the older girls. Later, she spent a
year in business college, and from there she enrolled in the
Muscatine Normal School. All this had been made possible (so
Mrs. Blankenberg was to testify) by the generosity of Lotta Crabtree.

Now, in a rented Willys Knight, Ida May set about calling on
her "foster" brothers and sisters. The oldest brother, John William Crabtree, was indeed surprised when she pulled up at his
house in East Dubuque. Truth to tell, he had not seen her in

thirty years, had long since lost track of her comings and goings, and couldn't imagine why, after all this time, she wanted to see him. The question was soon answered: Ida Blankenberg needed his help in "proving up her claim" to a $4,000,000 estate. At this, John William's interest perked up. The previous year he had suffered a paralytic shock and was no longer able to work (he had been a house painter), but this was no reason why he could not devote time to helping his sister look for evidence. Together they drove to the home of a sister, Margaret Anson, in Rock Island, where they spent the night. The following day they proceeded to the "home place," some eight miles out of town, in Drury Township. The farm was now run by Ida May's two bachelor "foster" brothers, Edmund and Joseph Abraham Lincoln Crabtree, who had bought the property from their father. They lived alone, doing their own housekeeping as well as the field work. Ed and Joseph were then in their mid-fifties, which made them about ten years older than Ida and twelve years younger than John William.

They, too, were unprepared for this unannounced appearance. It had been sixteen years since John William had come to see them, and a visit from Ida May usually meant that she wanted to involve them in a business proposition or borrow money; it was something of a relief, therefore, to discover that she merely wanted the family Bible. The possibility that she had traveled all the way from Oklahoma for the sake of any religious concern, however, struck Joseph Crabtree as extremely implausible, and he was not surprised when she told him that it was the family records that interested her. As to this, there was no doubt she had come to the right place.

Whatever the farm might lack in material comforts (and in this respect it lacked just about everything) was made up by an abundant supply of Bibles. There were three such in the house, but it is not at all clear that Ida May realized this. In any case, she asked for the original "Crabtree" Bible. Another, smaller, Bible had come into the family when Ann Jane Steckman had married the elder Crabtree. Known as the "Steckman Bible," it did not contain any Crabtree genealogy and would be of no help in proving a claim. The third, or "big," Bible—it measured ten and a half by twelve and a half inches—was a later acquisition, purchased when John Edward Crabtree's eyesight began to fail and he could no longer read the fine print in the other two. Quite probably, Mrs. Blankenberg did not know of, or had forgotten, its existence. In a sense, this was the master Bible, since it contained the family records drawn from the other two. As matters turned out that afternoon, Joseph Crabtree, who did most of the talking for the two brothers, decided that Ida May could not have any of the Bibles, and she left the farm empty-handed.

She did not, however, return to Tulsa empty-handed. When, a few days later, she again showed up in Woodson Norvell's law office, Mrs. Blankenberg not only had John William with her, but had a Bible purportedly given her by John William at the time she had called on him in East Dubuque. The old man explained that this book had been entrusted to his care shortly before his father died because "it contained something of value to Idy." He had been admonished to guard it carefully and under no circumstances to open it; but to those who came to know John William later, this warning seemed superfluous. Ida May, of course, did open the Bible, and what she found there in the handwriting on the flyleaf was proof that she was, indeed, the daughter of Lotta Crabtree. Norvell now decided to take the case and enlisted another Tulsa attorney, skillful in probate work, named Grover Cleveland Spillers. Together they planned the legal strategy, and it was at their request that Florian Arey of Boston entered his "appearance" for Mrs. Blankenberg on March 18, 1925.

In the meantime, Ida May made another trip to Illinois, this time successfully persuading Joseph Crabtree to let her borrow the family Bible. As she was leaving, Ida May also asked her brother for a loan of $20. He refused. Ida May next called on two other sisters, both of whom lived on farms, but between visits an unfortunate thing happened: the rented car had a flat tire. Mrs. Blankenberg went for help. When she returned, the Bible was gone. She presumed it had been stolen. . . .

On April 24, Judge Chase and one of Mrs. Cockburn's attorneys, James Hoy, journeyed to Hannibal, Missouri, which the court had designated as a convenient point for the taking of depositions. Mrs. Blankenberg and her Tulsa lawyers had come up from Oklahoma, bringing the Bible containing her birth record, and her older brother, John William Crabtree. It was at this session that the Chase forces first heard the full story of Ida May's alleged relation to Lotta. In view of the sheer detail offered, what they learned was not calculated to make the defense of the will any easier. Ida May's deposition ran to 176 legal-size pages.

The claim boiled down essentially to this: that Lotta had married a George Manning on Christmas Day, 1877. Manning had disappeared the following March, and Ida was born to Lotta in October, delivered by a Dr. Broadbent. (Through an English investigation agency, Chase ascertained that there were five Broadbents listed in the British Medical Directory for 1878.) As "proof" of her maternity, Mrs. Blankenberg produced the Bible John William had given her, with the entry of her birth.

Her story, if not immediately plausible in all its aspects, could hardly be disproved out of hand. A certain sympathetic element ran through it that could well appeal to a jury, for Ida May Blankenberg pictured herself as something more than a foundling, yet less than an acknowledged heir. The relationship between mother and daughter, Ida May claimed, had been a loving one, and not without its rewards; but it had also been largely a secret relationship; she had been disinherited by the mother in the end. The daughter was only claiming her due.

Born in an English manor house, the infant had been taken to Crabtree Ford in Illinois, just across from Muscatine, Iowa, to be placed in the keeping of John Edward Crabtree and his wife Ann.

Why this remote spot for the child of a famous actress? Such a choice of foster home for the infant Ida May might seem to be an act of cruelty rather than kindness, but it did serve to keep the fruit of Lotta's secret marriage out of the limelight. And besides, there were to be numerous rewards later on.

Frederick Chase was unable to shake her story, and he had no greater success with the other witnesses. A "foster" sister, Mrs. Elizabeth Brown, claimed to have been told by her mother that Ida was not her real sister, but that she must call her that anyway. And John William testified that he had met Lotta at the family homestead and that for the first several years of Ida's life the actress had sent him money for the child. But it was the Bible produced by Mrs. Blankenberg—the "Hannibal" Bible, as it came to be called all during the trial—that struck attorney Chase as the most damaging piece of evidence. Possibly it was a fake, but proving this to be the case might not be easy.

Upon his return to Boston, Chase began an intensive search among Lotta's effects for some clue to her whereabouts during the time she was alleged to be living (and getting married) in England. It was known that she had spent lengthy interludes abroad, for she had appeared on the London stage and vacationed in Cheshire, where her father had lived during the latter part of his life. That none of these periods might coincide with the date of Ida May's birth was something they hoped to establish.

Lotta's theatrical ventures in the California gold fields and in San Francisco and her New York stage triumphs in the gas-footlights era were traced. While much of this effort produced interesting sidelights on Lotta's career, from a legal point of view it was of little help.

For Raymond Baldwin, the trail led to the office of David Belasco; to the throne room of A. L. Erlanger, the flamboyant booking agent; to the Lambs Club; and to the Actors' Home on Staten Island, where a handful of Lotta's contemporaries lingered on. Unhappily, nothing much was learned.

One old-timer who had managed to stay out of the Home—by compiling a 370-page book of theatrical reminiscences which he sold for $1 a copy—was John R. Rogers, an ex-husband of Minnie Palmer, the soubrette who had once vied with Lotta for popularity. Rogers had known virtually every important theatrical personality of the latter half of the nineteenth century, including Buffalo Bill, Lew Dockstader, P. T. Barnum, and Harrigan and Hart. "Not one took any money, costumes, or scenery on their last tour," he reminded the actors of a later era, to whom he sold his recollections of those who had departed this life. Rogers was given the assignment of locating anyone who had worked with Lotta and who might still be living. He himself had played the clown in *Little Nell and the Marchioness* in Lotta's troupe in 1869, had known the Crabtrees well, and boasted that he had lent Lotta's brother George money on the not infrequent occasions when he wanted to redeem something from a pawnshop.

Meanwhile, both the Cockburn and Blankenberg forces were increasing their legal firepower. To the attorneys representing Carlotta Cockburn was added Sherman Whipple, a noted Boston trial lawyer who, in *Willett vs. Herrick et al.,* had wrung a $10,300,000-verdict out of a jury two years before, only to see the judgment reversed on appeal. Working with Jim Hoy, Whipple's strategy at this point was to get the Cockburn case before a jury, which would almost certainly prove more sympathetic than a probate judge. Judge Prest denied Whipple's initial motion to frame jury issues, however, and Whipple's next move was to petition for a "bill of discovery" to give him access to Lotta's papers. This, too, was refused.

For her part, Mrs. Blankenberg added to her battery of attorneys the former Attorney General of Massachusetts, J. Weston Allen. A prominent public figure, Allen lent a dangerous element of respectability to Ida May's claim that had hitherto been lacking, for it was regarded as unlikely that he would have taken the case were he not convinced that it had merit.

The cast was to be shuffled once more before the curtain rose, in a surprising way: Hoy and Whipple joined forces with the lawyers for the Estate against Weston Allen to try knocking out Mrs. Blankenberg's claim, for it was greatly to the advantage of the woman who said she was Lotta's niece to dispose of the rival who insisted she was her daughter. When this was done, they themselves could attempt to establish their client's claim of kinship and try to break the will.

While General Edwards's investigations continued—an English detective agency was put to work looking for heirs of "Dr. Broadbent" and the whereabouts of Chateau Crabtree—Mrs. Blankenberg's Tulsa lawyers pressed ahead. With Grover Cleveland Spillers concentrating on the legal aspects, Norvell took over the publicity, and he was unabashedly infected with the literary possibilities of his new role. "Back to the ancient hills of Merrie England and the crumbling walls of Chateau Crabtree, in Lancashire, which she left in babyhood . . ." he was quoted in the *Tulsa Tribune,* in announcing Mrs. Blankenberg's imminent departure to seek out additional family records.

But Ida May did not go anywhere, and Norvell was careful to keep her incommunicado—the "snooping Pinkertons" were everywhere. In Boston, Florian Arey, who had traveled to Tulsa to see what the case was all about, returned exuding confidence. Word from England, he announced to the press, had established the existence of a marriage certificate issued to Lotta and George Manning and a birth certificate issued for Ida May. "An effort is being made to obtain certified copies of the English records," Arey declared, adding that, if necessary, he would make the trip himself. However, Arey did not go to England either.

Chase was still hoping to discover a flaw in Ida May's story that would blow the case up before it came to trial. Unexpectedly, late in April, 1925, the necessary explosive for such a blast—so it seemed—was sent over from Judge Prest's chambers; it was a letter from Mrs. George Miltenberger of St. Louis, Missouri, who had read about the Crabtree story in the local newspapers. Mrs.

Miltenberger knew very well that Lotta could never have given birth to Ida May Blankenberg or, for that matter, anyone else. Why? In 1895, Lotta was still a virgin.

If true, this was, indeed, a remarkable break. The letter did not seem to be imaginings of a crank. In 1895, Mrs. Miltenberger had been a patient in the New York sanatorium of Dr. Walker Gill Wylie. While she was there, Lotta was admitted for the removal of a fibroid tumor. During the course of the operation, the hymen was found to be intact, a discovery that caused considerable stir among Dr. Wylie's staff, especially the nurses. Hardly supposing it possible for an actress to be a virgin, they had lost no time in passing the information on to the other patients. It was not the sort of gossip one forgets, and Mrs. Miltenberger, who thought the event remarkable when she first heard it in 1895, decided that it was even more unusual in 1925, now that Ida May had come forward with putative proof to the contrary.

By this time, Dr. Wylie's sanatorium had been closed for thirteen years. Its staff had scattered. In St. Louis, the Pinkerton office interviewed Mrs. Miltenberger. Although well along in years, she recalled that Rose Halsey had been Lotta's nurse. (It was she who had helped spread the news of the operation.) Through the nurses's registry, Miss Halsey was traced to Remsenberg, L. I., where Pinkerton Operative W.H.M. found her at work in her garden. "She has a neat cottage with considerable grounds, well kept. She invited me to the house, where I interviewed her at length. She stated that she was Lotta Crabtree's private nurse while Miss Crabtree was a patient at Dr. Wylie's hospital; that Miss Crabtree was a very exacting person and would not have anyone but her, Miss Halsey, attend her; that . . . Miss Crabtree was operated on for a tumor of the uterus, a major operation which was a success . . . also that she distinctly recalls Dr. Walker Gill Wylie making a remark that Miss Crabtree was a pure woman, which for an actress of her career was very much out of the ordinary. . . ."

Dr. Wylie had since died, but Miss Halsey believed that an

attending surgeon, Dr. David Ernest Walker, lived somewhere in North Carolina. She herself agreed to come to Boston and explain the whole business in court if she could "get someone to look after the chickens." Dr. Walker was located in Rock Hill, North Carolina, and, like Miss Halsey, recalled the operation vividly—indeed, perhaps too vividly, for when he was cross-examined by Mrs. Blankenberg's Tulsa attorney in Judge Prest's court, his inability to remember other operations of a similar nature weakened the testimony. Chase produced the former nurse and Dr. Walker as surprise witnesses on June 28, at a hearing in which he hoped to dispose of Mrs. Blankenberg's standing. Miss Halsey testified first.

"Did you hear Dr. Walker Gill Wylie say anything about the condition which he found as to—about Miss Crabtree's condition after the operation?" Chase asked her.

In a flurry of objections, Grover Cleveland Spillers did his best to prevent an answer. Judge Prest overruled him.

"Just what did he say?" Chase repeated.

"He said she was a chaste woman, a virgin."

Dr. Walker, taking the stand, confirmed this. However, on cross-examination, Spillers attacked his credibility. "Isn't it a fact, Doctor, that this is the only instance that you can tell this court that you remember after a period of thirty years that the hymen was not broken?"

WALKER: Yes, I shall have to admit that.

Had the fact of Miss Crabtree's virginity been put in the records at the time? Dr. Walker could not remember.

SPILLERS: Now, over the period of thirty years . . . since that time, you have kept clearly in your mind the remembrance of this hymen, have you not?

WALKER: I certainly have.

SPILLERS: Have you that recollection of any of your other patients?

WALKER: I can't say that I have. . . .

The skirmish ended in a draw. Actually, Dr. Walker was not

the only surgeon from Dr. Wylie's staff who had been traced by the Pinkertons. Operative W.H.M. had interviewed a Dr. J. Ives Edgerton, who, although he had not attended Lotta, declared, in the words of the Pinkerton report:

. . . no physician could take the stand and swear that a certain woman or women had never had sexual intercourse with man or men by an examination or operation. He cited a number of instances as follows: A young lady, daughter of a minister, called on him for treatment and confessed to him that she had given birth to a child quite a while prior to his examination of her; that his examination did not disclose same, which he would otherwise not have known as there was no evidence of same; that he knew of a married woman who had had three children without showing any evidence of same. Dr. Edgerton cited other instances of somewhat similar cases that came under his observation and terminated the interview by stating that any physician who would take the witness stand and attempt to prove that the virginity of a woman can positively be determined would be ridiculed and made a fool of by the opposition. . . .

Needless to say, it was Dr. Walker, and not Dr. Edgerton, whom Chase asked to testify.

Chase had two other witnesses through whose testimony he hoped to prevent Mrs. Blankenberg from pressing her case. The first of these was Mrs. Annie Fretwell, one of the admitted first cousins, who had come to Boston from Mexico City. Wearing a long black dress that hung down to her ankles and a bowl-shaped hat with white rim, from which a feather bobbed at the rear, and carrying a parasol and fan, Mrs. Fretwell rather resembled Queen Victoria—no one quite like her had been seen in the Suffolk County courtroom in some time. So far as Mrs. Fretwell was concerned, there were no next of kin except for the three American and three English first cousins. Lotta had never married, although she had once been engaged to a man named Bolton Hulme, who had died in 1872. She objected to going further into Lotta's love affairs but testified that Jack Crabtree, who had married Annie Harris of Boston in 1899, had left no children. Lotta's other brother, George, died in 1891. He never married.

The final witness of the day for the proponents was Miss Sarah Ann Crabtree, who had come over from England. A petite woman in her eighties, she was a bright, demure and engaging witness, establishing herself and her English brother and sister as the other surviving first cousins. At the close of the day's testimony, Judge Prest disposed of some sixty additional claimants, whose attorneys had swarmed through the courtroom all during the day—"all tracking round," as Morse had predicted. By their own admission, their clients were more remotely related than first cousins, and Chase's motion to strike their names from the record was granted.

It now remained for Judge Prest to rule on the standing of Mrs. Blankenberg. The important testimony was not that of Lotta's cousins—as beneficiaries, they were subject to prejudice— but that of Nurse Halsey and Dr. Walker. Could an intact hymen be accepted as proof of virginity? Such a fact had apparently not gone into the records of the sanatorium, and in any case, the records had been destroyed. Thirty years later it was all a matter of recall. For Judge Prest, it was a momentous, not to say unique, ruling; he was being asked to declare Lotta Crabtree a virgin. Nothing quite like this had ever come before the Boston courts.

Even without Dr. Edgerton's contrary opinion, the judge, at the end of the day, and after due consideration, solemnly announced that there was not sufficient evidence to establish Lotta's virginity—and virginity was something you either had or you didn't have. Thus it was that Ida May Blankenberg survived the purge. The case was set for trial two days later.

5

The Plaintiff's Tale

WHEN IDA MAY BLANKENBERG arrived in Boston on June 30, 1925, she was greeted by a sizable contingent of reporters, who, although inclined to regard her claim somewhat skeptically, accorded her the fanfare due to one who promised to produce some sparkling copy during an otherwise dull summer. A reporter noted in his account of the interview that the claimant was a grandmother "of middle height, with thick, rather reddish hair" and from all outward appearance a respectable American housewife. This impression was strengthened by Ida May's conservative dress and flat, Middle Western accent. Above all, she radiated confidence. It would be proved right off, she declared, that Lotta was her mother.

To do this she had assembled a formidable number of witnesses and hired no fewer than five lawyers. All in all, it was an expensive production for Mrs. Blankenberg, or more accurately, for her backers: an item in a Boston newspaper hinted darkly that a syndicate had put up the cash for the necessary expenses, and Mrs. Blankenberg herself was to testify later that she had promised her Tulsa counsel half of the money if she won the case. How much of it he would share with her senior counsel, J. Weston Allen, can only be guessed at, but Allen came high, his reputation was unassailable, and his presence gave the claimant a powerful advocate. The two had never met until Ida May arrived in Boston for the hearing, which opened on July 1.

Long before Judge Prest took his place on the bench, every seat in the gloomy, high-ceilinged courtroom was filled, while crowds, jamming the corridors, waited for a glimpse of Mrs. Blankenberg. Shortly before ten o'clock, escorted by her attorneys, she made her entrance, wearing a blue dress and a large-brimmed hat from beneath which burst a shock of conspicuously red hair. At length the doors were closed and Judge Prest stepped from his chambers and the court was gaveled to order.

The judge was in his mid-fifties at the time, a man of irreproachable conduct and inscrutable mien. To the considerable perturbation of counsel, he was to maintain his inscrutability throughout the trial. Facing him sat ten attorneys, in opposing phalanxes of five each: Stewart, Chase, and Baldwin, teamed up with Whipple and Hoy on one side; and, on the other, J. Weston Allen, flanked by the Tulsa lawyers Spillers and Norvell and two other Bostonians, Thomas Barry and Florian Arey. As the case progressed, this unwieldy cast was reduced to five principal advocates, Chase, Hoy, and Whipple vs. Allen and Norvell, with remaining counsel furnishing supporting roles.

At this time, Chase was fifty-five years old and had been practicing law for thirty-one years. As a young man he had taught at the Concord Reformatory, an experience that had left him intolerant of convicted criminals and had made him a stern judge of character. He had written a biography of Chief Justice Lemuel Shaw, the father-in-law of Herman Melville, and from 1911 to 1920 had served as judge of the Superior Court, resigning to resume his law practice. As a New Englander born and bred, he was conservative in temperament, with courtly manners which varied according to the occasion. "The core of his character and behavior," Baldwin recalled much later, "was the New England conscience of a boy who had been brought up without money." By the mid-twenties, Chase was beginning to have money in comfortable amounts, but he would still walk from North Station to his office, or ride the subway on rainy days rather than take a taxi. With almost $4,000,000 at stake, winning the Crabtree case became a matter of personal honor and, needless to say, involved a very handsome fee.

For their part, Hoy and Whipple were no less determined to head off Ida May's raid on the honeypot. They wanted the money for their client. Of the two, Hoy was the younger, and had been the leg man in chasing down witnesses for his side out west. (On one occasion he had shaken hands with Wyatt Earp, who was then in his eighties, and recalled that the Marshal's grip had almost felled him.) Fifty years old, he was a stocky six-footer with a shock of unruly brown hair, a ruddy complexion that extended to his rather large nose and ears, and a bull-toned voice that all but shook witnesses off the stand. One of Judge Chase's observations of the man was that he wore suits of no distinguished tailoring.

Hoy had enlisted Sherman Whipple, an adroit lawyer and celebrated Thespis of the Boston courts, in the hope that the case would go before a jury. On one memorable occasion, Whipple had hauled a barrel of apples from his farm to the courtroom, making certain that each juror had an apple to munch on during the deliberations. Perhaps it was coincidental, but he won that case. Skillful in cross-examination, he was known at times to compel the most truthful of witnesses to discredit himself. At sixty-three, he was the oldest attorney in court and sartorially the best turned out, the wingspread of his collar being equaled, it was said, only by that affected by the late Abbot Lawrence Lowell.

But it was Frederick H. Chase and J. Weston Allen who were to supply most of the thrust and parry of the day-to-day combat in *Blankenberg vs. Crabtree*. Allen was a short, square, aggressive man whose demeanor contrasted sharply with Chase's rather courtly manners, and he could usually be depended upon to spring a few surprises. One such "surprise" had already been leaked to the press in the form of a "mystery witness" who, it was said, would produce a photograph of Lotta's baby.

Chase was not especially concerned about this; more perplexing was a letter in his files that had been discovered among the actress's papers. It was from Lotta to her sister-in-law, Annie Harris Crabtree, dated 1908, and it included the following passage: "I know you will be surprised to hear that Florence has left me and is going to Kansas City with her father, but Ida, a splendid girl, comes to me tomorrow."

That this might be the same woman who sat facing the judge, waiting to tell her story, Chase very much doubted. The problem was to disprove it. General Edwards, who was also in the courtroom, looked at Ida May for familial proof of "the most beautiful ankle in the world," but unfortunately, a pair of high-button shoes concealed any clue to the evidence.

From the defendant's point of view, there was no unusual point of law involved, and Judge Chase recognized from the outset that the decision would turn on three major developments: the credibility of the witnesses, the authenticity of the Bibles, and Mrs. Blankenberg's own testimony.

Of witnesses, the plaintiff had an ample supply. This in itself was damaging. Would all these people deliberately perjure themselves in a court of law? They were a disparate lot, ranging from relatives who had grown up with Ida May to Bostonians and others who had allegedly known Lotta; at least two of the latter claimed to have seen the "child," and the remainder had been privy to the secret. It might not be easy to disprove their stories. One in particular, John William Crabtree, had, in deposition, provided a meticulous account of his dealings with Lotta.

The Bibles were another matter. There were four all told, and they were to be a source of endless confusion. One of these, the Crabtree "family" Bible, had been lent to Ida May by her brother Joseph, and purportedly lost. Another, the so-called "Hannibal" Bible, was in her possession. It contained the handwritten entry of her birth in Lancashire, England. The account of this birth, with the name of the attending physician, was persuasive, and it *looked* authentic. Then there was the Steckman Bible, which contained the records of Ida May's "foster" mother's family. Finally, there remained the "big" Bible, which, along with the Steckman Bible, was still in the possession of Joseph Crabtree. It contained no mention of Ida's birth in England and constituted, of course, a prime exhibit for the Estate.

The difficulty was that Joseph Crabtree refused to let either of these Bibles out of his keeping, and when the trial opened, he had not yet agreed to appear as a witness.

Mrs. Blankenberg herself was an unknown quantity. In certain obvious respects—her red hair, for example—she resembled Lotta; what is more, she had enjoyed educational advantages denied the other members of the family—thanks to Lotta, she insisted. If she was telling the truth, the evidence would support her. Chase promised the court that he would prove her an impostor, but promise and performance were not the same, and that was why they were all in court.

Weston Allen, Mrs. Blankenberg's star counsel, opened the proceedings by calling the "mystery" witness, a diminutive sixty-one-year-old spinster from Lynn, Massachusetts, named Mary Couhig. She took the stand carrying a sewing basket; later, she would produce the photograph of a baby said to be Lotta's, but not before Allen had drawn from her the story of Lotta's great secret, revealed in the days when Miss Couhig herself had nourished ambitions for the stage. She had been a student at Madam Russ's Dramatic School on Washington Street, in Boston, where Lotta from time to time came to visit. On one occasion she had given Miss Couhig the sewing basket; another time she had invited her to the Brewster. Alas! Miss Couhig's sister and mother died in a fire, and she had had to quit the Dramatic School. But she had gone to the Brewster, where Lotta had consoled Mary Couhig by revealing her own unhappiness. "Remember, little girl, you are not the only one to make sacrifices; we all have our griefs and sorrow. What would you think if you were in your teens, in a foreign land, and met somebody you thought perfect, but who deserted you when you most needed help? My husband left me stranded after two short months."

"Did she tell you anything about a child?" Allen asked.

"She said I could imagine her sorrow, coming to this country with a child in her arms and going west with it, where no one would ever know."

Out of the sewing basket came an embroidered lace handkerchief that threatened to disintegrate in Miss Couhig's fingers: a gift from Lotta thirty years before. This was followed by the tintype of a small child. It resembled a fat-faced boy rather fancifully decked out in a white muslin fichu. Chase smiled tolerantly. On cross-examination, he was unexpectedly gentle.

"She didn't tell you she left the child in a two-room log cabin on the banks of the Mississippi?"

"No," Miss Couhig replied.

"She didn't tell you that she was placed in a family where by reason of poverty the children were compelled to go to work at ten years of age?"

Miss Couhig seemed surprised. "No," she murmured again.

Not everyone in the courtroom missed the irony of Chase's line of questioning. In a slightly different sense, Lotta herself had been "put to work" at the age of eight.

Chase deferred to his adversary, and Allen thereupon called his "trump card," as *The New York Times* wrote the following day. This was the ailing John William Crabtree, the eldest of the children, who had arrived from the Midwest in a new, rather ill-fitting suit of clothes. Slightly deaf, shaking, and admittedly nervous, John William nevertheless gave a good account of himself. The *Boston Herald* called him "a unique character," echoing the general opinion of the courtroom, for whom the witness's illiteracy, added to his leathery, toil-worn appearance, seemed to preclude a talent for guile. "When I put my hand to the plow, I would have to walk all the way on tiptoe to reach the handles," he testified, describing his childhood. He had never gone to school, could not properly spell his sister's name. "I-d-e-a-," he said hesitantly when the court asked him to try.

"The new idea," Sherman Whipple, Mrs. Cockburn's attorney, announced *sotto voce*.

"Very much so," Chase agreed.

Under direct examination, John William expounded on his dealings at great length. A colorful account it was; if the old man were not telling the truth, he had been well rehearsed, for his testimony cloaked the skeleton of Mrs. Blankenberg's story like a suit of clothes. Lotta had first turned up at Crabtree Ford in the spring of 1879. John William was twenty-one that year, a house painter working across the river in Muscatine. He had come back home to get some ladders, and there, sitting in the parlor holding a baby girl, was a woman he had never seen before. "She called herself Lotta Crabtree, the actress."

"Weren't you introduced to Miss Crabtree?" Chase asked.

"No, my folks were not in the habit of introducing people," John William replied. And no doubt he was telling the truth. In any case, it had not been necessary, for Lotta had come right to the point. " 'This is my baby girl, Idy.' She was going to leave her Baby Idy-girl with my father and mother, and she wanted me to help them take care of it with her support."

As an earnest of her intentions, the actress had given John William $25. In the ensuing years, she had made him a go-between, sending money orders from time to time for Ida May's benefit. "Buy her clothes and school her," Lotta had written once, enclosing $50. Years later, she had run across John William in Davenport (Lotta, he said, was continually looking for him when she was on tour), this time giving him $100 to buy the growing child a horse "like what she wants." In John William's mind, the two sums—$50 for schooling and $100 for a horse—seemed about right for the purposes intended. When a chuckle went through the courtroom, he seemed puzzled.

One of John William's chief roles was to identify the small, worn "Hannibal" Bible which was offered in evidence the next day. According to Mrs. Blankenberg's deposition, he had been charged with the safekeeping of this Bible for Ida May shortly before his father's death. He had obeyed this injunction to a fault, for in the twenty-odd years during which the book had supposedly been in his possession, John William had never opened it. He was as surprised as everyone else, therefore, when Chase, leafing through the exhibit, discovered part of a torn envelope, apparently used as a bookmark, in Second Corinthians. On this bit of paper, the words

John E.—
Muscat—

were typed. Either the Bible had assuredly been in John Edward Crabtree's possession, or the slip of paper had been planted there to give that impression. The witness denied knowledge of it. Hadn't he wondered about the Bible? Chase wanted to know. "Weren't you a little curious why your father was giving you a book to keep for her?"

"I wasn't," John William replied.

"You weren't curious at all?"

"No, sir; I always did as my father bid me."

"Always did as your father bid you without asking any questions?"

"Never allowed to ask no questions," the witness assured the court. Not until Ida May had shown up unexpectedly in East Dubuque in March, 1925, did John William realize the importance of Pa Crabtree's foresight. It was then that he had turned over the Bible. John William had accompanied Ida May back to Tulsa. She left him there and then returned to Illinois to look for more evidence. When she came back the second time, he was surprised to learn that their brother Joseph had finally parted with the "Crabtree" Bible, which contained the official family records. But he was not too surprised to hear that it had mysteriously disappeared from Ida May's car. After all, it wouldn't be needed, now that she had the other Bible, which gave her birthplace as England.

There were two principal objections to this story, and Mrs. Blankenberg had realized this from the outset. The legal proof of her birth, as recorded in Illinois, contained absolutely no reference to Lotta Crabtree. And the "big" Bible owned by Joseph Crabtree included genealogy pages that set forth a different set of facts. To counter these, Mrs. Blankenberg contended that there was another Ida May Crabtree, the daughter of John and Ann Crabtree, who had died within a year of birth; it was Ida Manning who had been brought to Illinois and raised in her place. Chase had had the genealogy pages photographed, and now he produced them in court—to John William's consternation. Significantly, in these records, a child called Ida May had been born on schedule, but there was no record of her having died. That would leave Mrs. Blankenberg a log-cabin—rather than a chateau—Crabtree, and it was this that the attorneys for the estate hoped to prove.

Chase's strategy at this point was twofold. He would try to establish the accuracy of the family records in the "big" Bible, and to challenge the authenticity of the "Hannibal" version. Ink and handwriting experts would be produced, he told the court, to show that Exhibit A—the "Hannibal" Bible—had been doctored. For this purpose, Baldwin had secured the services of an ink expert named Joseph Wilbur. However, Wilbur had not yet seen the Bible, and Chase asked the court's permission to let him do so before testifying. In the meantime, Jim Hoy, Mrs. Cockburn's attorney, arranged to call his own expert, William Hingston, whose full title was "examiner of documents, handwriting, and ink." Both men awaited the call.

In the meantime, Chase handed the photographed pages of the "big" Bible up to the witness, and an effort was made to get him to read them. John William protested that he could see nothing without his glasses and, for that matter, very little with them.

THE COURT: Have you your glasses with you, Mr. Crabtree?

WITNESS: I got glasses but I can't see through them.

"What do you carry glasses for?" Chase demanded.

John William didn't seem too sure. "Because I want to carry them," he said at last, in a weakening voice.

Judge Prest was getting impatient. "Will you be willing to put your glasses on and try?" he asked the witness, leaning over the bench.

John William put them on, but got nowhere. Chase offered to let him try a pair of his own. This was rejected. "Where did you get those glasses?" Chase inquired.

The witness hesitated. "The five-and-ten-cent store in Tulsa," he admitted finally. The exhibit went unread, and John William was excused for the day. Judge Prest announced a recess and suggested that the time be used by the defense for its examination of the "Hannibal" Bible. (Since defense could not call its own witnesses until the plaintiff had finished presenting her case, the experts would not testify until later.) Wilbur and Hingston were sent for.

Ordinarily, they were on opposite sides of a case. Somehow, they had not been advised on this occasion that both would be testifying against the plaintiff. Hingston arrived first. With Jim Hoy, he was examining the Bible at a stand-up table in a room behind the judge's chambers when Baldwin entered. Wilbur had not yet appeared, but was expected soon. "That *is* artificially aged ink, isn't it?" Hoy said to Hingston.

The expert undid a small kit which he had brought along, took out a magnifying glass, and looked at the page. Then he produced a scalpel-like knife and delicately scraped off a tiny bit of ink. "Mr. Hoy, that ink is artificially aged," he declared with some confidence after a few moments. It was at this juncture that the door opened and Joseph Wilbur entered. Baldwin intercepted him.

"Will you kindly examine the writing on the end pages of this Bible and give me your opinion as to whether the ink is genuine old ink, or a recent entry made with artificially aged ink?" he said.

Wilbur nodded to Hingston and went at his job with even greater deliberation than his predecessor. After several minutes, he turned to Baldwin. "In my opinion that entry is genuine old ink," he announced dryly.

Jim Hoy gave a grunt of disgust. He pulled Hingston to one side. "The damned fool doesn't know which side of the case he's on," he said. "You talk to him."

The two experts went into a huddle. The embarrassed Mr. Wilbur asked if he might examine the entry again, and this time took even longer. "I was mistaken," he said at length, looking up. "That *is* artificially aged ink."

Hoy and Baldwin exhibited considerable relief; even so, they agreed that Wilbur was not the man for the job. Fortunately, Judge Prest had not been present. Now he called the court back into session briefly and then recessed it for the Fourth-of-July weekend.

The break was not much of a holiday for any of the principals; Mrs. Blankenberg was compelled to look after John William, whose two days on the witness stand had left him feebler than usual. While her legal battery held conclave in Boston, Chase and Baldwin spent much of the weekend planning strategy in the study of Chase's three-story brick house overlooking the Concord River. Preposterous as Ida May's story might seem, the two men realized that it would not necessarily fall of its own weight. Court records contained innumerable examples of claimed relationships even more improbable than this one, some of them successfully prosecuted.

The celebrated Tichborne case in England fifty-odd years earlier had demonstrated the extent to which an aggressive impostor could go under the most unlikely circumstances. In this instance, an enormously fat, unlettered Cockney, Arthur Orton, had presented himself as Sir Roger Tichborne, missing heir to the Tichborne baronetcy and estate. In spite of the most wildly contradictory evidence—lack of physical resemblance to Sir Roger being the least of it—Arthur had convinced even Lady Tichborne that he was, indeed, her lost son and therefore entitled to an income of £20,000 annually. True, he did not succeed in convincing the courts, but before he was convicted of perjury in 1874, he had cost the British taxpayers thousands of pounds and tied up the courts for eight months. Moreover, like Ida May, Arthur had had eminent counsel and a loyal society of believers, who supported the impostor in a life of relative ease while he pressed his case.

Yet desire for money apparently did not explain everything.

Ida May craved to *be* somebody. "I wanted to find out who I was," she had told Chase in deposition when he asked her why she had gone traveling around the countryside looking up family records. The discovery that she was, after all, the daughter of a celebrated actress, rather than the great-granddaughter of an imaginary "Lord Lewisgile," was comforting to the ego, and certainly promised more for the pocketbook. If, as Chase saw her, Ida May was thoroughly unscrupulous, she also possessed the kind of flamboyant imagination that he could not help but marvel at.

When Chase arrived at his office on the morning of July 6, among the letters waiting for him was one from Harry Houdini, the magician. Houdini had read about the case in the newspapers and offered to come to Boston to testify concerning Lotta's handwriting; as a friend, he had received a good many letters from her, and "being an expert in handwriting, I am at your service in any way possible."

Chase decided against it; the trial was turning into enough of a show without adding a magician. Mrs. Doremus of the Ouija Board had already suggested hypnotizing the witnesses to get the truth out of them; more than this, she had complicated matters temporarily by recalling that Lotta had been visited once by a young girl who declared that she was the actress's daughter. "Lotta and Mrs. C. were greatly amazed at her assertion," Mrs. Doremus wrote to Baldwin. "I am quite sure she had no papers or documentary evidence." Could it have been Ida May? Not likely, Chase decided.

Early in the trial, Mrs. Blankenberg's "Hannibal" Bible had been offered in evidence (technically, on Chase's motion, so that he might challenge its authenticity) as Exhibit A. The plaintiff's attorneys, however, had made facsimile copies of the colorful account of Ida May's birth at Crabtree Chateau, and these were distributed to the press. One effect of this, along with the publicity given the trial, was the appearance of a new supply of witnesses for Ida May. One can speculate that they had come forward hoping to be rewarded if Mrs. Blankenberg won her case but in the meantime quite happy to have a walk-on part in the high comedy that was packing the spectators' benches in the old Suffolk County Courthouse.

When the trial resumed Monday morning, the audience was more excited than usual; on the night of July 4, the Pickwick Club in Boston had gone up in a flash fire that had killed forty-three persons. Everyone was talking about it. Then, too, the newspapers were preparing their readers for the Scopes trial, which was soon to begin in Dayton, Tennessee. Judge Prest had a difficult time getting the courtroom to settle down. At last, Weston Allen called the first of his new witnesses; it would be his strategy to introduce their testimony at opportune times throughout the trial, and except for minor variations, what they revealed was remarkably predictable. Each seemed to remember that at some time in his past he had met Lotta and had been told about her marriage, the birth of Little Ida, and George Manning's desertion. Thus, Allen called up George A. Proctor, a retired lumber dealer from Cambridge, Massachusetts; Proctor was referred to as the "postcard" witness because he had originally volunteered his information on a penny postal to Miss Couhig, who had obligingly turned it over to Mrs. Blankenberg's counsel.

Proctor insisted, in a rambling account of his visits to York Beach, Maine, that he had met Lotta there in 1886 with a small child said to be her daughter. Chase was unable to shake his story, which, in any case, was uncorroborated. Next, a widow from Lexington, Massachusetts, wearing a small henna-colored hat, recalled that as a child of eleven, while visiting in Rochdale, England, she had been introduced to Lotta and a man she assumed to be her husband. "Why assumed?" Whipple demanded, boring in on cross-examination.

"Because they had been quarreling," the witness explained.

The stand was vacated for William Thompson, an engineer

who worked for the city of Boston. But Weston Allen didn't
know that Chase had information about Thompson, taken from
Attorney Morse's files, which was anything but favorable.

Thompson had been hired by Jack Crabtree to drill a well
underneath the Brewster; he was to be paid by the foot, and
Jack, needing money, was to share secretly in the profits. The
drilling continued for three hundred feet without producing so
much as a cupful of water, and Lotta threatened to call a halt.
Thereupon, water had begun to flow copiously; and although
Thompson denied it under Chase's biting cross-examination,
water had flowed because the engineer had piped it into the well
from a city main. And this, of course, is where the Brewster had
been getting its water all along.

At some point during the episode, Thompson testified, Jack
Crabtree had told him that his sister had been married and was
the mother of a child, but by this time the courtroom's interest
had shifted to Jack's complicity in the well. Lotta had discovered
the ruse, the deal had fallen through, and Thompson had gone
largely unpaid. About all that his testimony proved was that
Jack was a scoundrel; Whipple and Hoy were not at all unhappy
about this. They were looking forward to the time when they
might establish just how much of a scoundrel Jack could be.

On Thursday morning, July 9, the claimant herself took the
stand, wearing a black straw hat and a blue dress trimmed with
rhinestones. A courtroom spectator recalled that her lips were
thin and sharp, "savoring of aggressiveness." Her overall appearance, as Weston Allen pointed out, was markedly different
from that of the other Crabtrees in the courtroom, and to prove
it he called upon Mrs. Blankenberg's three "foster" sisters—a trio
of stout, ample-bosomed farm wives, one of whom gave the impression of being twice the size of Ida May—to stand beside her.
None of them had red hair.

As a witness in her own behalf, Mrs. Blankenberg exhibited an
impressive self-confidence. Under Weston Allen's skillful questioning, she testified that she first remembered seeing Lotta—"a

strange and beautiful lady"—at the home of an aunt when she was eight years old. The actress had taken her in her arms and rocked her to sleep, singing "Hush, my little baby, don't you cry; you'll be an angel by and by." Although titters went up from some of the spectators at the mention of the word angel, they failed to rattle the witness. "It is one of the sweetest memories of my life," she declared.

To the attorneys for the estate, this was an interesting, and even puzzling, bit of testimony. In preparing their case, they had employed a literary researcher to search the files of the theater collection at Harvard's Widener Library. One of the products of this search was a sheaf of songs which Lotta had made popular. Music publishers had seized upon these hits as quickly as Lotta had turned them loose on her audiences, and from 1868 until 1886 they had supplied the sheet music for Lotta Nocturnes, Lotta Polkas, Lotta Gallops, Lotta Marches, and Lotta Lullabies, in addition to a good many other songs, ballads, a yodeling number, and a sentimental piece called "Our Baby Beats 'Em All," which, under the present circumstances, Chase wished had not been written. Among the lullabies was "Hush, Little Baby, Don't You Cry." It had been copyrighted in 1884. By 1886, when Ida May Crabtree was eight years old, "Hush, Little Baby" was undoubtedly being sung throughout the country. The question was, who had sung it to Ida May?

The lullaby wasn't all that Mrs. Blankenberg remembered from that first meeting at the home of Aunt Eliza Underwood. "Lotta Crabtree said she had brought me a present, and she handed it to me; it was material for a beautiful white dress, white underwear, white stockings, white shoes, and a white slip, and she asked me if I was going to school, and I told her 'Yes,' and she asked me if I liked to go to school, and I told her 'Yes,' and in the evening she asked me if I would like to have her put my nightgown on for me, and I said 'Yes,' and that appealed to her something wonderful—"

Mrs. Blankenberg's voice broke. She took out a handkerchief, wiped her eyes, drank some water, and then launched into a performance that continued through four days of direct examination. In sheer imaginative detail, her recital of life with Lotta overlooked nothing. She had always supposed she was Lotta's half sister; and not until John William had given her the Bible, with its handwritten entry of Ida's birth, had she known the real truth, but even the lesser relationship had not been such a bad bargain. Upon her graduation from high school, Lotta had taken Ida May on a trip to Chicago and given her a gold bracelet "three hundred years old with the coat of arms of England on it." She was teaching school in Muscatine when she met Gustav Blankenberg, a young German who had emigrated to the United States with his family some years previously. Gustav had proposed, and Ida May brought her future husband over to Uncle Jim Underwood's house so that Lotta could have a look at him during one of her visits there.

Actually, Gustav remained outside in the yard; the young school teacher opened the back door "so as to give Lotta a good view." The net result of this visit was that the actress advised Ida May not to marry a man so young. In the present circumstances, it might have been better if she had not married him at all, for Gustav had from the first resolutely refused to take part in his wife's contest and was not present during the trial.

Mrs. Blankenberg's explanation for this was that her husband had never seen Lotta; as a carpenter, he was away for days at a time on construction jobs, so that when Lotta visited, he had not been home. These visits were accompanied by gifts of money; sometimes $200, once as much as $1,100. The Blankenbergs moved to Rock Island with the proceeds and settled into "a nice place in a reasonably nice neighborhood." There had been letters from Lotta, too, but unfortunately, they were destroyed in two separate fires in the attic of the house. (A check of fire records in Rock Island corroborated Mrs. Blankenberg's testimony in this respect, although there was no proof as to *what* had actually been burned.)

Soon after moving to Rock Island, Ida Blankenberg had set herself up in the real estate business, but she needed capital and in 1902 had gone with a Chicago realtor named Arthur Hardin to Boston, where Lotta entertained them. Hardin, she explained, was another go-between through whom Lotta's monetary gifts were channeled between personal visits.

"Was this a special invitation?" Chase wanted to know on cross-examination, referring to the Boston trip.

"No, I wanted to go on business, too."

"What was that business?"

"I wanted to see about getting a farm loan cheap."

"Cheap money in Boston?" Chase asked in some amazement.

The trip was not successful in this respect, but the two visitors accompanied Lotta to her summer cottage on the Hudson River, where, according to Ida May, they remained for a week and a half. The visit was productive. Ida May came away with $3,000 "to do with as I pleased." In 1905, Lotta had taken her on an extensive trip to the West Coast, Hardin accompanying them, along with the Blankenberg family doctor, who got off at Seattle to attend a medical convention.

"How much money did she give you that trip?" Chase inquired dryly.

"$5,000."

"Were you to buy land?"

"No, sir. She just gave it to me to do as I pleased with but gave me a little advice."

"She said buy land cheap and sell it dear?"

"No, sir. She said sell it at a reasonable profit. She said to keep it awhile and to buy in a good district, improve it, and it would be a nice way of making a good profit."

"You have never forgotten that wise advice?"

"No, I remember that particularly," Mrs. Blankenberg said cheerfully.

In the back of Chase's mind the thought kept coming forward that the sentiments attributed to Lotta were very close to the

truth. The Crabtree fortune had been built on just such investments.

Chase moved on to the question of the "lost" Bible, but
Weston Allen objected to calling it that. "Lost, strayed, or
stolen," Chase amended gently.

Mrs. Blankenberg laughingly declared that the Bible could not
have strayed because it lacked legs, whereupon Judge Prest, leaning over the bench toward the witness, suggested, "It might have
developed wings."

Jim Hoy, rising to interject a question of his own, suddenly
broke the mood of frivolity. "Did you buy the 'Hannibal' Bible
in a secondhand bookstore?" he asked bluntly.

The court was in an uproar as both Weston Allen and Spillers
jumped up shouting objections. Judge Prest overruled them, and
Ida May also leaped to her feet. For the first time, her composure
was shattered. "I'll vow to God I never entered a secondhand
bookstore to buy a secondhand Bible," she shouted over the noise
of counsel. "Excitement reached a high pitch," the *Boston American* reported later, but not all of Mrs. Blankenberg's perturbation was the result of Hoy's question. As she completed her testimony and stepped down, she saw staring at her from the front
row her brother Joseph. He had finally been induced to come
from Illinois as a surprise witness to testify against her. And not
for nothing were Joseph's middle names Abraham Lincoln.

6

⊙⊙⊙⊙

Contrary Evidence

FROM THE FIRST, Chase had operated on the assumption that if Ida May Blankenberg was an impostor, her deceit would be recognized most readily by a member of her own family. But there was a reason why exposing the claimant in this fashion might be difficult. Most of her brothers and sisters had nothing to gain by testifying against her, and quite possibly they had a great deal to lose. By the time the trial opened, the Pinkertons had unearthed information showing that Ida May Blankenberg was no ordinary farmer's daughter. People in Rock Island, in fact, might wish that she was not such "an interesting example of what can be accomplished by a woman in the business world," for Operative J.M.M. had ascertained that the claimant's final venture before leaving town had been to launch a highly speculative venture called the Lueagle Oil Company. Stock had been sold to local citizens and to all three of Ida May's brothers-in-law. All that was lacking was a well, and in 1922, Mrs. Blankenberg had gone west to drill one. So far as the stockholders knew, this had never been done, but some of them, at any rate, had stopped worrying when they heard that she claimed to be the daughter of Lotta Crabtree. A pipeline to a wealthy actress was as good as an oil well any time.

Even better, since, as time went on, the well stood less and less likelihood of getting drilled. Mrs. Blankenberg had run into trouble. Operative J.I.T., reporting from El Reno, Oklahoma, wrote that his quarry had arrived in nearby Hennessy some two years previously, where she had taken leases on about four thou' sand acres of farm land. Women wildcatters were not a very common sight in the oil fields, and at first there had been reluctance on the part of the farmers to take this fast-talking stranger seriously. She returned with a geologist from Ponca City, preliminary tests were made, and a drilling rig was brought in and set up on one of the farms. At that point, the money had run out, the farmers began clamoring for their lease payments, and Mrs. Blankenberg disappeared.

When she surfaced next, it was in Tulsa, where she had bought (on borrowed money) the erstwhile home of W. G. Skelly, president of the Skelly Oil Company—one way or another Ida May was determined to become an oil executive. This gambit, too, soon failed. Unable to meet the mortgage payments, she had lost the house, and the Blankenbergs now lived in modest circumstances in a nondescript section of town. A Tulsa source, interviewed by Operative J.I.T., described Ida May as "apparently a bootleg lease broker acting as a go-between in shady deals, or which were at least not desired to become public." Her credit rating was bad, but it had suddenly improved, in some quarters, with the news that she was contesting the Crabtree will.

Armed with this information about Ida May's brief and catastrophic career as a wildcatter, Chase hoped to discredit the testimony of those of her witnesses—and they were numerous—who had bought stock in the company. W. G. Brown, of Bloomfield, Iowa, Mrs. Blankenberg's brother-in-law, had been asked if the plaintiff betrayed any similarities common to other members of the Crabtree family; he assured the court that, indeed, she did not. "She was unlike them in every respect," Brown declared, in what was intended as a compliment. "In the first place, she was smarter . . ."

"How smart?" Chase inquired.

"She was a smart talker, smart as a tack."

"Smart as the sharp end of a tack?"

"Yes, sir."

"How much stock did you buy?"

"That's my business."

Joseph Crabtree, however, had not invested his savings in a nonexistent oil business. Perhaps he knew Ida May too well. Chase's visit to the Crabtree farm in March, during which Joseph Crabtree had produced the "big" Bible that contradicted Mrs. Blankenberg's story, promised the kind of proof he was looking for. The family records from the "big" Bible had been photographed, but this was not original evidence. The problem was to persuade Joseph to testify in person, bringing the Bible with him.

This was no easy task. By the middle of July, both Joseph and Edmund were busy harvesting the oat crop, and it was only through the most rigorous intercession of the Pinkertons' Chicago office that Joseph was induced to make the trip. He had seldom traveled anywhere, and was accompanied to Boston by agent E.J.C., who, upon their arrival, bought him a new suit of clothes and treated him to a hair cut, shave, and a "mustache trimming." Two Bibles—the "big" one and the Steckman—were carried in a small, banged-up valise which Joseph refused to let out of his sight. Thus, on the morning of July 14, all the living Crabtrees, with the single exception of brother Ed, were present in the courtroom. (Ed was "getting in the last of the oats.") For good measure, the Pinkerton agency had begun rounding up a pair of Steckmans, one of whom also bore the name of Lincoln.

The proceedings had now been going on for nearly two weeks. Even with the large windows open top and bottom, the courtroom was hot as Joseph Crabtree took the stand. A tall, gaunt man, somewhat uncomfortable in his new suit, he carried the satchel with him and, once seated, placed his soft brown hat on the shelf of the witness box where he could keep an eye on it. Speaking in what the *Boston Post* described as a "soft, Western drawl," Crabtree testified that when he was six years old, the family had moved from Crabtree Ford to Uncle John Steckman's farm, which his father had bought. It then consisted of twenty acres and was mortgaged. Now it belonged to Joseph and his brother Ed, consisted of one hundred and twenty acres, and was unmortgaged. "There was something of well-earned pride," Baldwin recalled, "in the way the witness straightened up, as though the day's plowing was done and he could notice the world again."

Joseph described the three family Bibles: the Steckman, which had been a wedding present to his mother from her family; the old Crabtree Bible which his father had owned and which had since disappeared; and the "big" Bible which had supplanted it about 1905. This lay on a table in the parlor, and Crabtree testified that he read it "sometimes three or four times a week." The Steckman and Crabtree family records had been copied into the "big" Bible by sister Ida, years before she had returned to Illinois and wheedled him out of the original. If this was true, then Mrs. Blankenberg had unwittingly preserved the evidence by which Chase hoped to refute her claim to having been born in England.

The immediate problem was to get this Bible offered as an exhibit. Joseph, who, on the whole, proved to be as stubborn as he was outspoken, refused to let it out of his hands. Weston Allen insisted. After all, the "Hannibal" Bible had been sur-rendered; the court had a right to this one. Crabtree could keep the Steckman version. There was, moreover, the matter of au-thenticity. Mrs. Blankenberg's lawyers wanted to have it ex-amined by handwriting experts. (The claimant denied that she had copied the entries, as Joseph insisted.) When the witness agreed to turn it over only if it remained in a bank vault over-night—the offer was made along with a suspicious glance at Ida May—Judge Prest readily assented. "I have more Bibles than I can use," he remarked.

Crabtree's testimony on direct examination was brief but damaging; he denied Lotta's visits to Uncle Jim Underwood's, denied that his sister had ever been given a horse. . . . Had he heard anyone sing "Hush, Little Baby, Don't You Cry"? Judge Chase inquired. He had. And who sang it?

"My mother used to sing it."

"To whom?"

"To my sister, Ida." Mrs. Blankenberg shook her head vigorously.

Suddenly, Chase noticed something different about her. He leaned over to Baldwin. "Look at the roots of her hair," he whispered. Baldwin did. The red was disappearing. When Joseph Crabtree stepped down, Chase lost no time in asking the claimant to take the stand again. "Mrs. Blankenberg," he said abruptly, "do you dye your hair?"

She looked at him sharply. For the second time, her poise weakened. She overcame a flash of anger, and then smiled. "Yes," she said at last. "I do."

Chase had another gambit. At his suggestion, General Edwards had assembled ten photographs of young women, all taken in the 1880s. One of these was an excellent likeness of Lotta, inscribed on the back in her own hand. The pictures were shown to Mrs. Blankenberg, face up. One by one she flipped through them— and Lotta went unrecognized. Ida May protested that the photograph was not a good likeness; how could she be sure of someone she hadn't seen for twenty years? But the damage had been done, and she left the stand obviously shaken. When court adjourned for lunch, her three older sisters came forward to speak to Joseph, who had retired to the front bench with his valise. "The meeting was not effusive," the *Boston Post* noted.

The three women were sworn in that afternoon. Although their testimony contained few surprises, the rustic embellishments with which they told their story gave it a crude ring of veracity. Could such doltish-looking people *not* tell the truth? "I was out in the barnyard piling up corncobs when I saw a lady carrying a baby up the path toward the house," declared Sarah Hobart, recalling her first glimpse of Lotta. The baby, of course, had turned out to be Ida. At fifty-two, Mrs. Hobart had borne sixteen children of her own. Weston Allen's strategy was to elicit from the witness the fact that the substituted baby had at first been called "Ida M," the "May" having been added later. Mrs. Hobart made quite a point of this. Chase waived cross-examination, and Allen called up Elizabeth Brown, a hefty, gray-haired woman who boasted of having thirteen children and a good memory, especially of Ida's arrival. "We've got a sweet little girl," her mother had told her. "It's not your sister, but you'll have to call her sister." Mrs. Margaret Anson, the third witness, and by all odds the largest, had been "working out" when Ida arrived, but she remembered that the child had been brought to the house where she was living on the Fourth of July, the year before Margaret was married. *That* marriage hadn't lasted; "I just got up and left him—I don't know why," she said nostalgically. She hadn't seen much of her sister after that until the oil company had been formed.

Allen called Joseph Crabtree back to the stand the following morning. Joseph's previous appearance had received a "good press," and an even better show seemed likely with the witness under cross-examination. For a brief time, there was some doubt as to whether he would comply; impatient to get back to his crops, he had threatened to take his Bibles and go home, thus removing essential evidence from the jurisdiction of the court. The crisis was averted by a telegram from a Pinkerton man who was standing by in Illinois. "Ed Crabtree states oats all in; he does not require help," the message assured the court. But the Pinkertons had made doubly sure of the farmer's continued presence in Boston by entertaining him the previous afternoon and evening: a trip to Bunker Hill, another to Revere Beach, and a movie at night.

Early on the morning of the seventeenth, agent J.O.C. met the witness at his hotel, accompanied him to the bank to get the master Bibles, and brought him to the courthouse. None of this solicitude had mellowed Joseph's attitude toward Boston, nor, for that matter, toward the halls of justice to which he had been ceremoniously escorted. "When the next earthquake comes," he began, ignoring Weston Allen's opening question, "I hope it utterly destroys this courthouse with its noise from automobiles and its gasoline fumes." Judge Prest admonished him not to make statements.

"When you speak of your brother, Ed," Allen resumed, "what is his name—Edward or Edmund?"

"I don't know," answered Crabtree.

"When you become loquacious, what do you call him?"

"When I get what?" asked the witness severely.

"When you talk dignified," Allen said. "What do you call him in that case?"

"Ed," Joseph replied.

"I don't think the witness could be called loquacious," Judge Prest put in. Weston Allen's question had not been irrelevant. If Joseph Crabtree didn't know the full name of his brother, with whom he lived and worked, how could he testify accurately about the correct names of a sister who was not half so close? Allen made a point of Joseph's admission that he had refused Ida Blankenberg a loan of $20; but the witness, pressed as to whether he was fonder of one sister than of the others, turned to Judge Prest.

"I don't see the necessity for such foolish questions," he objected.

Allen bore in, demanding that Crabtree compare the entries in the "big" and Steckman Bibles. After some prodding, the witness opened the valise. It had been the Estate's contention all along, and in his original testimony Joseph had maintained, that the entries on the left-hand side of the "big" Bible had been "drawn off" the family original, whereas those on the right side had come from the Steckman Bible. But now it appeared, under Allen's probing, that there were discrepancies in the consolidated entries which concerned places of birth. Allen made the most of these and Crabtree was forced to modify his testimony, a mildly damaging reversal.

Joseph Crabtree was to provide one final peep into the family history. A ferry boat, running from Drury Landing, Illinois, to

Muscatine, Iowa, was called the "Ida May." Joseph had been eight years old at the time, and he remembered his sister's birth very well, because naming her after the ferry had entitled the whole family to ride free for a year. During that glorious time, Ida had served as a ticket to Iowa. Mrs. Blankenberg frowned; brother Joseph stretched out his hand, pointed his finger at her, and smiled. Allen excused the witness and court was adjourned for the weekend.

Mr. Charles Wolters was a soft-spoken man in his late fifties whose uncle had owned the theater in Rochester, New York, where Lotta had appeared on December 25, 1877—the date on which she was supposed to have married George Manning. Wolters remembered the occasion because special trains had brought people in from the surrounding towns to see the show— *Musette* on the twenty-fourth, and *Zip* on Christmas. General Edwards had already appeared as a witness some days earlier, armed with playbills and programs covering Lotta's 1877-78 season, but it had been Weston Allen's contention that this proved nothing. Had anyone actually *seen* Lotta at this time? The assiduous Pinkertons had located Wolters, but he had been a child in 1877, had never seen Lotta afterward, and could not swear that the woman in *Musette* was really the actress.

Establishing, through an eyewitness, that Lotta had actually been in the country at this time proved difficult. Later in the trial, Chase was to produce a seventy-five-year-old member of the old Boston Museum stock company, George W. Wilson, who had played with Lotta in Boston in the late spring of 1878, and who entertained the courtroom with an account of his performance in *Zip,* during which he had accidentally nicked Lotta with a knife. Mary Ann had sailed into him after the show, but Lotta had come to his rescue, even though she had had to play the remainder of her Boston engagement wearing a bandage.

One thing Lotta had not been packing around with her at the time, Wilson assured the court, was a baby. This was vital testimony, because Chase was trying to offset the statement of an elderly stage doorman who had unexpectedly turned up as a witness for Mrs. Blankenberg. John W. Blaufelt, the doorman, had known Lotta when she had played in Springfield, Massachusetts, in the early '70s. Years later, on a snowy night in the winter of 1878, she had come to the stage door with a baby in her arms. "You remember me, John, I'm Lotta Crabtree. This is my little baby, Idy-girl. Her father, George Manning, deserted me and I am taking her out to live with cousins of mine in the West."

Blaufelt appeared not only to have read the facsimile from the "Hannibal" Bible, but virtually to have memorized it. Chase tried repeatedly to break down his story, but without success. The old man told it over and over, occasionally adding some new bit of information about the theater, or about other incidents in his own life. Finally, Chase leaned over to Baldwin. "The trouble with this witness is that he's read the papers and confused what he's read with something he remembers. It's an illusion, but he believes it." Whereupon he stopped his cross-examination. Jim Hoy didn't even try.

As the proceedings continued, witnesses for the plaintiff became more plentiful than even Mrs. Blankenberg could have anticipated. There was Timothy Manning, of Troy, New York, who informed her, by letter, that he was a cousin of "Frederick George Percy Manning," the man whom Lotta married. This was welcome news, indeed. Manning was rushed to Boston. Weston Allen was even more pleased to find that the witness, who had emigrated from England as a young man, spoke with a Lancashire accent, which held up somewhat better under cross-examination than the testimony. Lotta had come to his home in Troy in search of news of her missing husband, a "clog dancer." When she was told that George had died, Lotta wept, confiding to the witness that a child born to them was now being raised in Iowa. Manning placed this visit in 1902, but after he had left the stand, attorney Thomas Barry, one of Mrs. Blankenberg's second-string counsel, rose to inform the court, somewhat more humbly than usual, that the witness wanted to make "a slight correction." Manning thereupon revised the date to 1892, no doubt after it had been pointed out to him that the "child," in 1902, would have been twenty-four years old. "You call that a slight correction?" asked Judge Prest.

Undaunted, if not entirely unembarrassed, Weston Allen produced two more witnesses. Mrs. Helen Hartford, who had long ago worked as a chambermaid at the Brewster, had no trouble remembering dates. It was in 1908 or 1909, she testified confidently, that she saw Lotta throw her arms around a young woman, kiss her, and call her "daughter." Could she identify this woman? "There she is sitting right there," Mrs. Hartford declared, pointing at the claimant. This sent "an electric thrill through the courtroom," the *Boston American* reported. Mrs. Blankenberg obliged the gallery by standing up and smiling.

Barry concluded the plaintiff's case by calling a thickset, silver-haired man in his fifties named George Dietz. A painter, Dietz had been decorating the Ladies' Parlor at the Brewster when he had overheard an argument between Lotta and her brother, Jack. Lotta was being difficult about money, and Jack threatened to "expose" her as the mother of a child. The painter recalled that he had pursued the subject of Lotta's child on a later occasion during a conversation with Jack.

On a hunch, Chase asked him where this conversation had taken place. "At a restaurant called Charlie Wirth's," the witness replied, somewhat reluctantly.

This had been a shrewd thrust on Chase's part; conversations at Charlie Wirth's were likely to be well lubricated. "How many beers did you have?" he asked blandly.

"I object, your Honor," Dietz remonstrated angrily.

"You refuse to tell how many beers you had?"

"I was never drunk in my life," the witness protested.

After defending his sobriety at some length, Dietz stepped down. Chase's strategy had worked; the thread of the original testimony had all but disappeared. Dietz's honor was intact. And so, Judge Chase hoped, was Lotta's.

He produced two final witnesses, the Steckman brothers from Muscatine, Iowa. Like their cousin Joseph, they had been escorted east by a Pinkerton man, outfitted with clothes suitable for the occasion, and shown the sights of Boston. Lincoln Steckman—like Joseph, he had been named for the president—testified first. And like Joseph he punctured Mrs. Blankenberg's claim to have been substituted, as an infant, for a baby who had died. But it was David Steckman who revealed the origins of Ida May's story. There *had* been another infant named Ida May, he said, but she was a Steckman, not a Crabtree. The baby had lived six months, and during this time the Steckman family had also ridden the ferry free of charge.

Chase saw the "Hannibal" Bible—Exhibit A—as the denouement to the drama. He had no doubt that it was a forgery; a clever forgery, but one which could be exposed. What were experts for? He would show that the long entry pertaining to Ida May's birth was not in Lotta's handwriting (as Mrs. Blankenberg suggested) and that it had been doctored to give the appearance of age.

On July 23, Jim Hoy—Chase's colleague in this effort—produced his expert, William Hingston, the "examiner of documents, handwriting, and ink." Hingston compared the "Crabtree Chateau" passage with specimens of Lotta's writing and found it completely dissimilar. Weston Allen was unfazed: he reminded the court that it was Chase who had offered the Bible in evidence. (Actually, Allen had maneuvered the defense into submitting the Bible by refusing to do so himself. He did not want to offer it as an authentic document; aware that he was playing with fire, he did not intend to get burned if he could help it. So in order to challenge it, Chase had to submit the Bible as evidence.) After several objections on Allen's part, Hingston was allowed to testify as to the ink itself. In his opinion, he stated solemnly, it was of recent origin and had been treated with acid to make it appear old.

He was followed by Prof. Augustus H. Gill of the Massachusetts Institute of Technology. Gill was a replacement for Joseph Wilbur, who had gotten off to a shaky start in the preliminary Bible examination by putting himself on the wrong side of the case. Hoy took over direct questioning.

HOY: Have you an opinion as to whether or not it [the ink] is of recent origin?

GILL: I would like to refresh my examination and opinion by a rather cursory examination again but I have an opinion.

HOY: What is your opinion?

GILL: That it is of recent origin.

The professor based his statement partly on the fact that the "blue" in the ink when he first examined the document on July 6 had disappeared. Moreover, the "halo," which had been transparent at that time, was now opaque. Gill thought that both of these changes could be explained by the use of an alkali, such as caustic soda or potash, to artificially age the ink. To prove his point, he offered to submit the writing to an alkali test.

But Allen was not to let him carry out the experiment without challenging his competency. He produced a document purporting to date from 1778—the "Valley Forge Paper" signed by George Washington. Gill had no hesitancy in declaring that it had been written in iron gall ink, on "very old" paper.

ALLEN: What makes you think it is iron gall ink?

GILL: From the fact that it is so old that it shows evidence of iron rust in the ink.

It was with considerable glee that Allen promptly announced to the courtroom that the document in question had been recently purchased from Goodspeed's Book Store—a lithographed copy of the original. Although this setback disturbed the Crabtree Estate forces, it seems not to have bothered Gill, who went on insisting that the Bible was doctored. A chemical test would prove it. He had come into court with a testing kit, which was now handed up to him. As the apparatus was set up on the witness stand, Hingston and Allen's expert, a man named Schmitt, were permitted to observe the experiment at close range. Judge Prest, dropping his sphinxlike demeanor for the occasion, looked down from the bench with some fascination while attorneys crowded around the witness stand. Mrs. Blankenberg moved into the bar enclosure, where she watched the proceedings unperturbed. "The courtroom resembled a classroom in some chemical laboratory," the *Boston Post* commented.

The climactic moment had arrived. Gill took a scraping of ink from the flyleaf and dropped it in a test tube half filled with a chemical solution. He looked up, announcing that when another chemical was added, the entire solution would turn purple. An alkali would be precipitated, thus demonstrating that the ink had been artificially treated.

But to the professor's chagrin, Allen's delight, and Chase's dismay, nothing happened. The solution did not change color. As one observer noted, "It was Gill who turned purple." Mrs. Blankenberg nodded smugly as the witness packed his kit and hurriedly stepped down. For all that Gill had been able to prove, the Bible was as old as Ida May said it was.

Weston Allen was quick to seize the initiative by placing his own expert on the stand. A rigorous outdoor man in his early sixties, Charles A. Schmitt worked for the Carter Ink Company and lived in a camp near Reading, Massachusetts. His testimony was not surprising. After a lengthy dissertation on the different classes of ink, and on iron gall ink in particular, he was asked about the writing in the Bible. Allen's purpose was to show that it would be impossible to "date" the entry, as Gill had tried to do.

ALLEN: Is it possible, Mr. Schmitt, to state positively how long that ink has been upon that paper?

SCHMITT: No.

ALLEN: In your thirty-odd years of experience, do you know of any test, chemical or otherwise, which will definitely show how long ago that was written?

SCHMITT: No.

Under prodding from Judge Prest, the witness explained, however, that "it might be over ten years old; it looks old."

ALLEN: Is it conclusively shown now that there is iron in the ink?

SCHMITT: That is my opinion, yes.

Schmitt went further; he noted that the ink had not only gone through the flyleaf to the back of the page and impressed itself on the title page, but that it had gone through the title page, too. He deduced from this that the ink had been there a long time and that the Bible had been kept closed. Taken for what it was worth, the testimony apparently cleared Ida May of the charge of "doctoring" and implied that the record of her birth had been entered long before Mrs. Blankenberg could have known about Lotta's death. This was everything that Allen had hoped to get across, perhaps more for his own sake than his client's.

In a new burst of confidence, he loosed one more "surprise" witness before the trial ended. On July 29, a member of his staff turned up a nurse who had attended William Morse at his home in West Roxbury in 1923. Mrs. Cora Lane was obliging beyond all expectations. Taking the stand the next day, she testified to having seen Lotta Crabtree on two occasions, once when she had accompanied Morse to the Brewster Hotel. "I just received two letters from my little girl, Ida. I want you to read them," Lotta was overheard to tell Morse at the time. The lawyer had taken the letters with him. "This is strange," the witness quoted him as saying to her that night. "The writer of this letter is the daughter of Lotta Crabtree, but she doesn't know it." The name on the back of the envelope? "Ida Blankenberg."

With this, Allen concluded his case. Chase began his final argument at 11:15 on the morning of July 30, 1925. Speaking for an hour to a courtroom packed with spectators, many of whom had not missed a day since the trial had started, he impressed his listeners with the sympathy he showed for Ida May Blankenberg while, at the same time, denouncing her as a fraud. Chase pictured her as an ambitious woman who dreamed of great wealth.

"She believed she could do better than the simple man she married," he declared ruefully. "She went into business and prospered, but her ambition was not satisfied. She organized an oil company. The scheme failed. She became involved, receivers were appointed, suits were started. She was in danger of being evicted from her house."

Then, late in September, 1924, came word of the death of Lotta, a woman who, by coincidence, bore Ida Blankenberg's maiden name. Out of this a fantasy was born. The two-room cabin at Crabtree Ford became an English chateau. There were white dresses and lullabies, horses, schools, trips west, gifts, money—all the things that had been lacking in Ida May's struggling childhood. Now she was a middle-aged grandmother whose dreams had failed, but an impostor none the less. If there was any gall involved, it was not in the ink used in the Bible inscription, but in the claimant herself. "I shall ask your Honor to find," Chase told the court, "that Lotta Crabtree died as much a virgin as when she was born, . . . that Ida M. Blankenberg never had Lotta Crabtree for her mother." Brushing drops of perspiration from his mustache, he sat down.

There was silence in the courtroom, then a shuffling of papers as Weston Allen stood up. His was not an easy task; his client, nominally the plaintiff, had been maneuvered uncomfortably into the role of defendant. But the case was one of mystery, not fraud, he asserted. Seven persons had come forward to swear that Lotta had told them of the birth of the child, and two others had testified that Jack Crabtree said his sister was married. "Are all these witnesses of broken memory?" he asked, avoiding the question of perjury. Moreover, there was the Bible. Not even the experts for the Estate had been able to show that it was not genuine.

Allen made the best of a bad situation. Ida May's brother Joseph and the Steckmans had been too convincing. Her own exuberant witnesses were either stockholders in the ill-fated oil venture or people of dubious reputation. When court adjourned for lunch, Allen sensed that the gamble had failed. Mrs. Blankenberg was more sanguine.

Throughout the proceedings, with few exceptions, Judge Prest had displayed his poker-faced neutrality; if he had been entertained by the parades of farmers and their wives, by the versatile Ida May, the "eyewitnesses" and old actors, he had kept his amusement to himself. The scathing language in which he delivered his decision when court resumed that afternoon came as a surprise. "His words had the sound of the last judgment," Baldwin noted.

Although he did not pronounce an opinion as to Lotta's virginity (as Judge Chase had requested), he did declare Mrs. Blankenberg to be a "brazen adventuress," as well as a "corrupter of witnesses." "The case is pock-marked with fraud," he added. "The spots of fraud are as thick and as plainly visible as the spots on the flyleaf of the Bible. . . ." Judge Prest not only denied Ida May the right to contest the will, but ordered her to be held in contempt of court for perjury.

The courtroom sat in shocked silence. Mrs. Blankenberg started to rise, fell forward, and was caught by a young woman reporter sitting nearby. She had fainted—or so it appeared. Attendants helped her stretch out on a bench. As the courtroom was being cleared, Weston Allen rushed forward with unseemly haste to inform Judge Prest that he was withdrawing from the case. After all, a lawyer has his reputation to consider.

Mrs. Blankenberg was revived and taken to the matron's room, where she remained until bail was secured for her release. In a long statement to the press later on, she insisted on her innocence, resigned herself to a jail sentence, and expressed sympathy for John William, who had also been ordered to appear in court the following week. But he had long since departed for Iowa, and no attempt was made to extradite him. As for brother Joseph, Mrs. Blankenberg had no comment whatever.

The contempt hearings opened on August 10. Judge Prest, having received a number of anonymous letters threatening bodily harm, closed the court to all but the press and legal counsel. Mrs. Blankenberg sat alone on the front bench, a bottle of smelling salts in one hand and a glass of water in the other. All five of her attorneys had deserted her, and she was now represented by W. Jennings Patron, who took on the thankless task of trying to keep his client out of jail. He did not succeed. Ida May Blankenberg drew a sentence of six months. After losing an appeal, she served four months in the Charles Street Jail and was then released for reasons of ill health. She returned to Tulsa and lived there until her death in 1966, at the age of eighty-eight. Her husband, Gustav, died in 1962, at ninety-one. Shunning publicity, Ida May led an exemplary life as head of the Lueagle Oil Company—so exemplary that many Tulsans wondered if she had not been telling the truth after all. She insisted to the end that she was Lotta Crabtree's daughter. Chase himself remained puzzled by one aspect of the case: if the handwritten entry in the "Hannibal" Bible was not of recent origin, if Ida May hadn't doctored the Bible—and Professor Schmitt had seemingly demonstrated, with Gill's unwitting help, that the ink was genuinely old—then who had?

Grover Cleveland Spillers, Mrs. Blankenberg's Tulsa attorney, is still living, although retired from active practice. Spillers went on to try some of the most important cases in Oklahoma, but it is the Crabtree case that he likes to remember—and with good reason: it almost left him rich. As matters turned out, however, Spillers collected no fee at all.

If Ida May Blankenberg was an impostor, she was one of the boldest in the annals of American trial law. More than this, her performance paralleled the stage folklore that Lotta herself had made popular. The outlines of her own story closely resembled an early Lotta success, *Hearts Ease; or What's Money Without.* In this play a small girl, born of wealth in England, is taken to the California gold fields and abandoned by an adventurous father, only to discover her rightful identity several years later. Ida

May's version of the drama was a case of nature imitating art, with one or two notable differences. In *her* melodramas, Lotta interrupted the inevitable climb toward wealth and position with gunplay, dancing, singing, and above all, a solo performance on the banjo. But in the end she got the money, and this is what mattered. Lotta's plays were essentially materialistic in spirit. Mrs. Blankenberg, too, had cast herself in the role of the abandoned child; she wrote her own play, with real-life characters, hoping for a happy ending. Indeed, she had done very little that May Wylderose, in *Hearts Ease,* had not done in claiming her inheritance—except tell the truth.

It remained for the *Boston Post* to inquire, editorially, why the court proceedings had been allowed to continue beyond the first week in view of the "gross, clumsy, totally unconvincing lying . . . in the effort to wrest millions from the fine charities to which Lotta's will destined them." Legally, of course, Judge Prest had had no choice. A charitable view might be that Ida May was led on by her own attorneys. In any case, the "fine charities" were still a long way from getting their money, for the second act of "Getting Lotta's Loot," as Boston newspapers termed the affair, was yet to be played. The way had simply been cleared for Hoy and Whipple to try their hand at breaking the will.

On August 19, 1925, not long after Mrs. Blankenberg's contempt hearing, an important break developed in the Cockburn case. Throughout the summer, the Los Angeles office of the Pinkerton agency had combed the area for traces of the redoubtable Kate Taylor, Jack Crabtree's Tombstone acquaintance and proprietor of the San Jose House. Now, word was received that she had been discovered in Glendale, a Los Angeles suburb, where she was known as Mrs. Logie.

"Her house was located at 114 North Everett Street," Operative E.L.B. reported, in cipher, to Boston. "It is a small bungalow of five rooms and the outside is covered with vines." Conveniently, a "Room for Rent" sign in the window gave the operative an excuse to call. She later reported: "Age about sixty years [a bad guess; Mrs. Logie would have had to be nearer seventy], height 5′10″, brunette, heavy build, weight 175-180 pounds; wears false hair of chestnut brown and switches; wears silver-rimmed glasses and false teeth; has all the appearance of a broken-down sport." Kate Logie, it was also learned, taught a women's Bible class in the Methodist church a few blocks from her home.

"Endeavor secure room residence Mrs. Samantha or Kate Logie," Boston wired back. "Cultivate acquaintance."

Thus, on August 21, Operative E.L.B., a young woman trained in the art of investigation, and ordinarily employed by suspicious wives, moved in with Mrs. Logie, bringing her husband, Operative A.X. It was a challenging assignment. In the month that followed, she was to learn a good deal about Tombstone, Arizona, in 1880 that would be useful in *Cockburn vs. Crabtree*.

Book Two

BANJO ON MY KNEE

1

"Brave Wickedness and Splendid Folly"

MARY ANN LIVESEY was still in her teens when she left Cheshire, England, for New York with her mother, three sisters, and a younger brother in the 1830s. Of solid, middle-class stock and an adventurous turn of mind, the Liveseys had originally planned to seek their fortune in India. A few years before, Samuel Livesey, Mary Ann's father, and three of his four sons had set sail for the colony that was then becoming the diadem of the Empire; once settled, he would send for the others. But on the voyage out, their ship sank and with it all the Liveseys on board. The surviving family found itself overwhelmingly female and unexpectedly without support.

The Liveseys were not the kind of people whose women were accustomed to "working out." Mrs. Samuel Livesey could sew, but in England to become a seamstress was a step down. In America, it promised to be a step up. In a move almost as daring as her late husband's, the widow used her savings to buy passage to New York. She was no ordinary seamstress in any case, preferring upholstery to dressmaking. A business in slip covers, and the satin and velvet upholstery that was demanded by the "carriage trade," was set up in the living room of rented quarters in lower Manhattan. Mother Livesey lost no time in teaching her daughters the trade, and at seventeen, Mary Ann, one of twins, was fitting brocade on the rosewood chairs and Biedermeier settees that supplied the cachet of aristocratic living, if not always comfort, in the big houses uptown.

At nineteen, she met a bookseller on Nassau Street named John Ashworth Crabtree, a fellow immigrant from England. How he had wandered into the book business was unexplained; he did not read books and knew little about them. He drank more than was good for him, dressed elegantly, and barely scraped out a living: Crabtree's bookstore was more likely to be closed than open, while its owner tended to other matters in the nearby saloons. Nevertheless, in 1844, Mary Ann finally married him. A small woman—erect, red-haired, industrious, prematurely matriarchal—she was getting to an age when a husband was a necessity, and John Ashworth Crabtree had a certain undeniable charm.

The couple set up housekeeping, and to her husband's small earnings Mary Ann, still an upholsterer, added her own. One surmises that in this respect, John Crabtree got the better of the bargain; the added income made him somewhat lazier than usual. Mary Ann must have hoped that a family would spur him to better things, or at least settle him down—perhaps both. A daughter, Harriet, was born in 1846, but died almost at once. Lotta, named after her Aunt Charlotte, followed on November 7, 1847. But John Crabtree grew increasingly restless.

When gold was discovered in California, in 1848, he experienced the first of several urges to go west. The following year, letters from Forty-niners, trickling back east, were beginning to appear in the New York newspapers. "We are on the brink of an Age of Gold!" exclaimed Horace Greeley in the *Tribune,* whose office was just around the corner from the Crabtree bookshop. Everybody seemed to have struck it rich, or was about to.

Crabtree held out until 1851, then sold his bookstore, and made the trip without his family. Mary Ann had been skeptical from the first; although her husband's early letters were optimistic, even to the point of braggadocio, as he moved from Sacramento into the mountains, they arrived with less frequency and finally stopped. The silence was its own message. "Nothing would do but Crabtree must leave New York and dig gold in

California," Mary Ann wrote later, adding, "He never got any."

He would never be John after that, but simply and patronizingly "Crabtree." Then, in the spring of 1852, another letter came. They were to join him in San Francisco, although no money was included with which to make the trip—a characteristic omission. It was not an easy decision for Mary Ann to make. She would be traveling alone with a young child, and with no certainty that Crabtree could support them when they arrived. Mother Livesey was not happy to lose a daughter, who was also one of her best workers, but she thought that Mary Ann would do well to join Crabtree before misfortune overtook him, since fortune itself did not seem to be so inclined. Mary Ann was five months making up her mind. Once decided, she determined to go west by the fastest possible means, before Crabtree changed his.

California-bound pioneers in those days had a choice of three routes. They could go by wagon train, which took upwards of five months and involved the risk of attacks by Indians; they could sail by clipper around Cape Horn, a tediously confining trip of about a hundred days; or they could elect the Panama route. This last was the quickest, and although there were serious disadvantages, Mary Ann elected to take it. Debarking at what is now Colón, her party proceeded for twenty-three miles to Barbacoas on the uncompleted transisthmian railroad. The fare was fifty cents a mile, the highest known rate of any railroad before or since. From Barbacoas, the journey continued up the Chagres River to Gorgona in a dugout canoe propelled by Indian boys and roofed over with palm leaves to ward off the equatorial sun and tropical rain. This leg of the trip, however, was relatively comfortable compared to the final thirteen miles, over which Mary Ann and Lotta jogged by muleback to Panama City. The trail wound through some of the worst ravines and jungles in Panama and was marked chiefly by the graves of earlier travelers who had died of fever.

There was a premonition of survival, if not success, in having gotten this far safely. The voyage to San Francisco, on board the steam packet *Oregon,* was luxury, even though passengers were stuffed six to a cabin. Not all of the women, like Mary Ann, were making the trip to join their husbands, and not all of the men, who made up most of the ship's passenger list, were journeying to the gold fields to dig for gold. There were easier ways of getting it.

Crabtree was not on hand to meet Mary Ann and Lotta when the *Oregon* docked; indeed, it soon became apparent that he was not even in San Francisco. In a sense, this might have been to his credit; knowing the man's weaknesses, one would like to think so. An inordinate number of the city's 40,000 people consisted of saloon keepers, gamblers, gold speculators, miners in from the camps on a spree, Chilean prostitutes, gangs of Australian criminals known as the Sydney Ducks, Chinese opium peddlers, fugitives from justice, adventurers, and sailors who had jumped ship. An unofficial census that year turned up 743 bartenders, or approximately one for every fifty-three inhabitants, whereas ministers in the city totaled twenty-one.

Describing the San Francisco of 1853, the city's leading newspaper editor, Frank Soulé, could deplore the inhabitants' way of life while recalling, a trifle nostalgically, a time when it had been even worse. "There was still the old reckless energy," he wrote, "the old love of pleasure, the fast making and fast spending of money, the old hard labor and wild delights, jobberies and official and political corruption, thefts, robberies and violent assaults, murders, duels and suicides, gambling, drinking and general extravagance and dissipation. . . . Yet somehow the oldest residenters and the very family men loved the place, with all its brave wickedness and splendid folly."

Not a small part of the gunplay involved newspaper editors. The shortage of women—or at least the shortage of the kind that demanded an apology when insulted—meant that affairs of honor were usually limited to such civic outrages as political bribery, speculation, and trickery at the ballot box. An affronted politician would be less likely to sue for libel, or write a blistering letter, than to issue a challenge to a duel, and by 1853 such invitations had reached an all-time high. Duels were the polite way of settling a dispute, and to most of the inhabitants far preferable to the more customary practice of murder. Upwards of 300 killings a year were being recorded by the time Lotta and Mary Ann arrived, and by 1855 the figure was to reach 487. Moreover, gunplay in the theaters of San Francisco did not—as was customarily the case elsewhere—always take place on the stage. In his book, *Annals of San Francisco,* Editor Soulé reported a shooting assault at the corner of Clay and Montgomery Streets by a theatrical manager named H. L. Bateman. "A large crowd gathered at the spot, and the excitement was intense," wrote Soulé, and he was in a good position to know; Soulé himself was the target.

The incident exposed two unique features of local life which could hardly have escaped Mary Ann Crabtree: the cavalier and generally pardonable use of firearms (Bateman was let off with a fine of $300 by a sympathetic judge who remarked that the assailant had had ample provocation for his act), and the almost holy regard in which citizens held child actors, since indirectly at least this is what the shooting had been all about. Bateman, an energetic and hot-tempered man, and a fixture in the theatrical life of the United States and England for several decades, had arrived in San Francisco with his wife Sidney, a playwright, and his two daughters Kate and Ellen, eleven and nine years old respectively. These young girls were already celebrated in the East, where their debut had occurred five years before, with Kate (then six) playing Portia to Ellen's four-year-old Shylock. In 1851, Barnum took them on a tour of Europe, and by the time they came west, their repertory had been enlarged to include scenes from *Hamlet* and *Richard III.* Papa Bateman was understandably proud of his performing offspring, and just as touchy about his given name, which was Hezekiah Linthicum. A slighting reference to either his children or his name might provoke retaliation. (Bateman signed himself either "H. L." or "Henry.") Earlier that year, he had announced a contest for the best play suitable for his daughters, with the stipulation that it be written by a local author. The prize was to be $1,000. Although some twenty plays were submitted, Mrs. Bateman won the prize. There was understandable grumbling on the part of the losers, and when Soulé exposed the source of her play as a novel entitled *All's Not Gold that Glitters, or, The Young Californian,* by someone who called herself "Cousin Alice," the public, too, became indignant. (Mrs. Bateman had appropriated the story, but changed the title, rather fittingly, to *A Mother's Trust.*) Editor Soulé's comments on the matter had been scathing; what saved him was Hezekiah Linthicum Bateman's poor aim.

The Bateman fracas was not, strictly speaking, an affair of honor. There had been no challenge, and Soulé, although armed (most men in San Francisco carried revolvers, editors especially), had not fired back. The incident must have drawn Mary Ann's attention to the excitement that swirled around the theater. She and Lotta had stayed briefly with some English friends living near the Presidio; Crabtree still had not put in an appearance, and early in 1853 she rented a small house on Telegraph Hill. As matters turned out, this period was to provide valuable working capital for the future—the house was in the midst of a small colony of actors which included Junius Booth, Jr.; Dr. David "Yankee" Robinson, a New England physician turned showman; and the prolific Chapman family, but recently arrived in San Francisco after years on a Mississippi River showboat.

But it was the Robinsons whom Mary Ann came to know best. They had landed in San Francisco on the first day of January, 1847, after a tour of the East in Robinson's play, *The Reformed Drunkard*. The erstwhile doctor opened a small "Dramatic Museum" on Portsmouth Square. A tall, angular man with hawklike eyes and an acid wit, he wrote the skits, composed the songs, and acted many of the parts; frequently, he delivered a temperance lecture between the acts, and it is said that he created the door prize—an oil painting of an Italian landscape. When he decided to run for alderman in 1850, his campaign was conducted almost entirely from the stage of his Dramatic Museum, where he produced a series of satires on the incumbent city fathers. Robinson played all the parts himself, and with such success that he was easily elected to office.

From Mary Ann's point of view, however, "Yankee" Robinson was interesting mainly because he managed a child actress named Sue Robinson; managed her, moreover, with great success—the doctor and his wife swung through the mining towns once or twice a year with Sue as the leading attraction. Despite her name, she was not related to them. Under Robinson's tutelage, Sue had become the pre-eminent "Fairy Star" of the Gold Coast, where, in the smaller camps, the very presence of a child was cause for wonder, and where a child who could sing, dance, or recite might be a better investment than the average claimstake.

To what extent Mary Ann had already begun planning Lotta's career is a matter of speculation. We do know that after Crabtree had been located and mother and daughter had joined him in Grass Valley, Lotta was promptly enrolled in a dancing class, conducted in the annex of a tavern. We also know that Mary Ann had a shrewd sense of opportunity. The theater was hospitable to anyone who was ambitious, willing to endure its lunatic ways, and energetic enough to build a personal following; one need not be a Catherine Sinclair, a Matilda Heron, a James Stark, a Laura Keene, or an Alexina Baker, all of whom had achieved fame in the East before setting out for California. One could simply be a Chapman and dig in with the natives. The Chapmans were friendly with Dr. Robinson, and through his wife, Mary Ann knew them on Telegraph Hill.

Like herself, the older Chapmans were English-born, having come to the United States from London, where the patriarch of the tribe, William, had managed the Royal Opera House at Covent Garden for thirty years. In 1827, William packed his wife, three sons, and two daughters off to Ohio, where he converted a small side-wheeler into a showboat. He was thus able to combine his two passions in life, acting and fishing. From 1830 until 1840, "Chapman's Floating Palace," the first showboat on record, plied up and down the Mississippi, entertaining the river towns with everything from bumptious low comedy to Shakespeare. A large family was born; George Chapman, one of William's sons, married Mary Parker, a member of the cast, who, during her ensuing career, gave birth to twenty children. (She was to survive all but three of them.) Many of these were born on "Chapman's Floating Palace," and with their help the family became numerous enough to cast even the fullest Shakespearean tragedy. In 1840, the elder Chapman died, "having caught his last fish and acted his final part," as one account described his departure, and the family scattered. It was said that they smelled of fish for years after they left the showboat. Following a series of ups and downs in the East, they began drifting into San Francisco in the early 1850s.

It was William, Jr.—"Uncle Billy," as he was invariably called—and his sister Caroline who took up residence on Telegraph Hill. By 1853, when the Crabtrees had settled nearby, they had established a unique place for themselves, and Mary Ann could only regard with awe the speed with which the Chapmans had catapulted themselves into local prominence.

During the previous winter, Caroline, Uncle Billy, and a host of lesser Chapmans had made a tour of the mining towns with a repertory devoted largely to Shakespeare and Goldsmith. They were paid in coins and one of Uncle Billy's proudest boasts, when the family returned to San Francisco with the proceeds of the tour, was that a silver shortage had been created in the region that lasted until spring.

The success of the Chapmans gave them no off-stage airs, as was the case with many actors, and the Uncle Billy that Mary Ann Crabtree knew was an eccentric little man—he actually got smaller as he grew older, and was said to have shrunk four inches by the time of his death three years later—who rode down Telegraph Hill in a two-wheeled cart pulled by a mule. He preferred this to a horse owned by the whole colony. The horse was encouraged to drink champagne from a silver basket and often as not would carry his rider in the wrong direction, to North Beach. Uncle Billy was a master of low comedy who often preceded the show with a patter of songs, conundrums, and recitations; and Caroline, who could dance and play the hand organ, did not consider the evening a success until she had the audience standing in the aisles singing with her. In the summer of 1853, she was the rage of the city with her "Sweep Song," which had been injected into one of those extravaganzas that San Franciscans loved, *Taming a Tartar*. The lesson for Mary Ann, however, was not the artistry of the performance but the rewards that followed. As Caroline played the hand organ, quarters began to rain on the stage from the audience; dodging the shower, the little tambourine girl in the play dashed about picking them up—the perquisites of the child actor.

Part of the charm of San Francisco was its freewheeling and improvising spirit, an *élan* which overtook the stage as it infected everything else, and we may assume that Mary Ann, during the months that she and Lotta lived there the first time, appreciated its immense possibilities. In one sense, the theater typified the city's wild and freebooting kind of life, and, in another sense, it provided convenient, if momentary, refuge from it. In a place as primitive as San Francisco during the gold-rush decade, the theater mediated between the higher and lower impulses of the more sedate citizens who were determined to enjoy themselves, yet needed a sanction for their pleasures.

It was to be dominated for the next twenty-five years by a former hack driver from New York named Tom Maguire, a shrewd, if somewhat illiterate, Irishman who could not read the plays he produced and seldom bothered to sit through their performance. Maguire had built a number of theaters, starting with the Jenny Lind in 1850, all of which burned down at one time or another to be replaced in more resplendent fashion than before. "Temples of Thespis," the newspapers called them—no wild hyperbole, for they inspired awe if not reverence. "The theaters are the only civilized distractions in this new city," a French visitor, Bernard de Russailh, wrote in his *Journals*. Maguire's Jenny Lind III (the previous two had gone up in flames) commanded Portsmouth Square with its finely dressed, yellow-tinted sandstone imported from Australia. Inside, from a capacious lobby, patrons were admitted to the orchestra floor through seven arched doorways reminiscent of a Roman basilica. The theater seated two thousand, and it was Maguire's boast that the stage was large enough to drill a regiment on, should the need arise.

Dr. Robinson overtook Maguire with his American Theater. This was a bold step forward from his little Dramatic Museum, and a temple to end all temples, with its interior Corinthian columns that rose grandly from parquet to boxes, drapes to cover the walls, a gilt dome on which painted clouds seemed to float in space. "The carpets are thick and soft, and deaden your footsteps so that you can walk peacefully through the lobby and glance into the boxes without disturbing the audience," de Russailh wrote. Built in exactly twenty-five days, the American opened its doors before it had had time to settle. As Mrs. James Stark, the leading lady, boomed out the salutation customary at premieres, the theater sank several inches, carrying a surprised audience with it. But settled in place, the American would provide the city with a mixture of high culture and extravaganza for years to come, and Mary Ann Crabtree's introduction to theatrical life was here. To a young woman in her thirties, it was a fascinating world.

"What San Francisco was explains what Lotta became," a newspaper critic wrote years later. Novelties set the tone. Rowe's Pioneer Circus saw nothing inappropriate in staging *Othello* with acrobats, clowns, rope dancers, horsemen, and even horses in various suitable roles. At the California Amphitheater nearby, an Italian opera troupe sang Donizetti and Verdi between eques-

trian feats, and for a time, Captain John Sutter, still command-
ing Sutter's Rifles, played the role of himself in Dr. Robinson's
topical *Past, Present and Future of San Francisco*. This was an
extravaganza in which Caroline Chapman played ten different
parts, but what astounded audiences at the time was a panoramic
backdrop showing a bridge spanning San Francisco Bay. When
the curtain rose, this brought forth howls of laughter.

Brawls in the theater were not uncommon, and acting companies were especially concerned about spectators who arrived at
the ticket office carrying bags of fruit. The fruit might be eaten,
and then again it might not, depending upon the quality of the
performance. At the American Theater, Alexina and Lewis
Baker, a team of producer-actors, persuaded a stage-struck but
inept young man named Defries to play Hamlet. But audiences
who did not mind having Shakespeare tampered with in the
spirit of true parody, and who would fill the hall to watch a
minstrel company do a burnt-cork version of *Othello,* were not
inclined to sit through a fake *Hamlet* when the joke was on
them. On the night of Defries's benefit, they arrived with an
unusually threatening supply of fruits and vegetables.

When the would-be actor began the famous "To be or not to
be" soliloquy, an orange sailed onto the stage. Ordinarily, this
would have been a warning for any experienced Hamlet to take
cover, but the imperturbable Mr. Defries caught the orange,
peeled, and proceeded to eat it. During the rain of fruit that
followed, he stood fast. Wild cries went up, and finally the
aroused audience rose from their seats and started for him in a
body. Defries escaped by way of the stage door.

The whole affair was reasonably good-natured. It proved that
San Franciscans knew their Shakespeare. They wanted it either
very bad or very good; and Mr. Defries had not been bad enough
to make them laugh. This ambivalent attitude was to be true for
most theatrical entertainment in the city, and would help explain why, throughout the decade and into the sixties, both actors and audiences flitted from serious drama to spectacle, to

variety, to minstrelsy, and back again, sometimes all in the same
evening. A night's entertainment was seldom limited to a single
play. The program, which usually began at seven thirty, might
lead off with a patriotic peroration delivered by one of the stars.
If the main bill was *Othello* or *The School for Scandal,* it would
likely be followed by a short farce such as *Family Jars.* The
nature of this "afterpiece" was determined by the main feature;
tragedies were followed by farces, comedies as a rule by death
scenes, it being assumed that audiences would be in no condition
to go forth in a mood of unalloyed hilarity or hypnotic gloom
when the curtain finally came down at midnight. If there was
any question as to whether the spell had been broken, fireworks
might be exploded on stage to finish off the evening.

Actors, above all, were expected to have an elastic attitude
toward their profession. A classicist like "June" Booth could fill
out a sparse season by serving as commentator for one of the
panoramas that were flooding the city, those hand-painted trav-
elogues, sometimes half a mile in length, that were leisurely un-
rolled to music. At Maguire's San Francisco Hall, Booth was
giving the descriptive lecture for *The Grand Panoramic Play of
New York and San Francisco,* while his younger brother, Edwin,
was playing the banjo and Richard III with equal facility. This
young man, whose fame was still some years away, lived outside
of town with two fellow actors in a house built on stilts that
could be entered only by climbing through a trap door. When a
bugle was blown each morning, "the actors threw on serapes and
raced into town to rehearsal."

Here in Portsmouth Square, Mary Ann Crabtree discovered a
theater unlike that of any other in the country—wild, full of
local panache, equally at home with Shakespeare and minstrelsy,
above all infatuated with child prodigies. "A good show town" is
how old-timers were to remember it. Yet Mary Ann did not like
the easy virtue, the scandals, the insecurity. Dr. Robinson was a
highly moral man, but Maguire had a reputation for political
chicanery, and his Jenny Lind adjoined an elaborate gambling

saloon to which theater patrons might retire during the unduly prolonged intermissions.

The city itself, on the other hand, with all its "brave wickedness," danced with vitality. When Crabtree was located finally, in Grass Valley, a mining town in the Sierras, Mary Ann must have thought twice about leaving. Her husband had found no gold, but he was not without plans. They would run a boarding-house for miners. Or rather, Mary Ann would run it. This she knew from the first.

2

The Golden Hills

ONE OF THE popular satires at Dr. Robinson's Dramatic Museum in the early 1850s was a skit called "Seeing the Elephant." Written by the doctor himself, it lampooned the calamities of late arrivals to the gold fields with such good humor that the phrase itself became a byword throughout the mines. A man who had failed to hit pay dirt, had lost his shirt at cards, or been rolled by one of the Mexican bar girls (among numerous possible misfortunes) was said to have "seen the elephant." Some miners went so far as to have elephants printed on their letter paper.

By the late spring of 1853, John Crabtree had seen the elephant clearly. After drifting through the Mother Lode, panning a little ore, working for wages at some of the big mines around Grass Valley with nothing much to show for his efforts, he decided to try his hand at a boardinghouse. Mary Ann, of course, would cook.

How Crabtree discovered his wife's whereabouts in San Francisco is not known. But he wrote her, and shortly after receiving his letter (it apparently did *not* have an elephant stamped at the top, and she could have had no clear idea of what she was getting into), Mary Ann set out. By steamer up the river to Sacramento, thence by stagecoach through the hot, dry Sacramento Valley into the foothills of the Sierras, she and Lotta made the trip to Grass Valley. A flourishing hub of the Mother Lode, the town had a population of about 3,500, of which possibly 300 were women and no more than 15 were school-age children. In a diary he kept while traveling through the region, Edwin Franklin Morse, a new arrival, described "dance halls full of Spanish women in full blast," eggs that cost $6 a dozen, and "frequent fist fights, especially between the men of the Boston Ravine and the Irish colony." Even so, Grass Valley had its culture. There was a local minstrel troupe, whose patrons were shown to their seats by ushers in white gloves. The town played host to small stock companies, Fairy Stars (singing, dancing child stars), and one-man entertainers, all of whom beat their way through the region at some peril to themselves. Miners were known to shoot up a performance that displeased them, and although there is no record of an actor having been hurt, they were occasionally run out of town. Edwin Booth, who had gone broke the previous winter touring the Mother Lode with the Ben Moulton company, was stranded in Grass Valley and finally had to make his way down the mountains on foot to Sacramento. Booth was to have especially disastrous luck in the mining towns: during a subsequent junket, fire broke out in five successive settlements following his appearances, a chain of coincidences that earned him a reputation as "the fiery star." When the troupe reached Downieville, the sheriff attached their rolling stock. Unpaid bills as well as fires had followed in their wake, and Booth again hiked to Sacramento, where two benefit performances restored him to solvency.

Most of the entertainment in Grass Valley took place in the taverns. These were among the larger buildings in town; they also provided a ready-made audience. The Alta Saloon, for example, was fitted up with a stage, scenery, footlights, and, when the occasion demanded, a makeshift orchestra. Another, operated by a man named Bowers, had spawned a small dancing school for children, and Mary Ann enrolled Lotta in his class soon after their arrival. Piano music for the lessons had, perforce, to drown out the noise that rolled in from the saloon next door. Bowers' pupils learned their steps with a pronounced éclat.

There was one other cultural intrusion into Grass Valley, which overshadowed all else—the arrival, in the summer of 1853, of Lola Montez, the Irish-born Countess of Landsfeld, a title bestowed on her by Ludwig I of Bavaria. Lola had come west preceded by a series of *succès de scandale*. After a year in San Francisco impersonating herself in *Lola Montez in Bavaria* and dancing her celebrated Spider Dance, an amalgam of polka, waltz, mazurka, and jig which gave her an excuse to "kick high and shake her petticoats," as one critic pointed out, she married a young editor named Patrick Hull. By this time, San Francisco audiences had begun to mock her, and Dr. Robinson, at whose home she had lived for a short time, produced another of his painful parodies, this time with Lola as its butt. It was an innuendo-ridden play entitled *Who's Got the Countess?* in which Caroline Chapman played the part of Lola and danced a wild burlesque called "Spy-Dear." By the time Lola moved to Grass Valley, she was in full retreat.

Whether out of sympathy, proximity, or sheer curiosity, Mary Ann Crabtree became acquainted with Lola, the Countess's reputation notwithstanding. At thirty-six, she had been married five times. Her first husband, Thomas James, had been cast aside for Ludwig I, who was inconveniently driven from the throne as the price of Lola's political intrigues. A third husband, the young French journalist Dujarier, had been killed in a duel. The fate of her fourth, George Heald, was mysteriously uncertain. Patrick Hull she divorced soon after the couple came to Grass Valley, whereupon a mine official, Johnny Southwick, set her up in a cottage on Church Street, not far from the Crabtree boarding-house. "She furnished the place in great style for that day, spending three or four thousand dollars of Southwick's money," Edwin Franklin Morse reported. A bathtub imported from the East, sliding glass panels, and a marble fireplace came high. The Countess's pet bear cub was tethered in the yard.

Lola's reputation made her a controversial figure in Grass Valley. It speaks well for Mary Ann, always a fiercely independent woman, that she was not prejudiced by a mode of living which the female population found shocking, especially the smoking in public, her horsewhipping of the local newspaper editor, and the rousing all-night soirées at which she danced for her guests. (The miners, on the other hand, considered her presence an asset and named the highest peak in the nearby range "Mount Lola.") Moreover, Mary Ann was undoubtedly influenced by the actress's interest in Lotta. Legend has it that Lola taught the child to ride horseback and, more importantly, how to dance the fandango and Highland fling. But in later times, Lotta gave Bowers the credit for her precocious, if unwitting, debut as a child entertainer. Wanting to open a class at Rough and Ready, three miles away, the dancing teacher, without Mary Ann's knowledge, packed Lotta there by muleback to demonstrate that his system got results. Perching the child on an anvil in a blacksmith shop, he had her dance to the rhythm of clapping hands. A crowd gathered and cheered her on. In Grass Valley there was a kidnapping scare until Bowers returned with Lotta that night, but the incident seems to have left no ill feeling. The dancing lessons went on through the remainder of the year and into 1854.

In the summer of that year, John Ashworth Crabtree, Jr., was born—"Ashworth" he would always be within the family; "Jack," to outsiders. But Crabtree was getting restless and the elephant beckoned once more, this time to Rabbit Creek, "a small violent camp" some forty miles to the north, later to be known as La Porte. In the fall of 1854, the family moved to the new camp, where Mary Ann opened another boarding house. The following spring, Lola Montez, on her way to San Francisco, paid them a visit, with the purpose of taking Lotta on a tour of Australia as her protégée. Although flattered, Mary Ann refused. Still, it must have confirmed her faith in the child's talent and another dancing teacher was found.

Mart Taylor, a local tavern keeper, had come west as a strolling player. Aspiring to higher things, he had annexed a small log theater to his place of business and here, during slack periods at the bar, taught dancing, singing, acting, recitation, and the art of entertainment in general. A tall graceful man who wore his hair long and looked Oriental, although he was reputedly Italian,

Taylor convinced the mothers of Rabbit Creek that being a saloon keeper was not inconsistent with promoting the refinements usually lacking in a mining town. Long afterward Lotta was to say of him that he had landed in California "with all kinds of air castles packed up in his carpetbag. They toppled over as soon as he set them up, and he fell back upon music for a living."

Perhaps Taylor saw in the tiny Lotta another castle in the air, or at least a medium by which he could build his fortune; although the leap from star pupil to Fairy Star was a big one, the rewards were tempting. Child actors were then roaming the mountains in profusion; girls especially were in demand, and their mere presence in the more isolated camps was enough to bring tears to the miners' eyes, most of whom had left their families behind and were thus reminded of their own parenthood at no discernible sacrifice. In any case, they made up the bulk of the audiences and were easily entertained.

Child performers were by no means confined to California. The mid-nineteenth-century stage in America was replete with prodigies who battled to outdo each other in precocity. William Crane, a popular comedian, who was later to play Dick Swiveller to Lotta's Little Nell in an adaptation of *The Old Curiosity Shop,* recalled that he had first got the notion that he ought to be an actor when, as a boy in Massachusetts, he was mistaken for a child prodigy who had performed in town the night before. "I was sent by my mother on an errand," Crane revealed in his autobiography, "and taking the shortest way home, which led through the railway station, I heard one woman say to another: 'There goes the Infant Drummer.' I did nothing to disillusion them." From that day on, Crane dedicated himself to the stage, and although he never became a drummer, or even a prodigy, he bounded to fame as half of the successful comedy team of Robson and Crane.

It was in the West, however, that the child star phenomenon reached its apogee. El Dorado County, California, for example, had its Fairy Minstrels, with a chorus of fledgling girls and not one but several boy prodigies, including Master Charles, who was billed as a "boneologist," and Master Gus Howard, "the youngest jog dancer, tambourinist, bones player, and banjoist living." At Downieville, another mining town, "La Petite Clorinda" was filling the house. No circus was complete without at least one infant bareback rider, the most noted of whom was Little Lottie; she was three years old. Among the acting prodigies in the summer of 1855, none matched the fame of Miss Anna Maria Quin, who was playing Hamlet at the new Metropolitan Theatre in San Francisco to Uncle Billy Chapman's Polonius. (Uncle Billy's son, "Master Billy," at five years of age was to play an especially villainous Shylock two years later.) Miss Quin had been born on a Mississippi River steamboat near Memphis while her parents were en route from Ireland to St. Louis and was six years old by the time she reached California. She was particularly effective in male parts, seldom playing anything less demanding than Shakespeare, and then only the leading roles.

Lotta, who was already seven, and rapidly outgrowing the age when she might be considered a true prodigy, could hardly aspire to be another Anna Maria Quin. However, as Mart Taylor realized, there was room for more Fairy Stars in the isolated mining settlements, whose flourishing atmosphere had proved so hospitable to Sue Robinson, who had the three principal requisites of a good fairy—she could dance, sing, and impersonate; she also kept alive her mentor's vendetta with Lola Montez. Apparently not satisfied with his victory over her in San Francisco, Dr. Robinson pursued Lola right into the mountains, where young Sue ridiculed the Montez Spider Dance with a version of her own. Once, in Grass Valley, the child's dress caught fire from a gas lamp on the stage in what might well appear to have been a well-timed flash retribution. Unperturbed, Dr. Robinson and his wife put out the fire with their hands, and the show went on.

By the time Sue Robinson arrived in Rabbit Creek, Taylor had groomed Lotta as a competitor. This was no coincidence. Dr.

Robinson had had his troubles with Taylor, who he thought asked too much for the rental of his theater. As a result, he booked Sue into a dance hall across the road, and Taylor retaliated by announcing Lotta's performance for the same night. A reckless gesture, indeed; Sue Robinson was the Fairy Star supreme.

But for whatever reason, possibly out of loyalty to local talent, Lotta drew the larger audience. Half of California's foreign-born population in the fifties was Irish; Taylor made certain that his pupil could dance a jig, and he cobbled her a pair of brogans and carved a miniature shillelagh to go with the new breeches, waistcoat, and green hat put together by Mary Ann. The jig and the reel were followed by a group of sentimental ballads on the order of "How Can I Leave Thee?" and when the singing ended, a rain of quarters, Mexican dollars, and gold nuggets clattered down on the improvised stage. These Mary Ann collected in a shoe. A subsequent account of the evening, no doubt exaggerated, told of applause so loud that a good part of Sue Robinson's audience heard it and proceeded to Taylor's theater to see what they were missing. In any case, Dr. Robinson canceled the remaining performances and retired from town, leaving Lotta in possession.

Encouraged by her success, Taylor proposed a tour of the mining camps. Crabtree by this time had effected one of his periodic disappearances and was presumed to be looking for gold. In the fall of 1855, when it came time for the company to set out and he had not returned, Mary Ann left him a note, along with some freshly baked bread and a pot of beans, and took off.

The company headed north, in the direction of Quincy. Mary Ann was then thirty-five, petite and not unattractive; to all intents and purposes she had deserted her husband to take up with a strolling entertainer—at least a stranger might so infer—for the unexpected bounty from Lotta's performance at Rabbit Creek had showed her where gold was really to be found. Yet we may be sure that her relationship with Taylor was a scrupulously proper one; out of necessity, she had come to be more interested in money than men, and somehow, all the remainder of her life, men would be obstacles to, rather than the means of, survival.

"Romantic! Romantic!" Lotta was to exclaim to Minnie Maddern Fiske, reliving these nomadic days in her Boston hotel room more than half a century later. They could hardly have seemed so at the time. Of all the mining towns, those to the north were the most inaccessible. The route was hazardous, often no more than a mule trail that skirted precipices; in later years, Lotta recalled that on these journeys she had often been strapped to her horse. John Ashworth was carried by Mary Ann, riding sidesaddle. Beating his drum, Taylor led the troupe into town, exhibited Lotta as the principal attraction, and engaged a barroom, school, or grocery store for the evening's performance. The flimsy construction of these places, which sometimes consisted of little more than canvas and cloth, was an added nuisance. (Edwin Franklin Morse called the northern mines "muslin towns," and more than one traveler commented that when a bullet was fired, which was not infrequently, it might go through every building along the street before coming to a stop.) To put on an entertainment under these conditions was not easy, but Taylor could usually round up some sawhorses and planks for a stage. Although the troupe carried no scenery, a professional touch was added by blankets hung up for a curtain. The audience, almost exclusively male, and a long way from home, staked off places on the dirt floor and waited for the tears to flow.

Even the larger towns offered accommodations that were but slightly better. "The parquet [of the Marysville theater] is lined with calico," the *Sacramento Union* wrote, "and separated from the first tier by a long unplaned board. The seats in the pit are without backs. The roof of the theater is covered with the most expensive quality of canvas but has, unfortunately, at the present time a large rent in it, which was occasioned by lowering the bass drum of the orchestra through it, in consequence of the main entrance being too narrow. . . ."

Taylor's company, makeshift as it was, appears to have been quite adequate to these occasions. Taylor himself was an improviser in the style of Dr. Robinson, clever at making the miners laugh at themselves. He wrote many of his songs, danced, told the latest jokes out of San Francisco. But Lotta was the heart of the show. Impertinent, sentimental, bashful and bold by turns, she gave a surprising performance. If Sue Robinson had the more ineffable charm, Lotta was the better dancer, giving an unexpected turn to the most familiar steps. Bowers and Taylor had taught her these, but it was Mary Ann who, like a ballet master, imposed the discipline and, when the moment came, literally pushed her onto the stage. Since Lotta usually closed the performance, it was important that she "win over" her audience, for this was the point at which the men untied their money pouches. Even so, the troupe made a precarious living splitting the take. Since this often depended upon the miners' recent luck, either at digging or gambling, the total might barely cover expenses; or again, it might be an inundation, compelling Mary Ann to replace the shoe she usually used with a basket.

In this fashion they played Quincy, Rich Bar, Port Wine, Gibsonville, Forest City, Oroville, and dozens of straggling "flats" in between. The style of entertainment, to say the least, was anything but sophisticated. At Bear Creek, Taylor provided Lotta with a stovepipe hat without a top; when coins were tossed onto the stage, the child would pick them up and drop them into the hat—through which they clattered right back onto the boards. For some reason, Lotta used to say much later, the audience found the stunt extremely funny. Perhaps it even puzzled her at the time. But in any case, the act elicited even more coins, since the miners wanted to see it repeated. The stovepipe hat became a fixture of Lotta's burgeoning career.

A possible hazard of this first tour, apart from a poor box office, was an attack by Indians or, worse yet, highwaymen. Taylor and his troupe were spared these calamities, but they were not immune to competition from other entertainers. Itinerant performers of all sorts, dog and monkey shows, even temperance lecturers, beat their way through the mountains in considerable numbers. Another Taylor, who called himself "Doctor," traveled from camp to camp hauling a 3,000-foot-long Temperance Panorama to demonstrate the evils of liquor. His audiences were understandably slim.

That fall of 1855, Mary Ann discovered that she was pregnant again. What followed at this point is a matter of some uncertainty. In the "official" accounts of Lotta's early career that appeared during the peak of her popularity, it was disclosed that the company broke up in Weaverville. Taylor took the infant Ashworth to San Francisco, where it was arranged that he would stay with Mary Ann's brother, Thomas Livesey. Lotta was sent to Eureka, to be cared for by the family of James Ryan, a friend of Taylor's, while Mary Ann waited out her pregnancy in the mountains.

What really happened seems to have been quite different; and it is easy to see why the family suppressed this version of the story. When Taylor's company was disbanded and Mary Ann went into confinement, Crabtree, who had joined his wife, turned Lotta over to another troupe of players. "As soon as Mrs. Crabtree found it out, she sent word to Captain W. I. Reed, then sheriff [of Humboldt County], and had Lotta taken away from the actors," reported Mr. James R. Duff in an interview with the *San Francisco Bulletin* in 1915.

Duff's credentials make this account reliable; moreover, it is consistent with Crabtree's later acts. Duff's sister had married into the family of State Senator James Ryan, of Eureka, where Lotta was placed by Sheriff Reed. "The little thing remained there with the Ryan children until her mother was well enough to come for her," he said.

Nora and Molly Ryan (by 1915 Mrs. C. A. Worden and Mrs. O. P. Evans) corroborated Duff's story, adding a few details of their own. "We kept open house in Eureka," Mrs. Worden reported, "and when Ulysses S. Grant, then a captain, and other men who have helped to make history came there, we always used to get Lotta to sing her character songs and dance. Captain Grant and his friends always enjoyed this fascinating little child."

Twenty years later, Grant would take his place in the President's box at the National Theater when Lotta swept into Washington in *Zip* and *Musette*.

George Crabtree was born in 1856. When Mary Ann was well enough to travel, she and Crabtree and the baby took the stage to Eureka—the house in Rabbit Creek had been sold—and retrieved Lotta. From Eureka they went to Sacramento, and from there to San Francisco by boat.

It had been three years since Mary Ann had left the city, and the theater she found upon her return was, if anything, wilder than ever. Lola Montez, whom Mary Ann had championed in Grass Valley, was back from her tour of Australia, although without her manager, who had fallen overboard on the trip home, the latest casualty among her ill-fated male associates. Caroline Chapman, who by now had practically made a career of burlesquing Lola, produced *A Trip to Australia, or Lola Montez on the Fanny Major,* but the public's sympathy this time was with the Countess of Landsfeld, who had auctioned all her jewelry for the benefit of the manager's widow and children. The play flopped and Miss Chapman moved on to other roles, although one may doubt that they were an improvement over Dr. Robinson's parodies.

Whatever its apparent concern with mere entertainment, San Francisco in 1856 was not preoccupied solely with such topical diversions as Dr. Robinson's parodies and panoramas. Miska Hauser, the European violinist, played a triumphal series of concerts with an orchestra put together with musicians shanghaied from the gambling dens and variety halls. "I drilled them until they could play Beethoven's glorious 'Leonore' overture," Hauser wrote in his memoirs. "My twenty-sixth and last concert lasted fully four hours, for I was obliged to yield to the tempestuous demands of the gentlemen present . . . and repeat each piece three times."

The legitimate stage, too, was in good hands. In the summer of 1856, Edwin and June Booth were drawing crowds in a series of Shakespearean roles. Lola Montez is said to have introduced Mary Ann and Lotta to Edwin just before he returned east in September. And it is quite possible that Mary Ann, having tasted success, elemental as it was, would not have passed up a chance to meet someone who was making a name for himself, and money, too. Lotta, naturally shy, still had to be pushed onto the stage at times, but once launched she let herself go, seeking not so much the applause of the audience as her mother's approval.

That fall, Mary Ann found places in Mart Taylor's touring company, which was about to set out for the Valley of the Moon. Her twin sister Charlotte had recently moved to San Francisco and married a man named Vernon; and Mary Ann left her two boys with her. She and Lotta trouped through Sonoma, Colusa, and Tehama counties to Shasta. The reception Lotta got was beyond even Mary Ann's expectations. A correspondent who signed himself "An Old Miner," writing to the *Brooklyn Eagle* in the mid-seventies, recalled Lotta's appearance at Brushy Canon, in Placer County:

She was proclaimed the pet of the miners. Next day she was carried on the shoulders of the men to visit the then celebrated claims Little Hope, Washington, Dutch Pete's and the great hydraulic claims, which made Brushy Canon famous in those days. When she left us some of the boys followed the party a long way before saying goodby.

The "Old Miner" was constrained to add that "this is no fancy sketch, but a truthful statement of facts."

In Shasta, the new company arrived during an engagement of the San Francisco Minstrels; this troupe had opened the previous

season under Maguire's sponsorship and were now in demand by
miners who wanted to see end-men with gold-tipped bones and
interlocutors who told better jokes than those dished up by the
local talent. Charlie Backus, who, with Billy Birch, operated the
company, provided just such fare. One of Backus's most popular
stunts was to remove his dentures and go through his routine
toothless. ("We would state on the authority of Bones," the
Golden Era had written during an engagement of the troupe in
San Francisco, "that the Minstrels nearly equal the net receipts
at the door by the sale of buttons gathered from the floor after
each concert.") Backus, at Mary Ann's urging, permitted Lotta to
do her Topsy act.

Taylor viewed this appearance glumly; Lotta was his property,
so to speak, and he had no desire to lose her to Maguire. What is
more, Topsy was becoming one of Lotta's most popular charac-
terizations, and she was right at home in a full-fledged minstrel
show, which was built around Negro impersonations. Lotta
played the part—actually, a routine extracted from *Uncle Tom's
Cabin*—with the mixture of deviltry and innocence that was becoming her forte. "I's so wicked," she explained to Ophelia over
and over. She hadn't stolen the ribbon; it had just caught on her
sleeve.

Whatever her reception at Shasta—and there is no record of
it—she remained with Taylor. The company returned to San
Francisco in the fall, where Lotta entered school. From time to
time, Mary Ann got her a booking in a variety show. At the
American, she danced (obscurely, as it turned out) as "La Petite
Lotta." Perhaps the audience was too sophisticated, the whole
show an anticlimax; a man had been shot at the American only
the night before. Lotta's act was tame stuff.

In the spring of 1857, the indefatigable Taylor organized a
new company, the Metropolitan. With Mary Ann as "Arabella"
and Lotta, of course, as Lotta ("La Petite"), they set out by
stagecoach up the Sacramento Valley. In addition to playing the
triangle, Mary Ann took a leaf from Dr. Robinson's old book

and impersonated various notables. Lotta, too, had expanded her talents to include a complicated soft-shoe routine learned from a Negro dancer whom Taylor picked up on the way to Placerville. The tour was a success. Taylor augmented the profits by selling his *Gold Diggers Song Book* after the show, while Mary Ann sometimes gleaned $400 a night from Lotta's performance. By local standards, she had perfected a fairly versatile act—comic patter, a walk-around, the shuffle, and a full quota of sentimental ballads, indispensable for any entertainer who hoped to stake a valid claim in the hearts of the Argonauts.

The Metropolitans were on the road all summer. Crabtree, in San Francisco, had "kept house," after a fashion, with money that Mary Ann had dispatched en route. He dressed handsomely now: beaver hat, long cloak, leather boots scrubbed and polished. He carried a pistol, ostensibly for self-protection, more likely out of temperament. Anyway, half the male population of the city was armed. And he had gotten ideas of his own during his wife's absence. Lotta would play at no less a theater than Maguire's Opera House. When the two returned home in the fall, he proposed himself as an emissary in his daughter's behalf. Heretofore, Mary Ann had made such overtures, but Maguire was a different breed of manager. For one thing, he swore,* and Mary Ann detested profanity. For another, he had no office. Anyone who wanted to see Maguire on business simply waited his turn in front of the Opera House, where he held a curbstone levee every morning at eleven.

He was already being referred to as the "Napoleon of Managers," and the history of the San Francisco stage from 1850 to 1875, in the broad sense, is the story of Tom Maguire. What is remarkable about this man is that he had begun life as a hack driver in New York City, a little more than ten years before. His stand was on Park Row, and a good many of his fares were

* ". . . freedom from the rules of grammar makes his discourse original and striking," the anonymous *Lampaci Vagabundus* wrote in the *New York Mirror* twenty-five years later.

patrons of the old Park Theater. What impressed him was that people would pay a good deal of money to be entertained and sometimes even more to sustain themselves for the ordeal, for not a few of them, upon being driven home after the show, were in a state of elation that could hardly be attributed to the play they had just witnessed. The significance of this was not lost on Maguire, and in the winter of 1846-47 he bought a partnership in the bars of the second and third tiers at the Park—not as profitable a franchise as the orchestra location, perhaps, but a good beginning. In 1849, he joined the exodus to San Francisco.

For the next several years, Maguire never thought of the theater as being much more than a necessary adjunct for thirsty bar customers. His first Jenny Lind was fitted out over a saloon, and all of his subsequent theaters provided ample drinking accommodations. By the time the Opera House went up, he had prospered mightily. He sported an enormous solitaire on his ring finger, a diamond stickpin, and a heavy gold watch chain. A handsome man with prematurely white, pomaded hair, waxed mustache, and polished fingernails, he wore spats and a top hat and resembled the gambler that he instinctively was. Those who, from time to time, were called upon to defend Maguire's devotion to games of chance could later point out that it was the city's good fortune that his long reign in the theater was also dedicated to the succession of gambles, for when the Opera House finally got around to producing opera, it did so in a big, expensive, and splendiferous way.

However, in 1857, Maguire was still alternating Shakespeare, minstrel troupes, Professor Anderson (Wizard of the North), a Chinese theatrical company on its way to Paris, and popular melodrama. Customarily, he dealt in big names. Though Lotta was not yet a "big name," there is evidence that he had heard of her, for when Crabtree insisted that he hire her for one of his mixed bills, he disparaged her ability. The child might be good enough for the mining towns, but the "Magnificent Temple of the Muses" was no tryout theater for nomadic Fairy Stars who

Right: Jack Crabtree, Mary Ann, and Lotta in San Francisco, about 1879. *Below, left:* John Ashworth Crabtree, Sr. *Below, right:* Mary Ann Crabtree in a photograph taken at Attol Tryst.

Three early roles: Lotta as "The American Boy" in a Civil War skit (above); as Pat Malloy (above right) and as Mrs. Gammage, both in *The Little Detective*.

Left: Lotta as Paul, in *Pet of the Petticoats. Right:* As Mlle. Nitouche.

Left: Lotta in a "celebrity" picture. *Right:* As the Marchioness in *Little Nell and the Marchioness.*

Above: A scene from *Zip; Below:*
Lotta as Firefly.

Above: Lotta's fountain as it appeared in 1877.
Right: The fountain today, after many extensions.

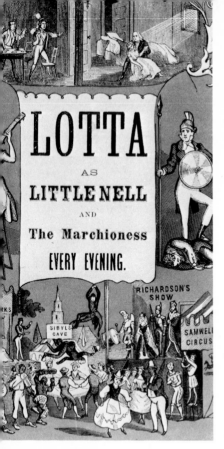

Left: An early playbill. *Below:* A studio portrait of Lotta, date unknown.

were accustomed to scraping their pay off the boards. It was an insult no father could ignore. Drawing his pistol, Crabtree fired a single wild shot. The bullet barely grazed the surprised Maguire, who sauntered away, unperturbed. Poor marksmanship was seldom punished in San Francisco, and Crabtree went free. In any case, Maguire bore the girl no ill will, for he not only hired her two years later, but gave her a piano in tribute to her talent.

In the meantime, it was apparent that Lotta would have to settle for something less than the Opera House. How much less was not apparent until Mary Ann, obviously more practical than her husband, got her a booking at the Gaieties, a "bit" theater on the Long Wharf, which ran from Montgomery Street to Pike Island. (Lotta had already made the acquaintance of this hodge-podge of junk shops, groceries, and similar establishments the year before, when she had danced on a platform at the rear of Michael Cohen's Auction Store. "Performances in the back room were continuous and the pay was small," a historian of the period has written. Admission was fifteen cents.)

The audience at the Gaieties consisted of gamblers, miners, rowdies, and teen-age boys, all of whom reeked of tobacco and exchanged jibes with the broken-down actors. The entertainment there was considered risqué by the standards of the 1850s and thus clearly in need of sentimental balladry to end the night on a purer note. Lotta was therefore engaged to follow the performance of *Brigham Young,* a play dealing with polygamy, in which Rowena Granice took the part of the "sultana," three other wives were played by juveniles, and the Mormon leader was enacted by an erstwhile acrobat. The production was so bad that when Lotta came on, after the play had ended, the audience was in an uproar. Her song—

> One summer even, with pensive thought,
>   I wandered on the sea-beat shore,
> Where oft, in heedless infant sport,
>   I gathered shells in days before. . . .

—failed to calm them. As the din mounted, Lotta grew hoarse and lost the tune. She fled the stage, the men began to quarrel among themselves, and Mary Ann, sensing that a fight was about to break out, whisked Lotta from the theater. However unfortunate the episode, it left no lasting scar.

3

◎◎◎◎

Melodeons, Benefits,
and Pleasure Gardens

IN 1858, Maguire's Opera House was expanded from 1,100 seats to 1,700. Two years before, it had been enlarged two stories without so much as interfering with a run of the San Francisco Minstrels, who were playing there at the time. (The new structure had simply been built around the old one while the show went on inside.) In 1859, further renovations were made. The chariot of Phoebus now raced across the proscenium arch, while frescoed cupids and angels chased one another about the ceiling. The most breathtaking feature of the theater, however, was still the drop curtain, considered by many patrons to be worth the price of admission. As befitted an opera house, it was a view of the Grand Canal of Venice, with domes and palaces in the background, ladies and chevaliers cavorting in gondolas up front. Sixty years later, the scene was still vivid in the mind of a callboy at the theater, Johnny Ryan. "It was like a ballet dance," he told an interviewer for a San Francisco newspaper. "No one didn't have any more elegant curtain. Oh, they ain't got no curtain in town like it."

By early 1859, however, the Opera House had yet to offer the public an opera. Maguire still leaned heavily on variety bills. These were actually bastardized minstrel shows, with a Tambo and Bones routine, grand olio and walk-around, comedy skits, monologues, and a "challenge" clog dance in which the performers competed for the applause of the audience. Lotta was catch-

ing on at this sort of competition; now she played a brief engagement at Maguire's, singing and dancing to Napier Lothian's
brassy pit band. Not quite twelve years old, she was the youngest
member of the cast.

Wearing boys' costumes on stage, Lotta had a habit of thrust-
ing her hands into her breeches pockets. Mary Ann disapproved
of this business as unladylike and sewed them up. Once, discovering this in the middle of a scene, the child broke into tears and
ran from the set. The incident became a minor turning point in
her career; she rebelled and Mama compromised. On stage, Lotta
could play the hoyden, but she would remain the young lady off.
The Liveseys had been "good people."

The previous autumn she and Mary Ann had toured the San
Joaquin Valley. By this time, Lotta had begun to play legitimate
parts; as Gertrude, in a creaky English import called *Loan of a
Lover,* she took the role that had previously served both the
youthful Sue Robinson and the aging Caroline Chapman. Gertrude was a singing part, of sorts; and Lotta had no great voice—
not, at any rate, a trained voice. In San Francisco, Mary Ann
arranged for an itinerant voice teacher to live at the Crabtree
house, part of the rent to be paid in lessons, the remainder in
cash. The family had settled on John Street, and Lotta attended
Miss Hurley's Spring Valley School—she was later to say that her
six months at Miss Hurley's was the longest uninterrupted span
of schooling in her life.

As time went on, the voice teacher found it harder and harder
to put his hands on money, and, as Lotta discovered, there was a
limit to the number of lessons even a rising star could profitably
endure. The rent went unpaid; Crabtree evicted him after exacting a promise that his music would be left behind, to be ran-
somed later upon payment of the debt. On the day of departure,
however, the luckless teacher smuggled the music out of the
house, and an infuriated Crabtree hauled him into court on the
rather unusual charge of stealing his own property. The com-
plaint was dismissed.

In any case Lotta had committed most of the songs to memory. Another teacher was hired who, sensibly, did not move in with them. Lotta's schooling, always subordinated to her career, was resumed, and there were banjo lessons from a smalltime minstrel, Jake Wallace. The regimen left very little time for play and no time at all for boys. A youthful neighbor, J. H. P. Gedge, whose back yard looked into the Crabtrees', recalled a good many years later that Mary Ann scattered would-be admirers with such vehemence that none dared return. Gedge himself harbored an infatuation for Lotta that expressed itself in a risky nocturnal tribute: "I felt it a duty to gather the prettiest rose in the neighborhood every day. . . . I'd wrap it carefully and throw it into her back yard after dark, for if her mother saw the act, woe to me!" Lotta became prettier as she grew older, but she was also, involuntarily, earning the reputation that was to be fastened on her a few years later in quite another sense—"Lotta the Unapproachable."

A good deal of her natural affection for others was directed toward her brothers, George and Jack, or Ashworth, as the family called him. They were a close-knit group, proud of Lotta's success, awed by her mounting collection of gold watches and nuggets, and tolerant of the elder Crabtree's peccadillos, his laziness and his fondness for the bottle, which was no great vice in San Francisco. Mary Ann, the manager and brains of the family, was no female martinet. She indulged her sons in the good things of life—both boys were later to attend private schools in Europe—and remained toward Lotta not bossy so much as overprotective. This may have been carried too far, but it was rooted in good sense, if not always expressed in good grammar. "Don't have a big family," she wrote, when she was a very old woman, to a niece in England—

Two is enough for any one mother to bring up and do them justis; for all people must have learning these days. If there not *learned,* there is no use in this world. Men can't teach themselves and work for a living at the same time. Now I wish to remind you and your husband never

to strike your children. *I never struck mine,* nor would I allow anyone
to strike them. Teach love. . . .

Lotta's high spirits, her irrepressible good humor on the stage,
reflected Mary Ann's boundless confidence in her; the child never
doubted who she was and what she had been put on earth to do,
which was simply to remain a child as long as possible.

As a focus for artistic endeavor, social life, civic pride, and, by
no means least, volunteer firemanship, the theater played a four-
square role in the San Francisco of the gold-rush decade. Theaters were among the few really comfortable buildings, public or
private, in the city, but they had been burning down with astonishing regularity ever since Maguire's first Jenny Lind went up
in 1850; many went up in flames not once but two or three
times.

Largely as a result of this, an unusual intimacy developed
between the volunteer fire departments and the various stage
companies. Theater owners were not only dependent upon the
speed with which a hose cart and pumper might arrive on the
scene, but the fire companies relied heavily on the acting profession for the money needed to buy equipment. There was no
greater honor on the San Francisco stage than to play the leading
role in a firemen's benefit, and with nineteen companies in existence, the benefits were numerous. Every traveling star was expected to give at least one during his visit to the city or risk
offending the arbiters of theatrical taste, not to mention jeopard-
izing the safety of his theater in case of fire. Moreover, since the
firemen themselves bought up a good share of the tickets—
sometimes bidding as much as $1,000 at auction for box seats—
the system tended to be uniquely self-liquidating. Everyone involved seemed to come out ahead.

These benefits were among the grander functions in the city's
social life during the 1850s. Firemen often marched to the theater
in full regalia, led by a brass band, to be welcomed before the
curtain went up with a peroration from the star. If the actor had

come to San Francisco from one of the large eastern cities, it was customary for firemen from that city to promote the benefit. The Booths, for example, who came from Baltimore, could look forward to a large contingent of men from Monumental Engine Company No. 6, made up largely of Marylanders. Hi-Toned No. 12, a Pennsylvania outfit, rallied to the support of the Bakers, Alexina and Lewis, a husband-and-wife team from Philadelphia. Edwin Forrest, who had been brought to San Francisco from New York by Maguire, quickly secured the loyalty of Knickerbocker No. 5, a company of native New Yorkers more rigidly exclusive than most, and which also boasted a mahogany fire engine.

Actors themselves frequently served as volunteer firemen. Jefferson De Angelis, a song-and-dance man whose father, Johnny, was playing the variety halls in San Francisco about this time, recalled the certificate of exemption, bestowed on the elder De Angelis after he had given a number of years to the cause, as resembling "a certification of military service in a European country. It is a huge diploma with a wide and elaborately copper-engraved border, picturing fire scenes and allegorical figures, including one of a bearded genius who is about to extinguish the flames of Hades by pouring water upon them from a large jar. . . ." Considering San Francisco's reputation during this period, the illustration was not inapt. Samuel Dickson, a historian of early San Francisco mores, reported that fire companies were to the city "what the Cossacks are to Russia," and, from some of the evidence adduced, this is a mild understatement. Social Engine No. 3, for instance—one of the earliest formed— raced to fires with cases of champagne on board. This was "to bolster the endurance of the men during a fire," Dickson records in his *San Francisco Is Your Home.* "They did not bother to pull the corks in the accepted manner; they knocked the necks off the bottles and drank while they fought."* Lafayette Hook and

---

* Social No. 3 later repented by organizing the city's first temperance group, the Dashaway Society, so named because its members "dashed away" the liquor instead of drinking it.

Ladder Company, on the other hand—a highly disciplined band of Frenchmen—marched to the fire in close-order drill, on the plan of the Parisian *sapeurs pompiers*. One conclusion San Franciscans drew from this heroic behavior was that fire companies sometimes put on a better show than could be seen in the theaters.

If the actors' benefits helped subsidize the fire companies, the firemen, in turn, put their endorsement to the actors. To be an honorary member of a fire company was the ambition of every notable actress in San Francisco, and not a few other women of social standing who were willing to chase the engines. This custom continued for some years. Lillie Coit, who gave the city Coit Tower on Telegraph Hill in memory of her husband, was attached to Knickerbocker No. 5 as a young debutante. So complete was her loyalty that she once deserted a wedding at which she was a bridesmaid when No. 5 raced down the street during the ceremony, and to the end of her life she signed her name as Lillie Hitchcock Coit 5.

Three years were to elapse before Lotta would take her place as one of the favorites of the fire companies. For a youngster in from the mines, the big playhouses were difficult to breach. True, there was her appearance at Maguire's, an occasional booking at the American, but these were one-shot performances. What counted was exposure; Lotta needed a personal following in San Francisco, a steady run.

In the late fifties, the city had begun to acquire those robust little theaters known as melodeons. Informal, raucous, with names such as What Cheer, the New Mammoth Melodeon, Tuckers, and Long Tom, they provided solid masculine entertainment, yet despite their rough clientele they were a cut above the "bit" houses like the Gaieties—melodeons charged the full twenty-five cents.

Mary Ann Crabtree knew a melodeon for what it was: a place no decent woman would enter. But by now, entertainment was her business—or rather, Lotta's. And business was business, even for a child. It was a measure of Mary Ann's determination that the poor repute accorded these places—many of them were stuck away in basements—did not stand in the way of Lotta's career. And she started at the top. The child was auditioned by the notorious Bella Union.

The "Belly Union," as it was popularly called, was not for everybody and, quite apart from the mildly risqué nature of some of the acts, had the reputation of being a tough place to work. It had started life as a gambling house in 1849, offering snatches of entertainment on the side; but in 1856, when gambling was officially outlawed by the city (like a good many such edicts, this one never quite caught on), the Bella Union switched to variety. Entrance was gained through an adjoining barroom or by means of a hallway commanded by the proprietor's wife, Madam Tetlow, who dispensed tickets from a table. It was said that newcomers to the Bella Union, confronting this imposing woman of stony countenance for the first time, were frequently so unnerved that they went back and came in through the saloon, stopping for a drink as they paid their admission. One way or another, the audience was primed and ready to whoop it up by the time the curtain rose. During one of Lotta's early engagements, a minstrel, Frank Hussey, killed his best friend while trying to frighten a drunk. The unusual aspect of the shooting was that it had been accidental. Most killings at the Bella Union were not.

It requires some imagination to visualize a twelve-year-old girl, small for her age, holding the attention of a group of randy men in a theater that boasted of its "frisky" entertainment. But it is all a matter of perspective; the show would be tame today. And Lotta, although still in short skirts, had one foot in adolescence. The "Old Miner" who remembered her from Brushy Canyon was surprised, during a visit to San Francisco, to see her skipping rope "in front of the Bella Union theater. I looked at the bills and saw that she was to perform that night. I went to see her; she was no longer the extremely comic and half bashful child, but a brilliant young actress, and I was glad to see her so well received and frequently applauded."

In any case, there was Mary Ann to keep order—at least backstage. Lotta never entered a melodeon without her mother being present. At Mary Ann's entrance, a churchly decorum came over performers not otherwise known for their gentility. Nora Ryan Worden recalled that when Lotta was accepted by the Bella Union in 1859, Mary Ann delivered an ultimatum to the manager: "If one vulgar word is spoken in the presence of that child, the contract will be broken." And since Lotta played the Bella Union off and on for several years, it can be assumed that Tetlow kept his word.

Whatever their crudities, as a training ground for local talent the melodeons were unique. They demanded versatility above all. Members of the cast were expected to sing, dance, act in the skits, play at least one musical instrument, and provide a personal cheering section to whoop things up during the grand olio. It was an exhausting schedule. The evening usually began at eight and ran until midnight. The "first part," generally speaking, was a musical program during which the cast might burlesque an opera. *Lucia di Lammermoor* thus turned up as "Lucy Did Sham Her More" and *Freischütz* as "Fried Shots." (Subtlety was not a strong point at the Bella Union.) Specialty numbers were followed by the olio and an intermission, during which patrons retired to the bar while the actors prepared for the comedy skits that made up the second half of the program. These were frequently in blackface and euphemistically called "Ethiopian drama." A juggler or acrobat sometimes performed; a comic might go through the familiar routine of removing innumerable coats and vests while another member of the company played Paganini's "Variations on *The Carnival of Venice*" on a tin whistle. The evening concluded with a vintage farce. Four hours of such frenetic activity convinced most customers of the Bella Union that although they might not have seen anything very frisky, they had indeed gotten their twenty-five cents' worth.

In later years, the melodeons would supply a devoted audience for Ned Harrington, Eddie Foy, James A. Herne, the Duncan Sisters, and Weber and Fields, but in Lotta's time they served to keep afloat a strange combination of theatrical castoffs and such emerging hopefuls as Johnny De Angelis, the Worrell Sisters, Annie Yeamans, and Joe Murphy. Lotta and Murphy proved a particularly felicitous pair of end men in the truncated minstrel shows that occupied the first half of the bills. Murphy had been a blacksmith before going on the stage and would later boast of having saved an inebriated young Edwin Booth from drowning in the tidal flats of the Sacramento River. When Lotta first knew him, he was accounted the champion bone player on the Coast. Another of Murphy's specialties was the combonicum, a comb covered with tissue paper, which gave off a nasal-sounding tune when he hummed into it. Although his usual partner was Johnny De Angelis, Lotta appeared opposite him on numerous occasions as the tambourinist of the company. The unlikely combination of the tall Irishman in burnt cork and an elfin redhead in a very short frock became a favorite with stage audiences. The two worked well together, and Murphy taught Lotta the kind of stage business, peculiar to minstrelsy, that was to characterize her eccentric style of acting.

The Worrells were another matter. For the next several years, Lotta was to compete with these celebrated "Juvenile Graces," Irene, Sophie, and *La Petite Jennie*—sometimes singly, more often in the aggregate—in virtually every melodeon, minstrel hall, and theater in San Francisco. With their father, advertised as "The Best Clown in the United States," they had come to the Coast in 1857, to appear in Lee and Bennett's Circus. The eldest, Sophie, was then nine. None of the sisters was very petite, and as they grew older they became so hefty that the label was soon dropped. In 1858 they were playing at The Melodeon, a hall that rigorously excluded women from attendance and supplied the men with cigars and brandy; a topical journal, *Varieties,* reported that "The Worrells have a *world* of wit in their heels, and their comic dances *heal* for the time the cares of the lookers-on."

They arrived the year before Lotta began her own climb to popularity in the melodeons and quickly achieved a following. When
the Melodeon closed temporarily, the whole company moved to
the newly opened Lyceum.

This was a far more elegant establishment, even presuming to
call itself a theater. It seated a thousand patrons and boasted two
bars, which did a flourishing business. Mart Taylor, Lotta's old
manager, sang the opening invocation:

> We're twenty-five performers here—
>   In his or her vocation,
> Each one will try their very best
>   To merit approbation;
> We only charge a quarter here,
>   In any kind of weather,
> So it only costs a cent apiece
>   To see us all together.

The Lyceum never quite made the grade as a variety house—
possibly it suggested too much respectability—and the manager,
John Wilson, soon switched to straight drama. Like the Worrell
sisters, Lotta was sandwiched in between runs of straight plays,
or cast in such afterpieces as *Our Little Treasure* or *Faint Heart,*
in which she played King Charles. Like the Worrells, she became
part of the rivalry between Wilson's Lyceum and Maguire's
Opera House. Wilson had armed himself with a first-rate cast,
which included Junius Booth, Jr., Joey and Adelaide Gougen-
heim (an inseparable team of sisters who were on their way back
to New York from Australia), the elder John Drew, and a reserve
battalion of twenty-seven child actors whose average age was just
under seven. There was little that Maguire could do that Wilson
wasn't prepared for. To counter a musical spectacle, *The Brig-
and,* he called up his twenty-seven child actors, who put Maguire's creakier company to rout. (Including the three Worrells,
Lotta, the twenty-seven infant brigands, and a later batch of
thirty Marsh Juvenile Comedians, the Lyceum's company housed
no fewer than sixty-one children at one time or another.)

The Napoleon of Managers decided that another outlet was needed for the lower forms of entertainment. Maguire liked to do things in a hurry, and his Eureka Minstrel Hall was completed in just two months and eighteen days. By way of celebration, many of the crew put down their tools, went home to clean up, and returned to see the opening show. Both Lotta and the Worrells were soon appearing at the Eureka, bidding for applause with their walk-arounds. Jefferson De Angelis, a popular operetta star later in the century, watched many of these performances from the wings as a small child, while his father, Johnny, danced and sang on stage. "The performers stood in a semi-circle and started off singing some nonsense patter such as

> Sun's going down, take a little rest—
> Wake, hi, Daddy, in de mornin

while first one and then another would strut or cakewalk around the circle and then break into a dance," he wrote in his autobiography, *A Vagabond Trouper*. Another denizen of the melodeons, John Jennings, observed that "demonstrations on the part of the audience were intense." Apparently they were also exhausting. "After the walk-around the house became almost empty," Jennings added. A star performer could be counted on to take a loyal and noisy following with her when she switched melodeons, and there was a good deal of raiding back and forth by managers, particularly when the variety houses began to multiply.

On December 5, 1859, Gilbert's, the newest and brightest melodeon in town, opened its doors on Market Street. As usual, the entrance was by way of the bar, but Gilbert also provided for thirsty customers who could not wait for the intermission in order to refuel. "To the back of each seat in the hall is attached a little shelf to hold the glasses containing the various beverages ordered by the audience during the performance," a gentleman calling himself "Wide-Awake" wrote to the *San Francisco Bulletin* in some surprise. "It is evidently no place for ladies." This

was indeed the case. The owner, Ferdinand Gilbert, was determined to put on shows even "friskier" than those at the Bella
Union. Lotta was hired, then the Worrells, and Gilbert's became
the battleground for an intensified warfare, especially after the
Lyceum burned down in November, 1860.

Consistently outnumbered in her rivalry with the nimble-
footed Worrells, Lotta labored under a handicap; a good deal of
the indefatigable kicking and jumping which later brought her
national fame was the result of making one pair of legs keep up
with three Worrells during the climatic walk-around. It was said
that Lotta wept in her dressing room when she came off second
best, which was not infrequently; only later did she discover that
Jennie Worrell, whose clog dances sounded like the roll of a
snare drum, had used trick heels. These had been hollowed out
to make room for a small, tin-lined box in which two bullets
were placed. The resulting clatter created the impression that
Jennie was dancing twice as fast as she actually did.

In this continued battle for public acclaim, a measurable cri-
terion of progress was who "topped the hangers," or, as it would
be called today, received top billing. The position of a performer's name on the handbills depended to a considerable extent on
her support at the box office. Sometimes Lotta topped the
hangers, sometimes all three Worrells did, but if only one Worrell topped the hangers, it was a black day in the Crabtree family. No exact count was kept, but Lotta seemed to be ahead in
the race until Papa Worrell took over the management of Gilbert's Melodeon a year or so later. Thereafter, until he relin-
quished the post, the Worrells always topped the hangers. (In
any case, Gilbert prospered: when he died in 1868, his estate was
valued at $400,000.)

How a performer was described on the playbills also figured in
the push for popularity, and in this respect Lotta forged ahead.
From "La Petite Lotta, the Celebrated Danseuse and Vocalist"
she became, almost overnight, and quite possibly at Mary Ann's
insistence, "Miss Lotta, the San Francisco Favorite." The new title

was by no means the result of mere press agentry. Her continual appearances at Gilbert's, with briefer forays into the Alhambra and Bella Union, had made her the best-known young entertainer in the city. When Johnny De Angelis decided it was time that his three-year-old son, Jeff, made his stage debut, Lotta was chosen to sponsor him.

The elder De Angelis was one of the regular performers at Gilbert's. On one occasion young Jeff wandered onto the stage during a performance and began imitating one of the dancers. The audience set up a din, and someone threw him a coin. The boy was only three at the time, and still in dresses; when he bent over to retrieve the coin, he exposed a bare backside. The elder De Angelis deftly interposed a tambourine but this made the crowd howl even louder. It was such a promising start that the father arranged for an official debut.

The occasion was opportune, but premature. Although Lotta's sponsorship was "widely advertised and sufficient to draw a packed house," Jefferson De Angelis recalled in 1931, "when she led me from the wings, my feet suddenly turned to lumps of lead. In vain did Lotta try to encourage me. . . . When it became certain that I was a flop, my charming partner was compelled to carry me, kicking and howling, off the stage."

The melodeons, valuable as they were as a training ground—a generation later they would be supplanted by vaudeville houses —also proved to be something of a dead end for Lotta. By 1861, the big theaters still eluded her. Suddenly, an opportunity came to go on tour, this time through the recently opened Washoe region, in what was then Nevada Territory. Gold had been discovered in the Comstock Lode; Maguire had already built an opera house in Virginia City. When Jake Wallace, the man who had taught Lotta to play the banjo, organized a small minstrel troupe to work the towns of the Washoe, Mary Ann signed her daughter on as a juvenile. There was, of course, the usual proviso that Mary Ann go along.

The entire company of seven, advertised as a "male and female minstrel company," was loaded into a single stagecoach. (An advance man had been sent on ahead to secure bookings.) But Lotta was the principal attraction—"She was really about the whole show when it came to popularity with the audience," Wallace recalled in a newspaper interview fifty-one years later.

The company had to contend with two unforeseen problems— the weather, which was bad, and the approaching Civil War, arousing as it did violent passions among the miners. At that time, the Washoe was ardently pro-Union, but parts of nearby southern Oregon were in outright sympathy with the South. A traveling show, therefore, was expected to adapt its patriotism to its itinerary, using particular discretion as it crossed the border into Oregon.

It had been raining several days when the troupe left Sacramento on the twenty-fourth of February, 1861. At Auburn, finding the roads impassable, they turned back, but the American River had come up in the meantime and the approach to the bridge had been washed away. Ned Whittmore, the driver, hesitated. Wallace, taking the lines from his hands, lashed the horses into the stream, then onto the tottering bridge. "Stay with 'em, Jake, stay with 'em," Wallace remembered Lotta yelling at him from inside the coach. Once across, Whittmore grabbed Wallace by the arm and pointed behind them. The bridge, settling into the water, gave a last lurch and floated downstream.

The whole trip was played to ominous thunder out of the South. At Iowa Hill, the main street was teeming with excitement. News had come that Sumter had fallen to the Rebels. "Cut loose all the patriotic airs you can tonight and everything will go smooth," a bystander urged Wallace. The minstrel "put in an hour arranging a patriotic song and dance," and the money "came down on the stage like rain."

In Roseburg, Oregon, the curtain rose on a hostile silence; the cast could sense they were being tested. Then a rebel yell went up. Lotta was perplexed. Her leading number, "Rally Round the Flag, Boys," would only inflame Confederate sympathies. When the moment came, she sang out, omitting nothing, hoping to win them over. Mutterings gave way to hisses; the hisses grew louder. It was a terrifying experience, "but she went straight through," Wallace said. There was no applause at the end.

Whittmore waited outside the schoolhouse where the troupe performed, the horses hitched and ready to go. When the curtain fell, no coins rained down to be scooped up from the makeshift stage. The cast beat a hasty exit, piled into the coach, and rattled out of town in the darkness.

Wallace also remembered that his advance man, in the flamboyant style affected by showmen of the day, wore a large diamond stickpin. Newspaper editors, dazzled by the glint of this mammoth stone, reasoned that the company must be unusually prosperous, and the cost of advertising went up accordingly. Wallace figured that he paid about twice what he should have until his agent was fitted up with a considerably smaller pin.

The tour was the last of its kind that Lotta and Mary Ann were to make. In San Francisco, the young actress settled in for a season of variety. At last came the ultimate tribute: she was invited to give benefit performances for the fire companies. This turn in her fortunes seems to have come about largely because she had acquired an agent, or "manager," one W. H. Smith, who was also a member of the cast in the Backus and Birch minstrel company. A smart operator, Smith put Lotta under contract; he was never very popular with Mary Ann, who resented the idea of paying commissions, but he got results.

In March, 1862, Lotta appeared at the Metropolitan "Temple of Drama" in a benefit for the Knickerbocker Engine Company No. 5, the outfit that Lillie Coit would chase through the streets in a bridesmaid's dress a few years later. The main bill was Tom Taylor's *Still Waters Run Deep,* with Charles Wheatleigh, Mrs. Judah, Frank Mayo, and John Wood. These were among the acting aristocracy of San Francisco, Mrs. Judah being a particular favorite, an actress who had come west in 1852 and was to remain active until 1879. Nothing daunted her. Twenty years before, on the way to Cuba with her husband and two young children, she had been shipwrecked. Lashed to a spar, she watched her husband drown and saw her children die of exposure before she was picked up by a passing boat four days later. Her present husband, John Torrance, managed the Metropolitan with Maguire. This was heady company for Lotta, whose name appeared on the bill as "Miss Lotty."

Other benefits followed rapidly. In April, on behalf of the Ellsworth Rifles at the American Theater, the rifle corps itself put on a full drill. On June 17—the anniversary of the Battle of Bunker Hill—a benefit for the National Guard. In August it was the Columbian Engine Company No. 11; Lotta appeared with Julia Dean Hayne, Mrs. Judah, and those "Terpsichorean wonders," the Worrell Sisters. Beside their individual specialties, they all acted in a comedy, *Serious Family*. Men threw money at the actors, then left their seats and rushed down the aisles to make sure it reached the stage.

Lotta seemed to mirror both the sentimentality of the people and their mild flirtation with bawdry. "The Captain with His Whiskers Gave a Sly Wink at Me," one of her most popular songs, was being sung all over San Francisco. Aroused audiences were brought to their feet cheering when she performed "Rally Round the Flag, Boys" in soldier's uniform, while "Dear Mother, I'll Come Home Again" restored them to their seats, and decorum. As Jenny Leatherlungs, Lotta burlesqued the famous Jenny Lind, "with mock shakes, trills and bravura," as Constance Rourke has pointed out; but she also did a parody song on the ballad "Belle Brandon," whose namesake, like Jenny, was becoming a popular name in California for locomotives and steamboats. Her dance routines blazed with hornpipes, Scotch flings, polkas, shuffles, and Irish jigs, any one of which she might perform to buck up a too-familiar farce. The informal partnership with Joe Murphy continued, and took her, along with the Worrells and Johnny De Angelis, into Maguire's Eureka Minstrel Hall.

But the camaraderie of theater life escaped her. Under the watchful eye of Mary Ann she was hustled to performances and home again. And although she was approaching sixteen, there were still no boy friends. Once, toward evening in the summer, a young man with horse and carriage called to take her riding. Mary Ann disposed of him quickly, but for days afterward, following dinner, Lotta contrived to sweep the front porch in case he should return. Unhappily, he did not.

Except for serious plays, there was very little now that Lotta could not do in the theater. Irish character parts, usually boys, became her specialty, probably because they provided so many opportunities for dancing. In the vogue of the period, she took on multiple roles; no actress could be said to have made the grade in San Francisco until she had played a variety of parts in a single play. Mrs. Alexina Baker played seven characters in the spectacle, *Three Fast Men of San Francisco,* but she was overshadowed by the brassy Adah Menken, who arrived in 1863 with a vehicle called *Three Fast Women.* The title did not go unremarked, for Menken was reputedly fast enough for all three parts. (Actually, she played nine, five of them male.) Lotta, in her first effort at this "protean" acting was cast in seven roles in the farce, *Object of Interest.* What set her apart from other virtuoso performers was that all seven characters, if need be, could play the banjo.

A good deal of the city's taste in this kind of entertainment derived from its affection for the low comedy that went on in daily life. No one ever spoke of Proper San Franciscans, and it is significant that the literary and artistic elite formed themselves not into an Academy but a Bohemian Club, presided over by a local man of letters, Charles Warren Stoddard. The streets were alive with strange characters. A deluded "George Washington," decked out in a frilled shirt, tricorn hat, and uniform, held forth as a fortuneteller at a corner table of Martin and Horton's saloon. Bummer and Lazarus were the town's most celebrated dogs, said to carry food to each other "in times of misfortune."

They also went to the theater with the Emperor Norton I, a Scottish Jew who had come to San Francisco in 1849, acquired a fortune in merchandising, lost it, disappeared for four years, and then made a re-entry in full regalia—pinchbeck decorations, epaulets, and, on state occasions, a high beaver hat bedecked with a bundle of turkey feathers.

Norton I was just the sort of odd castoff that actors found amusing, probably because, in playing one successful role for twenty-six years, he was beating them at their own game. In any case, he was taken up in the spirit of charity, and few theatrical performances from 1855 to 1880 opened without complimentary tickets for the first row of the balcony having been put aside for Norton and the two dogs. By the early 1860s, when a play chronicling his fabulous career filled theaters, audiences found it quite natural to have their drama transposed from the streets to the stage. The real-life story could hardly be improved upon. When the emperor died suddenly on the street in 1880, the city flew its flags at half-mast, and then provided thirty thousand persons for his funeral cortege. San Francisco was a show town that never made clear distinctions between hokum and art, and in a good many minds Norton I was an artist.

As a show town, too, it was expanding. Those who were reluctant to visit the melodeons could see many of the same performers, if not always the same breezy show, in the amusement parks. One of the earliest, Russ's Gardens, provided wholesome family entertainment as well as a steady flow of brew for the local German population. The Irish descended on Hayes Park for a more vigorous style of entertainment that included balloon ascensions, target shooting, and political clambakes. Hayes Park had one significant advantage over its competitors—it was reached by the Market Street Railway, a horsecar line owned by Michael and Thomas Hayes, who saw to it that most of the cars, no matter what their point of origin, terminated their run at the entrance to Hayes Park. Frenchmen in San Francisco favored The Willows, an elysian expanse of nature where the ladies could admire the shell walks while their menfolk took in the trotting races.

Lotta played all of the amusement parks, but it was at The Willows—closer in style to the melodeons—that she found her most enthusiastic following. With Joe Murphy, she had appeared there as early as 1859; four years later, she was a regular, playing *Melodramatic Sally, The Soldier's Bride,* or *Jenny Lind* during an afternoon, then rushing back to town for a night performance at Gilbert's New Idea. "The most talented juvenile actress California has yet produced," a critic wrote at the time.

When Adah Isaacs Menken arrived in the summer of 1863, she invited the friendship of the young girl that all San Francisco was raving about. Menken's appearance in San Francisco was a triumph for Maguire. She came high, but the notoriety already attached to her name made her worth the price. If there was any doubt in Maguire's mind that she would be *persona grata,* it was soon dispelled: the San Francisco Hook & Ladder Company made her an honorary member of its fire-fighting brigade, presented her with a red morocco fire belt, and serenaded her with its brass band. Lotta's introduction was possibly arranged through the writer Stoddard, who admired the young girl's dancing, and whose fondness for Adah Menken's acting led him to describe her as "a vision of celestial harmony made manifest in the flesh—a lovely and breathing poem that set the heart to music." Mary Ann Crabtree, who tolerated Stoddard's fatherly interest in Lotta, although she was careful to chaperone his visits, was also fascinated by Adah Menken, who she discovered was not half so wicked, and never as naked, as advertised. The important thing about Menken was that Maguire was paying her $500 a performance to act in *Mazeppa.*

Only twenty-eight at the time, she had already been thrice married: once to a musician in Texas, Alexander Isaacs Menken, under whose influence she had been converted to the Jewish faith; briefly to a California prize fighter named Johnny Heenan, otherwise known as the Benecia Boy, who had taught her how to box; finally to the political satirist Robert Newell, a pseudonymous individual who wrote under the name of Orpheus C. Kerr, pronounced "Office Seeker." For a time in New York, the

Menken had dabbled in literature, making the acquaintance of
Walt Whitman. This had been followed by a series of lectures,
and readings from Shakespeare, and then a vaudeville tour with
Blondin, the French aerialist who had crossed Niagara Falls on a
tightrope. Jimmy Murdock, her business manager, sensed that
Menken's reputation needed upgrading and suggested that she
enact the part of Count Olinska in *Mazeppa; or The Wild Horse
of Tartary*. Set in Russia, the play had been on and off the
American stage for thirty years—Joe Jefferson had parodied it in
The Fiery Steed; or the Wild Untamed Rocking Horse—and it
was about ready for a natural death when Menken decided to
play Olinska in flesh-colored tights.

The huge sensation which this created in the 1860s seems mys-
tifying today, but at the time it was considered a daring gesture
against convention—at least in the East. (Westerners, being used
to almost anything on the stage, were inclined to be blasé about
such matters.) The climactic scene of the play occurred at the end
of the second act, when Menken, a generously proportioned
woman, pretending nudity under a Greek chiton, was strapped
to the back of a horse and sent up an incline. It was no accident
that the path was circuitous, or that the horse took his time—
sometimes fifteen minutes—to negotiate the ascent. Menken
wanted the audience to get an eyeful, and ordinarily they followed
her hazardous journey with popeyed wonder. To her surprise,
however, many California reviewers were fascinated more by the
horse's performance than the rider's. In part this typified the
drollery that local critics were in the habit of injecting into their
work, but it was genuine to the extent that horsemanship was a
second language in San Francisco, and a well-executed ride could
be more noteworthy than a naked lady. The sorrel steed, Sweep-
stake, was generously applauded. In any case, the stunt was not
without its dangers; Menken had fallen once in Albany and hurt
herself, and a horse that would get her off the stage safely for
sixty consecutive performances was to be commended. (In London, she fell again when the horse stumbled and threw her into

the wings against a scene shifter. When the manager went before the curtain and asked if there was a doctor in the house, every man in the audience reportedly raised his hand. Some raised two. "The scene shifter has been hurt," the manager added, and the hands fell.)

Maguire's gamble had paid off; Menken's success in San Francisco was complete—so complete that at one time during her stay six rival productions of *Mazeppa* were in performance simultaneously, including one at Gilbert's that employed a mule. A local newspaper columnist remarked that so many horses were hired from livery stables for these shows that they absolutely refused to be mounted by anyone wearing clothes.*

Years afterward it was said that Lotta learned to smoke from Adah Isaacs Menken. Possibly Lotta herself encouraged the legend—long black cigars became her trademark off the stage— but it is unlikely that Mary Ann would have allowed any such deviation from propriety in a girl of sixteen.

Lotta played the aspirant to Menken's success. She was coming to an age when a career beyond California seemed feasible, and the older actress had shown how triumphant such a life could be if one overlooked the marital complications that attended fame. And there is good reason to suppose that Menken enjoyed being idolized by an innocent young comedienne for a change.

The two went horseback riding, watched the carriage racing on the highlands by the Cliff House overlooking the Bay. No doubt Lotta was flattered by this relationship. Talented juvenile though she might be, this was not the same as being a "real" actress. Adah Menken inspired Lotta, as she seems to have inspired all of San Francisco, with a conception of the theater that was startling and unorthodox. "Along with the flock of *Mazeppas* that spread over the country, she perhaps unleashed a larger

* There were other reverberations, too. A scandal sheet, *Mazeppa*—so named to justify the picture of a nude on the cover—listed the city's houses of assignation under the rubric: "Establishments to Stay Away From." So that the reader would know *which* houses to stay away from, an address was given for each.

freedom," Constance Rourke has written. In her own fashion, Lotta hoped to swim into national fame on this liberating current.

At least Mary Ann was ready to gamble on it. She would settle for nothing less than New York, leaving San Francisco to the Worrells. Junius Booth, Maguire's actor-manager, had announced his departure; so had Joe Murphy. Menken's stay was coming to an end. Why not sail with the tide?

It was a momentous decision. San Francisco had made Lotta; her public by this time could not get enough of her. Now she would be heading into strange waters, facing audiences that had never heard of her. Yet to delay might be fatal. It was national fame she wanted, and she was young enough to seize it. If Lotta herself had doubts, Mary Ann was boundlessly confident.

A heady excitement built up during the early months of 1864. Then Maguire announced that Lotta would take her farewell benefit at the Opera House with Joe Murphy, following benefits for Booth and Menken that same week. Fifteen hundred dollars rolled in as Lotta's share of the single night's performance to a jammed and jangling house. It was a tearful farewell, even for Mary Ann.

On April 23, the Crabtrees left for New York—via Panama—on the steamship *St. Louis.* Murphy was on board, and Junius Booth, Jr. Booth's benefit had gone to pay off debts, and he was taking his family east with money sent by Edwin. On another ship that day Menken departed with Orpheus C. Kerr; she later cast him adrift in Panama, proceeded to New York, and later to London, Paris, and a pauper's grave. Of all those who sailed, Lotta alone would be remembered as belonging to San Francisco.

Book Three

THE TRIUMPHS

1

Western Wonder

NIBLO'S SALOON was at Broadway and Prince Streets in New York, and it was not to be confused with Niblo's Garden. The Garden had once been the grand showcase of the Metropolitan Hotel, until the hotel burned in 1854. Adelina Patti sang there as a child soprano of eight; among other notables, Edwin Forrest, Joseph Jefferson, and Charlotte Cushman had drawn fashionable crowds to Niblo's, and the crowds had been drawn there in carriages direct from the Astor House, at no charge, by arrangement with the owner, Billy Niblo, an Irish immigrant who had once peddled turtle soup on the city's streets.

The Saloon, however—salon would be a more up-to-date description—was something else; like the Garden, it had survived the fire, but it was smaller, less prestigious, and, more importantly, easily rented. It was for rent in the summer of 1864, when the Crabtrees arrived east from San Francisco. Mary Ann took over the Saloon for the month of June and installed Crabtree as manager.

This smaller adjunct to the Garden had been used chiefly for string concerts and recitals; an atmosphere of musical decorum clung to it. Lotta's bill would be decidedly different. She would sing, but irreverently, burlesquing Jenny Lind (in *Jenny Leatherlungs*). Niblo's had no regular acting company, and a small group of actors was assembled to support her in *Jenny* and a short play called *The Mysterious Chamber*. Beyond this, she would perform on the banjo and do her clog dances.

On the night of June 1, 1864, as the curtain went up at

Niblo's, a sixteen-year-old girl blinked across the footlights at a great many empty seats. She had been nervous for the past hour; word had come that "the critics" would attend. But she had not been prepared for such a tiny audience. For an anxious moment, she wanted to turn and flee the stage.

Suddenly, there was a burst of cheering. It came from one section of the hall, and was the nearest thing to a claque that Lotta could count on to sustain her during the whole dismal evening. This was a group of "Argonauts," young men returned from the gold fields, who had seen and worshipped "Lotta the Unapproachable" in San Francisco.

Yet she sensed from the first that her debut was a failure. The louder the ex-Californians cheered and stamped, the more indifferent and cold the rest of the audience became. Her clog dances brought forth little applause; the attempted repartee with those in the front seats fell flat. It was a losing battle. From time to time the young gold seekers angrily berated those around them for their failure in appreciation; the auditorium grew noisy as they tried to rescue their favorite, but nothing could restore Lotta's confidence. When it was over, she left the stage in tears. What had been her magic in California, where she could "cram the biggest theater out," as her ardent admirers reminded others, was a puzzle to New Yorkers. "Miss Lotta . . . possesses any amount of aplomb—a graceful French word for the more vulgar English word, brass . . . ," the *Herald* critic concluded the next day. The weekly *New York Clipper* reinforced the insult: "Her style is certainly not intended for a first-class audience, concert halls being her proper stamping ground."

Lotta struggled through five more nights at Niblo's and then gave up. The audiences had grown smaller, and there was a limit to the number of former San Franciscans who might turn up to pay tribute. The gloom that at first settled over the Crabtrees was followed by a post mortem. Financially, the debut was no great disaster; Niblo's Saloon came cheap and Mary Ann had taken only modest advertisements in the newspapers. Crabtree himself had tended to business for a change, even though there had been little enough of it.

Characteristically, Mary Ann saw Lotta's failure in terms of external circumstances: the time of year was not the best, and what competition there was in town—Mrs. John Wood doing *Pet of the Petticoats* at the Olympic, Mlle. Vestvali next door at Niblo's Garden—was formidable, all of it in shadow to the great performance that was being put on by General Grant, who was laying seige to Richmond. It never occurred to Mary Ann that her daughter was not yet ready for New York, although it must have seemed so to Lotta, at whom the reviewers' barbs were aimed.

The critics notwithstanding, one man who saw Lotta regarded her "style" as an asset. B. F. Whitman was a smalltime manager who operated in New York only intermittently, but he was there in June, 1864, and he had connections. Exactly two weeks after Lotta closed at Niblo's, he secured her the lead billing at a one-night benefit performance for A. H. Davenport at Tripler's Hall. This was a concert hall all right, one of the largest in the world, having been erected for the New York debut of Jenny Lind, although Jenny came, sang, and conquered elsewhere—the Hall had not been ready by the time she arrived.

Lotta as "Jenny Leatherlungs" was no substitute for the real thing, and in any case her fellow performers, with the exception of Davenport himself, did not add up to an all-star cast: Mrs. F. S. Chanfrau; a stock company Edwin Booth named George Boniface; Mr. Robert Heller, proprietor and chief attraction of Heller's Salon Diabolique, whatever that was. Lotta was "the fairy artiste from the shores of the Pacific." Davenport, father of the soon-to-be-famous Fanny Davenport, was the beneficiary of a well-filled hall and a fat purse, and Lotta undoubtedly benefited from her appearance with this respected tragedian, although not financially. The appearance was donated, but at least she was "exposed" to an audience larger and more sympathetic than that at Niblo's.

Still, Whitman concluded that New York was not ready for Lotta; he cheerfully resisted putting it the other way around. Mary Ann liked him—he was a "gentleman"—and turned over the managerial reins. More accurately, he was a booking agent. The theater had not yet fallen under the domination of the large central agencies, and actors, or their managers, made their own bookings, often on short notice. Whitman found a place for Lotta—five places, rather—in an extravaganza called *The Seven Sisters,* which was to open later that summer at McVicker's Theater in Chicago. The Crabtrees headed west.

Since no one at McVicker's had seen Lotta perform, her employment was largely an act of faith, arranged on Whitman's recommendation. Not even the manager of the company quite knew what he was getting; Lotta was carelessly billed as "Miss Lotts." But it was apparent during rehearsals that Lotta belonged in this kind of spectacle show, and she belonged in the lead role of Tartarine.

The Seven Sisters, sometimes known as *The Seven Daughters of Satan,* had been written by H. B. deWalden and Robert Jones. Possibly it can be described as a kind of Civil War musical comedy. When first produced, in 1861 in New Orleans, the plot was decidedly Southern in its sympathies, but as the war went on, and Northern feeling hardened, the story line was modified. By the time Lotta played in it, there was no doubt where the authors' sympathies lay, nor which version commanded the bigger box office—after all, the North was winning.

The show opens in Hades—not a bad locale for a war play— where Pluto reigns supreme. Soon, however, a number of "spirits" escape, make their way to Dixie, and join the Union army. Their activities from this point on, as the play was produced throughout the Civil War, depended largely upon the course of the actual fighting; in August, 1864, coincident with Grant's campaign in Virginia, the "spirits" were put to capturing the outerworks before Richmond.

The Chicago performance, which ran for three weeks, was im-

mensely popular; Lotta transformed *The Seven Sisters* into something very close to a minstrel show. She played Tartarine in
blackface, strummed the banjo, danced breakdowns, jigs, and
hornpipes, and took over four other roles in a protean exhibition
of versatility. All of this must have been something of a surprise
to the audience, who knew the play as a "grand fairy spectacle"
full of delicate footwork, gauzy females, and flimsy scenery that
was never intended to stand up to a minstrel band. Perhaps they
were reassured by the "Lake of Silver," which consisted of 71,820
square feet of plate glass mirrors ("baffling all description," a
newspaper observed), or by the final "grand transformation"
scene—"The Birth of Cupid in a Bower of Ferns." It had absolutely nothing to do with the Civil War.

Lotta was instantly acclaimed. One admirer, male, rushed
down the aisle to present her with what later reports described as
a "$300 watch" tied up in a handkerchief. Since it is unlikely
that the gift carried a price tag, possibly Mary Ann had it ap-
praised. In any case, it was the first of dozens she was to receive
throughout the next twenty-five years, most of which she kept,
and few of which agreed on the time. There is a legend that, in
her years of retirement, Lotta was either early for appointments
or late, depending upon which watch she chanced to be wearing.

The Seven Sisters closed August 20. Whitman by this time had
formed a partnership with a Colonel Woods, proprietor of
Woods Museum on Randolph Street, and he now found a place
for Lotta in the Woods stock company. John Dillon was the star
comedian, and May Howard, a former teacher at the Female
Baptist Academy in Tennessee, played the leading lady. Dillon
was known to Lotta, having been an Irish character actor employed by Maguire in San Francisco. Miss Howard, who had
come north when the shooting got too hot in Tennessee, was
later to become a famous burlesque actress, which is not quite
what the term implies today.

Woods Museum was not in the same class with McVicker's,
being a theater that had been smuggled, so to speak, into the rear

of a curio hall. In large part, this arrangement was a sop to puritanical elements in the city that still regarded the stage as the Devil's own trap—the famous Boston Museum had begun its career on exactly the same principle. "When a person was seen going into a museum, that person was obviously seeking an education," Robert Sherman, a Chicago theatrical historian, has written. An education, however, was not necessarily what he got, for he was encouraged to keep moving right into the "lecture hall," where another admission was extracted to see the drama. It was here that Colonel Woods' stock company held forth.

True, Lotta was not the star, but the repertory was good experience. She played *Nan, the Good for Nothing* and the role of Topsy from her California days, while *Mr. and Mrs. P. White* and *Our Gals* were new to her. This was typical stock company material, and there is no reason why playgoers should have had to pay extra to see it, but they did and the Museum thrived until it burned down in the Great Fire of 1871. Lotta's connection with the company terminated late in December, 1864, when Whitman and Colonel Woods dissolved their partnership. Mary Ann had never been reconciled to Lotta's supporting roles, and Whitman apparently thought she could do better on her own. Early in 1865, the Crabtrees hit the road again, working east through Ohio, Pennsylvania, and upstate New York.

At that time, one of the most popular actresses in the country was a tiny, piquant young woman named Maggie Mitchell. Ten years older than Lotta, she had made her reputation playing gamin parts—Oliver Twist was an early success—with sufficient vitality to conceal what many critics thought was a lack of real dramatic ability. In 1860, she first played her famous role of Fanchon, in an adaptation of George Sand's novel, *La Petite Fadette*. By 1865, it had become her trademark, but Whitman saw no reason why Lotta should not cash in on the public's enthusiasm for the play, and in a bold move she took on Fanchon for herself. It was polite burglary, and presumptuous to boot; nobody played Fanchon like Maggie Mitchell, nor would any actress (except Lotta) have attempted it, just as no reputable male actor would have taken on Rip Van Winkle so long as Joe Jefferson could hold a blunderbuss. But Lotta "got up" the part, as she wrote to a friend, Miss Billie Vosberg, in San Francisco, and made a hit.

"I am a continual success wherever I go. In some places I created quite a theatrical furor as they call it . . . I got up the far-famed play called 'Fanchon' to play in Buffalo. The people were delighted and the theater not big enough to hold them . . . Why, friend Billie, your heart would jump with joy to see the respect I am treated with here among the theater people. I'm a star and that is sufficient, and making quite a name."

An advertisement in the local newspaper declared that Lotta was "justly acknowledged to be the best on the American stage"! Not even Mary Ann was willing to go that far. Still, Lotta was re-engaged for an extra week and by the time she had quit Buffalo had appeared in eleven plays. One of them was John Brougham's burlesque, *Po-Co-Han-Tas*. Lotta took the part of the Indian.

But *Fanchon* was later dropped. Lotta saw no reason to capitalize on another's popularity, even though the box office reflected the uncertainty as to just who this "western wonder" might be. A four-day run of *The Seven Sisters* in Albany took in only $1,558, and considering the production costs it could not have been a very profitable engagement. Lotta was a "star," as she had boasted to friend Billie, but she was not yet a highly paid star, and throughout this maiden tour of the East Mary Ann often thought of giving up and returning to California. W. H. Smith, Lotta's old manager in San Francisco, was importuning them to come back, but Lotta was against it. Smith was coarse, too "western," lacking in polish. "When anyone tells you that Smith is going to bring me back, you can tell him that you know better; we have not seen him and if we did we should not speak to him," she wrote Billie Vosberg. But Whitman—all the Crabtrees approved of him. "He is . . . a man of money. His wife travels with him, and a more ladylike person we never had the good fortune to be in company with. . . ."

Travel they did, although hardly in style. At best, they put up in second-class hotels, sometimes in boardinghouses. By June, 1865, they had reached Columbus, Ohio, and in July were in Buffalo for the second time. The tour had begun in Providence, early in March. There was a jump to Albany, a swing into Pennsylvania. No city was too small for a one-night stand, but it was a metropolis such as Columbus, Ohio, that dangled the big money. By August, the Crabtrees had reached the westernmost limit of their itinerary at Indianapolis and then circled back. It was a grueling schedule, made worse by the vagaries of local railroads. A trip from St. Louis to Detroit, by way of Columbus, required fifteen different changes of trains, the final 231 miles, on the Toledo, Wabash & Western, lasting some twenty-three hours. Yet few towns with a local stock company were too small to play in; it was better than "laying over," even though the support might not be much better than amateur quality.

The theater in those days was a rigidly formal hierarchy, and the acting parts went to those who had been hired to play specific types of roles, regardless of suitability. When Lotta arrived at a theater, she would be confronted by a cast that she had never seen before; at best, there would be time for two or three run-throughs before the performance. "Personal adaptability for any role was never taken into consideration," Clay Greene, a San Francisco-born playwright declared in 1915, reminiscing on the mid-nineteenth-century theater. "If the comedian happened to be 50 years old and the principal comedy role was a boy, he played the boy, under the mistaken notion that he could 'make up to look 16.' "

This did not make for verisimilitude, but for that matter, neither did the sets. These, too, were furnished by the local theater—a fancy interior, a plain interior, kitchen, palace arch scene, palace vestibule, one or two street scenes, a landscape or two painted on an olio. Literally hundreds of different plays, from Shakespeare to *East Lynne,* were produced with the same basic scenery, and the locale of the play made no difference.

There were advantages to this system: Lotta needed only costumes and a banjo. But there was not much time for rest, and none at all for romance. In Oil City, Pennsylvania, she visited a certain "Bishop," "the famous mind reader." August Pitou, an actor in the Sam Jack stock company there, went with her. Separately, they had their fortunes told, but Lotta refused to confide to Pitou what she had asked of her future. "When shall I be married?" he teased her. It was the same question that all girls asked. "Will my married life be a happy one?" Lotta said nothing. She was not yet eighteen.

In January, 1866, the Crabtrees made their first assault on Boston. This bastion of high culture welcomed the young "artiste" like a breath of fresh air from the West, which may have been just what was needed in a city where theatrical fare still ran heavily to uplift. The Grand Italian Opera Company was in town; at the Music Hall, Professor Bowers lectured on "Coal Formation in Pennsylvania," while the Horticultural Hall had been taken over by Chang and Eng, Siamese Twins, along with a covey of "Wild Australian Children." True, William Warren held forth at the Boston Museum, but he could be seen—and was—almost any night of the year. Lotta came for two weeks, and stayed three. The audience at the Howard Atheneum—it had once been a Millerite Tabernacle—found in her an actress close to the common things of life. She danced the MacGowan Reel and sang "Mickey Dear" in an Irish brogue. She did Boucicault's *Irish Assurance and Yankee Modesty.* She burlesqued Lola Montez. *Uncle Tom's Cabin* was offered straight, and although one critic reported that "it has never before, in our mind, been so well presented in Boston," he found her impersonation of Topsy "peculiar," which is just what Lotta was striving for.

What is easy to overlook is how much hard work went into this. In nineteen performances, Lotta romped through thirteen plays, in some of them taking as many as six different parts. *The Seven Sisters,* which began the second week, inspired the *Boston Post* to comment rapturously that the final scene of the birth of

Cupid "equals, if it does not surpass, anything yet seen upon a Boston stage. Everyone should see it." Yet considering that right up to Saturday of the previous week the theater playbill advertised for "25 ballet girls—apply at stage door between 10 and 12 o'clock A.M.," one wonders how much time could have been given to mounting this extravaganza; or, for that matter, how good the dancing was.

The Howard Atheneum stock company, new to some of Lotta's material, found the actress as enchanting as did the audience. A benefit on February 9, the next-to-last performance, set the house to ringing, and huge baskets of flowers were rushed onto the stage at the end of the first act. Benefits were nothing new to Lotta (and they were frequently a device to produce extra revenue for the management), but it is significant that as early as 1866 she began to turn over her share to charity. When a St. Louis newspaper, in September of that year, advised its readers to "give her a parting and substantial token," the notice was not as mercenary as it seemed—the money was to go to the Newsboys' Home. "There is a touch of pathos in this," the paper added. Lotta's most popular roles were precisely these gamin types who lived by their wits, and since her ingenuity in such parts was considerable, the newsboys and bootblacks were all admiration. On one of Lotta's later visits to St. Louis, a packet was tossed onto the stage of DeBar's Opera House from the "Boot and Peanut Brigade," which, when unwrapped, proved to be a marble dove. The management wondered from where it had been stolen.

All that year, the Crabtrees were on the road. In June, Lotta played for the first time in Washington's National Theater under John T. Ford, whose Ford's Theater had been closed following the assassination of President Lincoln. Curiously, Lotta's leading man had been a soldier in Lee's army. The next stop was Buffalo, where brother George, ten years old, was placed in a private boarding school run by a local minister. Cincinnati followed, then Columbus. In Philadelphia, the stock company star at Mrs. John Drew's Arch Street Theater exclaimed, "Who is this Lotta person?" when the visiting actress shared top billing. "Starred the same as I am? Ridiculous! *She* must open the bill. I'll follow."

Actors hated to "open the bill" because attendance and appreciation were usually scant. Lotta, who distrusted conceit, and was surprisingly lacking in false pride, agreed to open the bill. Mrs. Augusta Kidder, whose husband later managed Lotta for a time, recalls that there was only a fair house, but that it rang with laughter and applause, which dwindled away when the local favorite appeared later. This added to the veteran's fury.

"Tomorrow night *I'll* open the bill. This Lotta can have the leavings," she insisted.

"It was so advertised," Mrs. Kidder continued. "The first part of the program drew very few spectators, but when Lotta's farce came on, she played to standing room only, which lasted throughout the engagement."

Once, when Lotta shared the program with another troupe, the manager of the theater came to her for help. His ingenue refused to play the bit part of a maid in an afterpiece. Would Lotta do the simple walk-on?

Mary Ann was summoned and a council held; she was not opposed to the arrangement so long as her daughter be given a contract to play the part for the entire week. The manager pointed out that all Lotta had to do was bring in a tray, set it on a table at which two lovers were sitting, and go out. There was not even a line of dialogue. But Mary Ann insisted, and a contract was provided.

On opening night, Lotta made her entrance, spotted the lovers, and stopped dead. She advanced a bit, shyly, as though trying to get up her nerve, then paused, as if fearful of destroying the love scene in front of her. Again she advanced, again she hesitated, building her simple entrance into a climax of suspense over nothing. Finally, placing the tray down quickly, she turned and fled, pausing at the exit for a little backward kick at the audience.

It was the high spot of the evening, and so noted in the reviews

the following day. The ingenue and leading man were furious—
not without reason: a bit player had stolen the scene and made
them look ridiculous. The actress who had refused to play the
part demanded to be reinstated. Mary Ann, who could wave a
contract with authority, remained adamant. Lotta finished her
run.

The incident revealed something that was at the core of
Lotta's success as an entertainer. To her, stage love, as it came
across the footlights of the day, *was* ridiculous. In all her later
triumphs she mocked it, sometimes with a wink, more often with
a kick, and always with an inimitable sense of being Lotta, of
standing outside the play and laughing at it. When the Crabtrees
first came east, Lotta had ambitions toward serious drama. Mary
Ann took her to see the famed tragedian Charlotte Cushman in
one of her heavier roles. As Lotta described the occasion later,
"I saw at once that I was not large enough or strong enough, and,
if I ever had to set my chin to pronounce the dramatic passages,
as Miss Cushman did, I'm sure I'd giggle."

Lotta finished 1866 and began the new year at the St. Charles
Theater in New Orleans, where *The Seven Sisters,* despite its
unhappy connotation for Southerners, was well received. The St.
Charles, a fine theater in the French style, with a portico supported by delicately filigreed wrought-iron columns, had been
renovated the previous year by Ben DeBar, an actor-manager
who also ran the Opera House in St. Louis and commuted between the two cities by steam packet. DeBar was a celebrated
gourmet who thrived on the elegant fare provided by the Mississippi River passenger boats and played Falstaff at both ends of
the line with conviction. A statue today honors him in St. Louis.

But the real achievement of Lotta's 1867 season was her discovery by John Brougham, one of those heroic figures for whom
the nineteenth century seemed tailor-made. A Dubliner by birth,
he had come to America from London in 1842. He thought nothing of writing three or fours plays a year (his total output, by the

time of his death in 1885, had climbed to at least 125) and acting in as many others. For a time he ran his own theater. On one celebrated occasion, Brougham performed in both New York and Philadelphia on the same night, changing his costume on the way. Of course, the New York performance concluded early, and the Philadelphia show started late. Both plays, incidentally, were his own.

Brougham was fascinated by Lotta, whom he had seen several times on the road. She seemed to him ideal for the part of Little Nell in Dickens' *The Old Curiosity Shop;* and for good measure he wrote the part of the Marchioness for her, too. As matters turned out, it was as the Marchioness that Lotta scored. The adaptation, dashed off in the winter of 1867 and called *Little Nell and the Marchioness,* was produced for the first time at Crosby's Opera House in Chicago, but since Crosby's had no acting company, Lotta assembled her own—without Whitman, who no longer managed her—from among the groups at McVicker's and Woods.

The engagement came at an opportune time, for Crosby's had just been sold by lottery and was reaping the benefit of some unique publicity. The theater, which fronted on Washington Street between State and Dearborn, had been built two years before by Uranus H. Crosby, a millionaire with social ambitions. In those days, there was no surer way of gaining admission to the local Four Hundred than to put up an opera house, especially if the builder, like Crosby, was at the disadvantage of having made his fortune in the whisky business. (Pike's Opera House in New York, for example, belonged to the notorious Wall Street plungers, Jay Gould and Jim Fisk, Jr.) Crosby had a long way to climb, and his Opera House proved it. The cost was $600,000. An art gallery was attached to the theater, and patrons were invited to spend their intermissions in the presence of yet more culture rather than at the bar—surely the supreme gesture of sincerity on the part of Uranus Crosby.

But the whole enterprise had become a colossal white elephant, and Crosby conceived the idea of raffling it off at a dollar a ticket. Six hundred thousand tickets were printed and sold all over the Midwest; as a bonus, a chromo of one of Crosby's paintings was sent to each purchaser. George P. Upton, a Chicago musical impresario of the period, remarked that "this accounts for the profusion of Huntington's 'Mercy's Dream,' which may still be found hanging on parlor walls all over the western prairies." The winning ticket was held by the proprietor of a meat market in Prairie du Rocher, Illinois, named A. H. Lee. Lee, however, had not been present at the drawing, and "it was several days before he was discovered and identified," Upton reports, whereupon an excited band of night riders descended on the town, dragged Lee from his bed, and informed him of his good fortune.

Thus Lotta arrived at the Opera House in the midst of the raffle excitement not quite sure whether she would be working for a distiller or a butcher. As it happened, Lee, who had considerably less reason to own an opera house than Crosby, and who was quite astonished to discover that he had won, sold it back for $200,000. In effect, the owner recouped $400,000 and the elephant was no longer quite so white. High finance and high culture, in Chicago at least, were agreeable companions.

Lotta, who presented ten plays during her seventeen-day engagement at Crosby's, followed a series of lectures by Clara Barton. She opened with *Uncle Tom's Cabin*. George L. Aiken, the adapter of the novel, and an actor in the Woods stock company, came over to play Tom to her Topsy. *Little Nell,* sandwiched in among such stock items as *Family Jars, Nan, the Good for Nothing,* and *Ireland As It Was,* seems to have created no special stir; Brougham was still tinkering with the play, and possibly the version that Chicago saw was not the dazzling show that Lotta was to make it later.

From Chicago, the Crabtrees worked their way east while Lotta wrestled with a major decision. Should she try New York again? Brougham was eager to see *Little Nell* done there, but Lotta vacillated; it meant facing the critics, and she had not forgotten their patronizing attitude from three years before. On the other hand, Clifton Tayleure, a playwright and manager, offered to sponsor her reappearance. Tayleure was then managing Kate Bateman, another ex-San Franciscan. The adapter of *East Lynne,* he was an important theatrical figure in New York, and for ten per cent of Lotta's earnings he proposed to book her into Wallack's Theater for six weeks, beginning July 29. Tayleure drove a good bargain: Lotta was to receive half of the gross receipts after an initial deduction of $400.

She would be up against some familiar names. Miss Bateman had made a reputation in *Evangeline,* and it was said that her father, the man who had once taken a pot shot at editor Soulé in San Francisco, attended every performance to start the applause—"rousing the audience to their duty," in the words of one of Miss Bateman's supporting actresses.* Mary Ann could hardly do better.

The main competition, however, came from a daring spectacle play called *The Black Crook,* probably the first real "leg" show in the United States. True, the legs were encased in black tights, but they were visible enough, dangling in plain view as their shapely owners were whisked over the stage by a complicated mechanism of pulleys and wires while the largely male audience, most of whom sat with their hats on, ogled the sights. All this took place at Niblo's Garden. Ministers denounced *The Black Crook* from their pulpits, the good people of the city were shocked, and the play ran on and on.

In the face of this excitement, Tayleure mounted an elaborate promotional campaign to publicize Lotta's appearance. Not many New Yorkers had seen Lotta, but her success out of town

* The actress, Catherine Reignolds-Winslow, recalled, too, that when "Evangeline (Miss Bateman) slept upon the stage while the moving panorama behind gave the effect of motion to the boat . . . Papa Bateman saw only his child, and with a burst of joyous enthusiasm, he turned gratefully to an applauding neighbor with 'No woman can sleep upon a bench like my daughter.'"

was beginning to be talked about. Posters and handbills were plastered on the sides of buildings, curbstones, omnibuses, and ferry boats. Shops and hotels displayed Lotta's photograph. She was called the "western wonder," a "canary bird," a "sunbeam," a "kitten," and a "sparkling ingot." The young Argonauts who had shouted their opinion of her acting three years before at Niblo's saloon were vindicated; Wallack's was not the biggest theater in the city, but she "crammed it out" and many first-night patrons were turned away.

She opened in *Pet of the Petticoats,* in which she played six parts. According to the critic for the *Spirit of the Times,* the curtain came down on "storms of applause." Yet, "for the proprieties and unities and august traditions of the stage, [Lotta] shows a reckless contempt. . . . She says 'Damn it!' with spirit and gusto. The audience . . . likes to hear a woman swear on the stage." As Liddy Larrigan, in *Family Jars,* her "crowning success —the triumph of the night—was her banjo playing. It was Lotta, though, not Liddy Larrigan, who played it."

Little Nell and the Marchioness, which opened the following week, brought Lotta even wilder acclaim. "Rarely in the history of New York theatricals has a summer engagement proved so profitable," Colonel T. Alston Brown wrote in his *Annals of the New York Stage.* The run was extended for a week. Receipts averaged $1,100 a night, and Lotta's share of the twenty-eight days totaled almost $10,000. New York had at last been conquered!

There is no record that Dickens, who came to America for a series of readings the following year, ever saw *Little Nell and the Marchioness,* but if he did, he must have wondered what it was all about. For not only had Brougham freely adapted *The Old Curiosity Shop,* but Lotta had freely adapted Brougham. She was continually inserting new business, to the surprise of the resident company at Wallack's. At one point the Marchioness and Dick Swiveller take a mutton bone that has been picked clean and turn it into an imaginary feast; suddenly, Lotta grabs a banjo and breaks into a tune while her partner rattles the bone in the style of an end man. The fair at Highgate employed the Sable Minstrels—a local blackface troupe—as the chorus for Lotta's jigs and breakdowns. Acrobats tumbled about the stage, Quilp was made to walk a tightrope, gypsies gathered, clowns paraded, and men fought with broadswords in a grand climactic spectacle. In the final scene, Nell is hoisted into heaven as Grandfather Trent kneels at her grave. The audience wept but Lotta always thought it rather ridiculous.

Wallack's was packed at each performance. Brougham, who was playing at the Olympic Theater in *David Copperfield,* to houses not nearly so enthusiastic, was torn between envy and admiration. Lotta was outdrawing the great Brougham himself—and in his own play! "Like California wine, bright, sparkling, piquant . . . ," *Frank Leslie's Illustrated Magazine* wrote. Not wine, but something stronger, Brougham insisted; Lotta was a "dramatic cocktail."

There had been repeated curtain calls on the opening night, and when the audience had finally left the theater, Mary Ann and Lotta looked for Crabtree. The family had rented a house on Amity Street (now Third Street) for the summer, and he was to take them home. Midnight came, and Lotta and her mother found themselves in an empty theater, surrounded by a vast silence, with only the night watchman for company. Mary Ann fretted; all the triumphs of the evening seemed gone. Finally the two walked alone to Amity Street, twenty blocks downtown, only to remember that Crabtree had the door key. For two hours, on this night of triumph, Lotta and her mother sat on the front steps in the deserted street, waiting for the errant Crabtree to return.

2

Arrivals and Departures

THE END of September, 1867, found Lotta in Chicago playing repertory at McVicker's. *Little Nell* opened the following month, with McKee Rankin as Brass and the English actress Mrs. Cowell as Sally Brass. This was more solid support than Lotta was accustomed to; she no longer had to be "set off" by inferior actors. The play, moreover, was her own. It had been written exclusively for her, bought and paid for as was the custom of the day, and, as investments go, it proved a small gold mine.

Yet this kind of good fortune had its own built-in trap. Nineteenth-century audiences, by and large, preferred their favorites to enact one role. They came to see the actor, not the play, and as a further refinement they preferred to see him in the same part over and over again. Sometimes a single scene was all that mattered—"Wake me up when Kirby dies" was a byword for years at the old Bowery Theater, where the melodramatic tragedian J. Hudson Kirby held forth. Once death had come, it was not unusual for a good part of the audience to rise from its seats and beat a noisy exit without waiting for the end of the play. Brougham himself was a victim of this curious loyalty; it was his custom to improvise witty speeches between the acts. Fans who had seen the play before might dally in the lobby for most of the evening, then hurry to their seats during the intermission.

As both Little Nell and Sophronia, the Marchioness, Lotta might have settled into a lifelong role; as the years went on, there would be striking examples of how profitable this could be—and how confining.* But at twenty, Lotta was far too young to fall victim to a single great success. What she wanted was not one famous role but a dozen. Although the role might change, she did not, nor did anyone want her to; she would always remain Lotta. In *Little Nell,* she was continually inventing new business, changing her lines, adding dances. These variations were not always intentional but Lotta made the most of them. During a road stand, stagehands accidentally pulled off the bedroom set too soon, exposing the graveyard scene in back. As the ragged Marchioness, Lotta was dancing for the ill Dick Swiveller, who lay in bed playing an asthmatic flute. Suddenly, she found herself dancing wildly to the tombstones while Swiveller tootled to the empty skies. At one time, she would have fled the stage. Now the ludicrousness of the situation appealed to her, and she insisted on playing out the scene while a baffled audience watched in fascination.

"Reader, I know *Little Nell* is not lively, but Lotta was," George C. Odell wrote of her second New York appearance in the play. This was in January, 1868, at the Broadway Theater, a huge barn of a place that seated 4,300 persons. That summer, the San Francisco Minstrels, now permanently installed in their Hall on Fourteenth Street, burlesqued Lotta's Nell as a tribute to her success. ("People buying ladders to peep in at the windows," boasted the advertising posters.) With Wallack's company, she took over the Brooklyn Academy of Music, then went on to Boston at the invitation of June Booth. Still called "The Fairy

* For example, John T. Raymond became an eternal Colonel Sellers in Mark Twain's *The Gilded Age.* John E. Owen would play Solon Shingle for eighteen years, and Frank Mayo was a celebrated Davy Crockett from 1872 until two days before his death in 1896. Mayo came to hate the play, and stopped counting his performances after the 2000th. The record, however, would go to Joe Jefferson, who first played Rip Van Winkle in 1865 and continued in the role, with occasional lapses into other parts, until his retirement in 1904. During this thirty-nine-year span, he wore the same suit, patching it as he went along. But considering the character he was playing, this was not difficult.

Lotta," she filled the immense Boston Theater every night, her clogs "rattling like a merry hail storm." Booth's wife, Agnes Perry, was in the cast, along with Walter Leman, another California trouper. The great Edwin Booth himself followed Lotta in *Macbeth*, with Madame Janauschek playing Lady Macbeth in German—to smaller houses than Lotta's.

Earlier in the year she had performed in the first legitimate play to be produced at the ornate new Pike's Opera House in New York. Owned by the flamboyant Jay Gould and "Jubilee Jim" Fisk, like Crosby's in Chicago Pike's was intended as a showcase for opera, and it must have been a letdown to all concerned when this magnificent structure reverberated to the banjo playing and clog dancing of *Uncle Tom's Cabin* just two months after it opened. But this is what Lotta chose to put on, although the excitement on stage could hardly hope to match the intrigues, financial and moral, that took place in the owners' offices, and in Fisk's private apartment adjoining. But then, Lotta was to bail out a good many top-heavy Temples of Thespis during her career.

At Wallack's later in the summer, she introduced an adaptation of Ouida's novel, *Under Two Flags*, written to order by Edmund Falconer; that is, written to Lotta's order—Ouida was not mentioned and, since she was English, she was not paid either. The play was called *Firefly; or The Friend of the Flag* and sailed under the colors of a "grand Military Drama." Grand it was, filled with French Legionnaires, Arabs, marching bands, cannon, and wild ponies; but it was also interminably long—five acts comprising seventeen scenes—and, to audiences overwhelmed with the spectacle, somewhat perplexing. "We entertain the hope that future generations may be equal to the unraveling of its various ramifications," an anonymous reviewer complained.

But future generations did not have much luck with it either. (Other adaptations of the novel were produced as late as 1909.) What held *Firefly* together was Lotta. Like Brougham, Falconer seized upon her eccentric talents and fashioned a story around them. The basis of the play is the voluntary exile of an aristo-cratic Englishman under a false imputation of forgery (a crime actually committed by his brother). As Vivandière, or "Cigarette," Lotta falls in love with this nobleman, who is condemned to be shot for insubordination; but between their first meeting in Scene One and the shooting, sixteen scenes later, Lotta per-formed a whole gamut of variety entertainment for the benefit of the Foreign Legion.

Firefly was never taken very seriously by the critics, but it packed theaters wherever Lotta played. It ran for seven weeks at Wallack's; the *Times* reviewer duly noted that a good deal of its appeal lay in the star's sheer muscularity. For one thing, Lotta, tiny as she was, picked up a beefy soldier and carried him off stage. For another, she hardly ever stood still. "What punctua-tion is to literature, legs are to Lotta," the reviewer wrote. "Sometimes she aggravates a sentence with a dozen antics; at another time, an entire paragraph may escape with a single kick."

The play moved to Philadelphia, and then into the Boston Theater, which seated 3,150 patrons and boasted an enormous stage that was particularly well suited to anything written to the scale of *Firefly*. In another military drama produced there, *Youth,* a tallyho coach drawn by four horses was driven onto the stage and circled about, to the astonishment of the audience, this seeming to be the sole reason for the scene. Real Gatling guns were also discharged. It was the opinion of spectators, however, that Lotta in *Firefly,* made more noise on the snare drum. One of the high points of the play comes in Act Three when the desert camp of the Legion is attacked by Arabs. The regimental drum-mer being *hors de combat,* it falls to Vivandière to call the troops to arms. To prepare for the role, Lotta had taken a series of drum lessons, and by the time the show opened, it was generally acknowledged that no one outside the United States Army could execute a roll with more bravura than Lotta Crabtree.

The long, rattling flourishes, slowly building to a crescendo as the tempo is stepped up under threat of attack, continued for several minutes. The pit orchestra was silent, while the stage throbbed with marching boots. In the audience, Civil War veterans were known to rise from their seats and parade up and down the aisles. Women cheered. In later years, General Sherman seldom missed a chance to witness *Firefly,* both in Washington and New York, and after one especially thrilling performance he sent Lotta an autographed picture of himself, in full military dress, standing atop a battlement surrounded by cannon balls.

The fact that Vivandière later rescues the French flag from the Arabs, and that she throws herself across the breast of the Sidney Carton-like nobleman to save his life from a hail of bullets—all this was something of an anticlimax. Lotta's drumming even overshadowed a rather risqué cancan. "The impression made by the performance is one that nearly fifty years have been unable to efface," a Bostonian, reminiscing in 1917, wrote in the *Transcript.* General Edwards, who was to become the executor of Lotta's estate, saw the show in Boston while still in high school; and although it is perhaps too much to say that it inspired him to enter West Point, from which he graduated in 1883, he still recalled his excitement in 1919 when he visited Lotta at the Brewster. The Boston engagement, too, carried a touch of nostalgia. Napier Lothian, Maguire's conductor in San Francisco, had come east a few years before and was leading the orchestra at Booth's. He was to remain there for forty years, and in later life grew so absent-minded that he sometimes fell asleep while conducting. Lotta always turned one performance over to a benefit for Lothian, who, in turn, would lay down the baton, hop onto the stage, and take part in the show.

The Crabtrees' domestic life at this time was almost as turbulent as some of Lotta's plays. The principal reason seems to have been money. Mary Ann kept her husband on a short leash, or tried to, but Crabtree, who no longer had any managerial role, was not a man of uxorious temperament and the two battled it out from Boston to Cincinnati. Crabtree had always contended that, as Lotta's father, he should share in her earnings. But the money seems to have been under Mary Ann's control, and she doled out just enough to keep her husband fashionably clothed and not too inebriated. Sometime during the early summer of 1868, before Lotta brought *Firefly* into New York, Crabtree proposed a separation, contingent upon a substantial settlement that would permit him to return to England and open a pub. Mary Ann refused. In Cincinnati, her husband pried open the iron-bound trunk that held the receipts of the tour, the key for which was never out of Mary Ann's possession. He then went on a spree, and when the time came for Lotta and her mother to depart, Crabtree was still missing.

However, he returned to New York on June 3, apparently having advised Mary Ann of his impending arrival, for she swore out a warrant for his arrest, and he was taken into custody as he stepped off the train. Lotta was upset. The incident had gotten into the newspapers, and to her father's well-known intemperance was now added a charge of theft. At Police Headquarters, a conference was held, and, from what can be pieced together of the matter, Crabtree promised to return the money. In any case he was released. He did not, however, keep his promise, and a week later Mary Ann had him arrested again, this time at his room at the Metropolitan Hotel. District Attorney A. Oakey Hall, later to become mayor, and a man of considerable theatrical aspirations himself, granted commitment for trial, and Crabtree was locked up in the Tombs. Brought into court "to inquire into the cause of his detention," he finally surrendered the money and bonds and was released for a second time.

Crabtree without any money was an even knottier problem than Crabtree with too much. As Lotta's reputation grew, his antics proved an embarrassment, especially on the road, where social invitations were extended to the Crabtrees by distinguished local patrons of the theater. Mary Ann could never be sure, at such times, whether her husband would appear drunk or sober or if—happily—he might not turn up at all. A compromise seems to have been reached following the Tombs episode whereby she would provide a more generous allowance in return for which he surrendered any claim on Lotta's earnings. Although he rejoined the family, he did not travel much with them and, until his banishment to England four years later, remained a rather obscure figure.

The rage for Lotta had begun to approach that degree of frenzy which today is reserved for rock-and-roll singers. All over the country men and women were skipping to the "Lotta Polka" and the "Lotta Gallop." The appearance of the young actress in person was the signal for a spontaneous outpouring of admirers, chiefly male. Barely twenty-one, she had matured in the strange, childlike innocence that would always be her style; beauty radiated from her diminutive, bouncing person, and she was eminently marriageable—or so men liked to think. After the manner of the Menken craze a decade earlier, they unharnessed the carriage horses that waited for Lotta at the railroad stations and, seizing the shafts, pranced her through the streets to her hotel. Mary Ann, who was invariably the other passenger, made certain that although a serenade under Lotta's window might follow, such tribute was not extended into the hotel itself. "Lotta the Unapproachable," a press agent's phrase to set Lotta's star apart in the theatrical firmament, came to have quite a literal meaning.

She finished the year 1868 at McVicker's in Chicago, staying on into January. By March, she was back with June Booth in the Boston Theater doing *Little Nell, Firefly,* and *Uncle Tom's Cabin.* "If anything more queer, graphic or natural could be placed upon the stage, we have yet to see it," the *Post* said of *Tom.* Along with these plays went a protean piece written for Lotta, *The Little Detective,* in which she sang a "hoopty-doodendoo" and danced a "burlesque pas seni." The former number was a Swiss yodeling song; the "burlesque pas seni" seems to have disappeared from the literature of the stage—charitably, one suspects. To read *The Little Detective* today, a play in which Lotta played six parts, is to suffer. But audiences loved it.

The big event for Lotta in 1869 was her return to San Francisco for the first time in five years. She had left there a child actress; she was coming home as an actress who played children's parts, which was not quite the same thing. The city, which had been well informed of her triumphs in the East, would expect much of her, and she resolved not to disappoint it. The challenge was frightening: William C. Ralston, the financier, had built the California Theater for John McCullough and Lawrence Barrett; determined to outdo Maguire, he assembled the finest stock company in the country, a group of fifteen men and nine women which included, in addition to Barrett and McCullough, John T. Raymond, Emilie Melville, Willie Edouin, John Wilson, Henry Edwards, and the redoubtable Mrs. Judah.

Lotta was nervous at the thought of returning to San Francisco under such auspices. Barrett himself would play Dick Swiveller to her Marchioness. She could hardly grasp the fact that she was the star among such men and women, luminaries in their own right who would content themselves with featured roles.

Her long absence was explained largely by the difficulties of travel. Not until 1869 did the first transcontinental railroad link California with the Middle West. Soon after it was completed, the entire Crabtree family departed from New York, via Pullman, for the ten-day journey that would be interrupted by a stopover at Brigham Young's theater in Salt Lake City.

They were leaving the East in the wake of a personal tragedy. A short time before, Lotta's youngest brother, George, then thirteen, had run away from his boarding school in Buffalo, apparently with the idea of joining his mother and sister. Attempting to hop a passing freight car in the Buffalo yards, he miscalculated and fell; the wheels severed the toes of his left foot and his right leg just above the knee. Lotta was playing in Philadelphia at the time, and Mary Ann, who was with her, rushed to Buffalo. By the following month, George had recovered sufficiently to join his family, and early in July they entrained for the West.

But it was with subdued spirits that the Crabtrees set out for the scene of Lotta's early triumphs. Arriving in Salt Lake City, Lotta and Mary Ann were lodged in one of Brigham Young's numerous cottages, while Crabtree and the two boys, Jack and George, went on to San Francisco.

Mary Ann looked upon the visit to Salt Lake City with a certain skepticism. A few years before, the popular California actress Julia Dean Hayne had come to Salt Lake City for an extended engagement and had so impressed the Prophet with her beauty and talent that he invited her to become one of his wives, along with Eliza the Poetess, Harriet the Pale, and Amelia the Magnificent. Presumably, Mrs. Hayne (she was divorced by this time) would be Julia the Actress. Unfortunately, she was not a Mormon, had no intention of becoming one, and nothing came of the romance. However, a touching reminder of her visit remained: Brigham Young's sleigh was named the *Julia Dean*. It held all of his children, and required six horses to pull it. Thus it is not surprising that Mary Ann, who was suspicious of men on general principles, took a guarded view of Young's hospitality. Yet she must be careful not to offend him; the Mormon leader could virtually make or break an actress's appearance in the edifice he had built seven years previously—with 3,000 seats, it was then the largest theater west of Chicago. If he disapproved of a play or performer, he would send messengers about the city telling people not to see it. He disapproved of tragedies and in his dedication speech had thundered against them. "I want such plays performed as will make the spectators feel well," he had declared, and for this assignment Lotta was an ideal candidate. She was a hit in spite of the rather amateurish support she received from the local company, some of whom were Young's daughters.

Lotta was fascinated by the Prophet's theater, which was quite unlike anything she had played in. An imposing structure of classical proportions on the outside, it resembled a cross between a county courthouse and a Southern mansion, while the interior, with its long, pewlike wooden benches, suggested a church. Here, the elders and bishops, surrounded by their wives, children, and the ordinary people of the town, took their places, many of them sucking peaches while watching the performance. In the center of the parquet was a huge, upholstered rocking chair usually occupied by Young himself, or possibly one of his wives. The rocking, as well as the peaches, proved a minor distraction to Lotta, yet she seems to have enjoyed the unexpected novelty and engaged in her usual lighthearted banter with the audience. Some few years before, she had worked up a titillating bit of business, after her curtain calls, of extending one ankle from the wings and wriggling it daringly. At the time, this was considered an audacious gesture, and audiences responded with yells of delight. But in Salt Lake City there was a heavy silence. Perhaps the Mormon elders failed to see anything remarkable about another female ankle.

Mary Ann was disturbed by something else. Admission to the theater was sometimes paid for in merchandise—sausages, kegs of applesauce, wheat, corn, hams, even wolf skins. Once a live pig had been tendered, and chained in the box office. To Mary Ann's relief, when the manager settled up with her at the end of the week, Lotta's share was in cash.

San Francisco was a home-coming. Mrs. Vernon, Mary Ann's twin sister, came to the station; the Livesey girls, Sophia and Elizabeth, were there. W. H. Smith, Lotta's one time manager, was now stage manager at the new California Theater, where John Brougham was appearing in his burlesque, *Shylock, or Much Ado About the Merchant of Venice.* The city had grown, and the California Theater was proof of it.

Built only six months before, at a cost of $150,000, it had been paid for in bullion composed of 800 bars of gold, 90 of silver, and 107 of copper. Perhaps it was no coincidence that the opening-night play was entitled *Money*. The season was then in the midst of an unbroken run of three hundred nights. Since January, Booth had been there, Edward Sothern, Modjeska. . . . This was heady company to follow; yet Lotta was booked for six weeks, and filled the theater at every performance.

The engagement opened with *Little Nell* and was followed by a play new to Lotta, Tom Taylor's *Ticket of Leave Man*. Then came some old favorites—*The Irish Diamond;* her travesty of Lola Montez, *Governor's Wife; Family Jars; The Pet of the Petticoats. Firefly* was given an especially lavish production; the young Lawrence Barrett played the English nobleman who is saved by Vivandière, and Lotta rode a real horse.

In every sense, Lotta's return was a fashionable civic event. The new social elite came to see her. Men buckboarded in from the mining camps who remembered Lotta as the "Fairy Star" of their prospecting days, the child who had trouped through the mountains with Mart Taylor, who had skipped rope in front of the Bella Union before going inside to dazzle male audiences with her "high flavored and gamey" performances. The city was simply claiming its own. Her public had watched her depart for the East as a diverting comedienne and a minstrel. They welcomed her back as a polished entertainer and a national celebrity.

In at least one of her plays she was thought to be too diverting. This was *The Ticket of Leave Man,* in which she took the part of a fifteen-year-old boy, Sam Willoughby, and ran away with the show. As one of the earliest "convict" dramas, set in the slums of London, with an outcast for a hero, it marked a significant transition in the development of the socially realistic theater. It is remembered today for its introduction of the first famous stage detective, although it was not until many years later that he, too, ran away with the play. This was Hawkshaw. "Old actors still go through the motions when they utter the name," Wilson Disher, a historian of the nineteenth-century American theater, relates. "There are three movements: one is for the left hand to remove the cap at the words 'I am,' the second is for his right hand to take off the wig while pronouncing 'Hawkshaw,' and the third is for the hand with the cap in it to unfasten false whiskers while he says 'the detective.' " John T. Raymond played Hawkshaw at the California Theater while Barrett took the lead part of Bob Brierley.

Lotta's difficulty was that she had too much fun in what was really a melodrama. Comic relief could be carried only so far: Willoughby was a befuddled type, with a broad Lancashire accent, but the author of the play was making a comment on contemporary low life that was basically serious. Lotta's limits as an artist were defined too conspicuously; in the future, she backed away from roles that did not permit her the widest latitude in the escapades which her public expected.

She took her farewell benefit on September 10, "the house being densely filled in every part," and the harvest including a diamond-studded tiara and a packet of gold eagles. There followed a brief vacation. Tom Thumb and his wife, who had been on the program with Commodore Nutt at Platt's Music Hall, came to visit; Molly Ryan, in whose home Lotta had stayed briefly as a child when Mary Ann was pregnant in the mountains, journeyed down from Sacramento. Before leaving San Francisco, Mary Ann hired a colored maid, "Aunt Jane" Boyd, who was to be a servant in the Crabtree ménage for the next fifteen years. One of her duties was to carry the love letters. Somehow there was never room for them in Mary Ann's trunk; and besides, Lotta did not like to mix money with romance.

Time was to prove that this was impossible. Time was to show, too, that the letters did not always mean what they said. Many of them came from men Lotta had never met; of those she knew, few qualified in Mary Ann's eyes as suitable—or so the legend went. The truth probably lies in the practical difficulties of courtship on the run. Except during the summers, Lotta seldom spent more than a few weeks in one place. Dexter Smith, editor

of *The Folio,* a small musical paper in Boston, entertained Lotta
without making much of an impression on Mary Ann, who de-
cried his lack of worldly goods. Their engagement was said to
have been terminated by Mary Ann; proof is lacking. But *The
Folio*—and its successor, *Dexter Smith's Magazine*—went on
praising Lotta long after its owner had given up hope of marrying her.

For that matter, who didn't entertain Lotta? "Bolt" Hulme was
the handsome scion of a rich Philadelphia family. He followed
her everywhere, even to San Francisco. The two exchanged lock-
ets, each bearing a miniature. And whatever might be said of
Hulme's flashy habits, he was no typical stage-door Johnny. The
Hulmes were respected Philadelphians, and Philadelphia was a
city that looked upon theater people with remarkable tolerance.

J. Bolton Hulme had met Lotta in New York sometime in
1868. In his native city, he called for her nightly at Mrs. John
Drew's Arch Street Theater. Hulme sat through *The Pet of the
Petticoats* so many times he could almost recite the lines. His
photograph showed him to be blond and very handsome; the
gold locket that housed it indicated his wealth. What neither
revealed was a weakness of character that Lotta would discover
later. He drank (although not in Lotta's presence), and he
gambled—unfortunately, with Lotta's money. But she seems to
have been genuinely in love with him, and until the misuse of
funds came to light, Mary Ann approved, too.

But this is looking ahead. Edmund Falconer, who had done so
well with *Firefly,* wrote a new play for Lotta called *Hearts Ease,
or What's Money Without.* The grammar was questionable, but
no more so than the plot, which, in broad outline, was reminiscent of Lotta's early life in California. Lotta took the part of May
Wylderose, an Englishman's daughter who is taken to the California mining fields as a child and abandoned. Pale shades of
Crabtree! Most of the action is comic melodrama, punctuated by
the crack of six-shooters, for May Wylderose was well armed. (A
photograph of the period shows her holding two crossed revolv-

ers.) In one scene she is lowered into a canyon on the end of a
pulley to foil the villains; in another, she defends a buried cache
of gold. At last she discovers her father, whom she has not seen
since she was an infant; the two are reconciled and return to
London, where May is betrothed to a proper gentleman, although not before she executes some snappy numbers on the
banjo.

Hearts Ease was one of the few plays of Lotta's with a primarily American locale and theme, and it was her major production
throughout 1870. By this time, she had assembled the nucleus of
her own company, depending upon local actors only for minor
parts. In Boston, a pack of wild animals literally growled at the
company's heels, for Minnie Wells' production of *The Lion of
Nubia* followed her, and the collection of beasts—lions, pumas,
an elephant, and two camels—was housed backstage. It was for-
tunate that Lotta's company did not follow them, for *The Lion
of Nubia* played to disastrous houses, and the company disbanded, leaving the animals behind, "unwelcome and malodor-
ous guests."

From Boston, late in May, she went to New York for one of
those monster benefits that were virtually a command performance. Colonel T. Allston Brown, drama editor of the *New York
Clipper,* a theatrical and sporting paper, was retiring to take up
a career as an actor's agent. Brown was a powerful figure in New
York theatrical life, and members of the profession who had
quaked in apprehension of what he might say about them as a
critic now rushed to his aid in view of what he might do for them
as an agent. In any case, the Colonel needed money. He not
only organized the benefit—for which the capacious Academy of
Music was turned over to him for May 31—but subsequently
reviewed it in the *Clipper*. "His account . . . is naturally out of
proportion to its intrinsic value," Odell was to comment later,
but even so, as showmanship in the grand manner, it was highly
successful.

For one thing, it began at two in the afternoon and ran, with a respite for dinner, until almost midnight. The entire orchestras of three minstrel troupes entrenched in New York—Kelly and Leon's, Bryant's, and Hooley's—occupied the orchestra pit and overflowed onto the stage. Minstrel bands were not known for the delicacy of their music—a high proportion of the instrumentation was brass—and the combined volume of three bands, with the innumerable trombone smears called forth by the nature of the performance, turned the Academy of Music into a boiler factory. But the entertainers were equal to the occasion, if the audience was not. Brown himself, who watched the show triumphantly from a private box, wrote later that "there were more performers in the first part minstrel scene than ever before or since witnessed in America," and very likely he was right.

Some of the great minstrels of the day—Dan Bryant, Tony Pastor, and Billy Emmet—were there; Lotta performed in the evening, doing her indestructible one-acter, *Nan, the Good for Nothing*. On the same bill was Rose Massey and her British Blondes. The show closed with a walk-around of 123 performers, each of whom danced his specialty. The result of this marathon spectacle was that Colonel Brown was nearly $2,000 richer, and the audience was exhausted. Perhaps Lotta was too, for on the very next day she and Mary Ann sailed for a vacation in Europe.

Appearances of this sort, no matter how charitably intended, did not help her reputation with the critics. She had been thrown back into the milieu of minstrelsy, competing for applause with a troupe of hefty burlesque queens from England. There was further unfavorable reaction the following year when Richard Robertson, Edwin Booth's partner, engaged her to do *Little Nell*. Audiences would follow Lotta into any theater now, even as solemn and high-minded a temple as Booth's. Booth was decidedly unhappy; his beloved theater was to be profaned by a clog dancer. But Lotta herself seems not to have minded the tragedian's animadversions. Their paths crossed on tour; there was the kind of mutual respect that exists across a very wide chasm, although Booth could not appreciate Lotta's eccentric style and found it hard to accept the fact that she often drew larger houses.

But the truth was that Booth's ideal audience was lacking in New York, and he spent more and more time on the road earning money for his ailing theater. Robertson, an albatross around Booth's neck, was right about Lotta, even though Booth resented her presence; the money rolled in, and he was able to pay off some of his creditors.

Little Nell played for four weeks. John T. Raymond, who had come east from San Francisco, took the part of Dick Swiveller. The *Times* reviewer, describing the scenery as "exquisite," was less charitable about what took place on stage. "Questionings as to the potency of an ill-built play and of a pretty and mischievous little person would be repetitious only of earlier references to the same subjects and of failure in getting a reply." The poor man had seen *Little Nell* four times, in four different theaters, and was becoming weary.

The Worrell Sisters had come east, naming theaters after themselves in both Boston and New York. But the old rivalry was gone. Grown up now, Jennie Worrell refused to wear boys' breeches in an adaptation of Henry Ward Beecher's *Norwood*. Not so Lotta. She played stage urchins so convincingly that their real-life counterparts worshipped her, and in turn were rewarded. Very much a child at heart, she was genuinely shocked by the condition of these children. It was said that she clothed "from head to foot" every homeless newsboy in New Orleans. In New Orleans the "Lotta Baseball Club" had been formed, and all over the city young boys could be seen wearing the Lotta insignia on their uniforms. It was the only decent outfit some of them owned. On New Year's Day, 1872, she was made honorary president of the club, presented with a gold medal, and told that she was not only the pet of the petticoats but the pet of the breeches in the house, too. The pit was filled with them.

As time went on, such openhandedness was extended to all the major cities in which she played. One unforeseen result of this was that the newsboys became a permanent, nationwide claque—although this had never been Lotta's intention. As admirers, they were not only ardent, but on occasion threatening; on newsboy night, spectators seated in the parquet were careful not to withhold their applause at the proper time for fear of the young urchins who sometimes paraded through the aisles to assure an even greater ovation than the star expected.

New Orleans always held a special niche in Lotta's affections. The previous January, between impersonations of Corduroy Bill in *The Rainbow* and Vivandière, she had been baptized there. An Episcopal minister, the Reverend Mr. Leacock was called to Room 175 at the St. Charles Hotel; friends of the Crabtrees acted as sponsors in baptism, and Lotta, gowned in black silk, with bretelles of light blue thrown over the bodice, became a Christian at the age of twenty-three. There was no longer any social obstacle to marriage with Bolton Hulme.

In 1872, Lotta remained in New Orleans through the Mardi Gras. The Grand Duke Alexis of Russia was making a celebrated visit to the United States and had come to New Orleans for the carnival. He, too, with his retinue, was staying at the St. Charles. Twenty-three years old, he was handsome, unmarried, and had a strong attraction for the ladies, some of whom had pursued him during a buffalo hunt out west.

He chose February 14, St. Valentine's Day, to see her perform. He could not understand a word of the play, but Lotta captivated him. His aides had already fended off a covey of New Orleans society belles who wanted to meet him. Now he let it be known that he desired an introduction to Miss Lotta.

Lotta was flattered, of course, to be the object of royal attention. What made the meeting awkward—it took place in one of the hotel's private lounges—was the colossal disparity in the heights of the two principals. The Duke was almost seven feet tall, and Lotta barely five; when she curtsied, it was like going down at the foot of a tree. And when Alexis responded by kissing her hand, he was almost forced to his knees. He insisted that Lotta must visit his "ship," which turned out to be a small passenger boat furnished by the United States government. At a banquet in her honor, the Duke permitted each of his officers to take turns sitting at Lotta's side.

The Grand Duke sailed off, and Lotta went to Memphis with DeBar's company. It was her first appearance in this city. "Lotta was the Curiosity and the Shop," the *Appeal* said of *Little Nell.* "[She] borrows nothing and lends everything to the author. Even Dickens is her debtor. . . ." A few nights later, Lotta was making one of her lightning changes from Grizzie Gutteridge into Harry Racket in *The Little Detective* when the house manager rushed backstage with a telegram. Mary Ann took it, saw that it was not from one of the customary unknown admirers but the Grand Duke himself, gave a little yelp of surprise, and thrust it into Lotta's hand. Alexis had left orders for a bracelet to be sent to her in Memphis. The play picked up at once.

The dazzling arrangement of diamonds, opals, and pearls came a week later, in time for Lotta's farewell benefit. As with all of Lotta's jewelry, Mary Ann took custody of it, and eventually the bracelet went into the same box as the gold medal from the Lotta Baseball Club.

In April, 1872, Lotta was back in San Francisco, this time at the Metropolitan Theater, which had just been renovated. The *Alta California* noted that the opening of the New Italian Opera Season at Maguire's "was not more than half full . . . owing to special attractions elsewhere." Yet Lotta could hardly have relished her success at Maguire's expense; he was the only manager in San Francisco willing to take cultural risks, losing from twenty to thirty thousand dollars a year in the attempt. But the public flocked to the Metropolitan for another bout of Lotta—she was always in good form on her old proving ground.

Crabtree was in town, as well as the two boys, who were living with their aunt, Mrs. Vernon. At eighteen, Jack had begun to exhibit some of the wildness that was to make him both charming and irresponsible later on. Lotta was sterner than Mary Ann, and Jack looked upon her as something of a crank, albeit generous enough with her money. Corralling her husband and sons, Mary Ann brought them all to the empty stage of the Metropolitan one afternoon; with Lotta present, a photographer posed them against some Arcadian scenery for a portrait. Perhaps Mary Ann had a premonition, for it was the last time they would be together as a family. That fall, Crabtree went to England with the understanding that he would receive an allowance of £5 a week as long as he stayed abroad. He thus became possibly the only British-born remittance man forced to remain on his native soil. Except for two visits to the United States, he remained in England until his death in 1894. Money was provided for a trotting pony and an American buggy, and it was generally understood around Cheshire, where he settled down with a fictitious air of wealth, that John Ashworth Crabtree had made a killing in the California gold fields.

3

The Way to the Fountain

A SPEECH in *Hearts Ease,* describing the reclamation of the waif, May Wylderose, might have been applied to Lotta herself. "She has since been laboring to acquire the accomplishments that are looked for in the drawing room. Resolutely bent upon self-education, she has visited nearly all the places of note in Germany, Italy and France and devoting a great deal of time to study, has become an accomplished musician and can speak both French and Italian with ease."

Lotta could not yet speak French and Italian "with ease," but as time went on she would try. In the fall of 1872, the family, minus Jack, who had been sent to school in Heidelberg, went to England. Lotta's cousin, Louis Livesey, accompanied them; Crabtree was deposited in Altrincham, Cheshire, while Livesey and George Crabtree were enrolled in a private school in nearby Bowden. (A fellow student recalled that the two cousins slept in the same bed. "Livesey was short and dark with an extra-large head, which the boys explained by saying that he had been shipwrecked when very young and some insect had crawled into his head and out through the top.")

Meanwhile, Lotta and Mary Ann went on to the Continent for a sort of semi-grand tour of Italy, Switzerland, Germany, and France. It was the most extended vacation Lotta had had, yet she could not let herself relax. "O, how I do study French and music," she wrote to Dexter Smith. "It keeps me as busy as a long rehearsal would." Back home, the rumor had been circulated that she had died "in the South of France, of a slow decline . . . which

followed an overworked youth." The report, published in some
newspapers, was more than slightly exaggerated, and very likely
had been engineered by her manager at the time, W. R. Floyd, as
an ill-advised means of keeping Lotta's name alive with the public;
it was the first season she had not toured. Dexter Smith was "happy
to state" that the actress "is enjoying better health than for many
years." "At a good meal, I am a match for the smartest huntsman
in the chase," she had written him.

Mary Ann soon returned to England while Lotta remained in
Paris with a Boston friend, Mrs. Stratton. Lotta had a French
tutor, but the chaperoning Mrs. Stratton saw to it that he was
not alone with her, and in the end he was replaced by a talking
machine. Lotta missed Mary Ann. "My friends were very kind
but what is home without a mother? So I started for England and
here we all are, in a beautiful place called Yarwood, Cheshire. I
can, and do, walk four or five miles, and think nothing of it. . . . I
have had many offers to act in the best theaters in London, but
Mother says: 'No, you came here for rest, recreation and study,
and you shall not act,' and Mother is right, I guess—mothers
always *are* right." But Lotta had surprised Mother by arriving in
Cheshire with the French talking machine *and* the tutor, who
confined his activities to improving Lotta's accent.

Mother and daughter returned to New York in the spring of
1873, leaving George Crabtree and Louis Livesey in school at
Bowden. Jack had left Heidelberg before the year was over,
returning home without acquiring either an education or a duel-
ing scar. As for Lotta, the six months abroad hardly made up for
sixteen years of educational neglect, for the catch-as-catch-can
schooling she had been able to grab on the run, although it gave
her a veneer of culture that equaled that of most young ladies
who had been to Europe. What most young ladies did not have,
at least through their own efforts, was $300,000.

The money was managed by Mary Ann, with help, from time
to time, from Robert Dunlap, owner of a fashionable men's hat
store on Fifth Avenue. It was here, above the store, in an apart-

ment next to the Dunlaps, that the Crabtrees now lived. The two families were to become intimate friends, a valuable connection in view of Dunlap's rather unique entrée in the world of capitalism and power. His custom included J. P. Morgan, General Grant, Mayor Oakey Hall, Jay Gould, and other carriage-trade notables for whom the proper headgear was a social necessity. He cultivated the good will of these financiers and politicians by maintaining a private file of the shapes of their heads, noting the various protuberances and peculiarities that might make an ordinary topper seem ill-fitting. Dunlap, however, did not manufacture ordinary hats. Hand-crafted, they fit the most intractable cranium. And they were expensive. And so Dunlap rubbed shoulders with the mighty, felt their heads, and pried loose a good many "inside" tips which he later put to his own use. Some of these were passed on to Mary Ann, who was forever admiring the progress of the rich. "The original Cornelius Vanderbilt's fortune amounted to about $100,000 . . . his parents were poor," she scrawled in her item book, noting that Cornelius's grandson, the Commodore, had since parlayed the sum to $300,000,000. Inspirational data such as this, which gave her something to shoot at, cluttered a book ordinarily devoted to keeping track of the interest on Lotta's bonds, important birthdays, bits of poetry, and tax records.

Dunlap's advice was not always heeded—indeed, it was not heeded often enough—and the 1870s proved to be a challenging decade for Mary Ann's commercial ventures. She became involved in a number of get-rich-quick schemes, in which she invariably lost money; she acquired dozens of parcels of real estate, became the owner of a theater in Boston, the backer of a New York theatrical producer, part owner of a cotton brokerage firm in Fall River, Massachusetts, and, in 1880, partner in a livery stable in Tombstone, Arizona, a town in which she never set foot. The climax was reached in 1878 when, the victim of a confidence game, she found herself owner of a nearly worthless gold mine in

La Porte, California. Except for the livery stable, all of this was done in Lotta's name.

When she was not buying gold mines or cotton mills, Mary Ann "studied economy," as she liked to put it. It was the small, daily items of housekeeping on which she economized; big expenditures, especially if they promised big returns, were no problem. In a sense, money isolated Lotta, and no doubt that was one reason why she gave more and more of it away. "Charity is what is needed in this world," she told a reporter in 1874.

She was utterly sincere. And she had been stung by suggestions that her wealth, her newly acquired "culture," had made her too much a lady—she was beginning to "refine," a Cincinnati writer asserted in the *Enquirer*. "When last here, she was already becoming a shade too much of a young lady of breeding and high tastes to seem quite in place in her old characters . . . as she lost her hold upon the galleries, she gained friends in the dress circle."

Lotta resented such imputations, but the conflict was all too real. She wanted to be the "pet of the pit," yet it was the dress circle that filled the coffers of the box office, and she would compensate by showing compassion, by "identifying" with those who believed in her most. She took up the practice of visiting prisons and jails, and hotel bellboys, like the newsboys, acquired a special call on her bounty—it should be noted that they really were "boys" in those days, and Lotta treated them generously.

Whenever she was playing, Lotta always napped for two hours in the afternoon; at such times, her mother was a familiar figure in the hotel corridor, where, seated in a chair, she guarded Lotta's door and hushed any noisy guests who might be passing by. In New Orleans, Lotta was surprised one afternoon by a delegation of brightly caparisoned youths who had breached Mary Ann's defenses. The bellboys had waited until she left her post, knocked, and when Lotta appeared, presented her with a small package done up in ribbon. One of the group mumbled some words of esteem, but Lotta, not fully awake, and thinking that the gift was simply being delivered from an admirer, tipped the young man and dismissed him.

Inspection of the package revealed it to be a one-volume edition of Oliver Goldsmith, inscribed to her by the boys. Just who chose the book was never revealed, but Lotta rectified her gaffe in a letter: "I was never so surprised as when yesterday I was handed a lovely book. I did not understand it at first, in fact, I could not make it out until the boys had left the room, then I saw that it was a present . . . for which I thank them a thousand and one times."

Such gifts were a wholesome contrast to the torrent of mail from crank lovers, and from the gold seekers fended off by Mary Ann. A man in Chicago, who wrote Lotta faithfully for five years without ever receiving a reply, finally sent her a chart of his head. Lotta showed it to Robert Dunlap, who expressed his opinion that "it was a very fine head," or at least would fit well under a Dunlap hat, a fact which failed to sway her; she refused to meet him.

These were her "idiotic admirers," as she called them. In Boston she was compared to the Empress Josephine by a correspondent who identified himself as Napoleon "silently watching the star of destiny." Although gratuitous cakes with Lotta's name spelled out in the icing were usually eaten, the letters were consigned to the wastebasket, or given to Aunt Jane Boyd for her amusement. "I do wish that a man of a little sense would admire me for once," Lotta exclaimed to an interviewer.

Already, there was an underlying note of sadness about her relationships with men. Bolton Hulme had died unexpectedly in 1872, although not before he had repaid the $6,000 of Lotta's money that he had gambled away. No theatrical personality was the subject of so much speculation as Lotta. It was suggested that something had died in her with Hulme, and in part, this was true; she could forgive his escapades with money—indeed, she was to see much worse in brother Jack—but the fates that brought about Hulme's death, on the very threshold of his life, and after the noble act of repentance, she could not absolve.

This is how matters stood upon her return from Europe, when a letter arrived from a Harvard student named Francis L. Wellman, who seldom missed a Lotta performance in Boston. He, too, had been stirred to dreams of military glory by the romantic bravura of *Firefly*. Unlike Clarence Edwards, he did not enroll in West Point, but instead sought a meeting with Vivandière herself. Rather than turn the letter over to Aunt Jane, Lotta gave it to brother Jack with instructions to call on the young man and ascertain if he was a gentleman. Jack proceeded to Cambridge, looked up Wellman, and came right to the point. The student assured him that he was not only a gentleman, but a direct descendant of one of the signers of the Declaration of Independence, Francis Lewis. This was good enough for Jack, who brought him around to meet his sister.

She was still grieving over the death of Bolt Hulme, and Wellman was a pleasant distraction who gave her elaborate dinners, partly in order to impress his Harvard peers, and partly, too, so that he could hold Lotta's hand under the table, since their less formal meetings were always chaperoned. Lotta was older than Wellman, but this was no obstacle; he could never quite separate the real person from her youthful roles. The two were intimate friends for the next five years, even after Wellman became engaged to another girl—much to Lotta's annoyance, it should be added. "We were very fond of one another," Wellman reminisced in 1925, four wives later. (By this time he had become a prominent attorney and the author of several books on the law.) "My father, of an old Boston family, was afraid I would marry her."

Lotta had recently purchased a play by a popular dramatist, Frederic T. Marsden, the pen name of William Sliver. Marsden had "studied the whims and vagaries of Lotta, and made up his mind that he could write a play for her," *The Theatre* told its readers, and *Zip; or Point Lynde Light* was ushered into

Booth's—again to the anguish of the great man—in the spring of 1874. Marsden's object was to keep Lotta on stage as much as possible, on the theory that no matter how bad the play was, Lotta would make it entertaining.

A brief résumé of the plot reveals how shrewd a critic Marsden was of his own work. As Zip, Lotta lives in a lighthouse with an old man she supposes to be her father. He has been all but killed by villains who are out to lure an incoming vessel onto the rocks so that they may claim its treasure. What Zip does not know is that the ship also carries her real mother, who has come from the ancestral estate in England to seek the daughter.

One hardly needs to be told that Zip foils the plot. There is a good deal of thunder and lightning, decoy flares are lighted, and the ship is headed for disaster when the young girl climbs the rocks, swings across the foaming chasm with the aid of a rope, and lights the beacon while men fight with three-legged stools below. The crisis is averted. "The situation which caps the first act is really thrilling," the *Times* critic admitted.

The scene changes to England, and the final two acts are devoted to sorting out various documents, including the mother's marriage certificate, as well as foiling a new set of villains intent on gaining the inheritance. Here, too, Lotta finds a banjo. In the end, after a song-and-dance routine with the footman, she marries the right man, whom she meets in the intervals of a walk-around.

The only lasting influence of the play was the lighthouse, which suggested the fountain Lotta commissioned the following year. Yet the plot, however outmoded it seems today, had a secure hold on the nineteenth-century audiences. The theme of the child unaware of her own identity occurred in many of Lotta's plays from *Hearts Ease* in 1870 to *Pawn Ticket 210* in 1888. It was to crop up again, when Ida May Blankenberg cast herself in the role of Lotta's daughter, born at "Chateau Crabtree" and taken to a farm in Illinois to be raised by others.

In effect, these were Cinderella plays. Lotta's appeal lay in the exuberant manner in which cheerfulness could persist in spite of adversity. But Lotta was not only cheerful; she was saucy, pert, gamey, devilish, mischievous, unpredictable, impulsive, rattle-brained, teasing, piquant, and rollicking—to cite a few of the ad-jectives applied to her by the critics. She could bang the drums, strum a banjo, do a clog dance, and sing; and although there was considerable doubt that she could act, no one really cared. Lotta was Lotta, and for respectable, middle-class audiences she made low life acceptable because it was really high life in disguise.

It never bothered her that she was not a conventional actress like Clara Morris or Rose Coughlin; and after a time, it ceased to bother the critics. "A poor player," the Shakespearean actor E. L. Davenport wrote of himself in the guest book at a reception in Chicago. Following him in line, Lotta took the pen, read what he had written, and after her own name wrote: "A good banjo player."

Musette; or Little Bright Eyes, another Marsden play, followed later that year, and, as one observer commented, Lotta's eyes were indubitably bright. *Musette* was a slight, colorful extrava-ganza in which Lotta played a gypsy girl who, before winning her rightful estate, is chased across the English countryside by a lech-erous baronet. But the heroine is by no means happy at "Red-mond Hall," and her good-humored antagonism provides room for the usual Lotta antics. These, in fact, are what people came to see.

For some reason, which was certainly a mystery to London playgoers who saw it ten years later, *Musette* became one of Lotta's most popular plays. When she took it to Louisville, Ken-tucky, the *Courier* advised its readers that "it is the moral duty of everybody to go today," advice which was heeded, although probably not out of moral duty. The longer it ran, the less it resembled Marsden's original; a Moody and Sankey hymn tune was inserted and burlesqued as a specialty number, and toward the end of the 1870s, Lotta added a medley of songs from *Pina-*

fore! Marsden was outraged with the manner in which the star tampered with the script and in later years refused to see it, although the royalties poured in and made him a reasonably wealthy man.

These were the years of highest success for Lotta, and of the hardest work. She was what is called in the profession a "slow study"; memorizing parts was difficult. To handle them all—her repertory in any one year was never less than a dozen plays—was a problem which Lotta solved by improvising freely, a practice that was sometimes hard on the members of her cast. Once, in *Musette,* she substituted real molasses for the usual stage imitation and for three nights running smeared it into the hair of an actress who played the part of Maud. The woman did not find the incident funny, but others in the company, who escaped these mischievous assaults, took a philosophical view. "May it not be that this impulsiveness . . . was the keynote of her success?" one of them noted.

They could tolerate their star's unpredictable behavior in the spirit of professionalism. For one thing, they were always paid on time; and for another, the company never went broke on the road, a hazard so common with many troupes that the *New York Clipper* regularly listed the whereabouts of stranded players as a service to their friends at home. Although from time to time Lotta's company included actors of stature, such as Charles R. Thorne, Jr., James K. Hackett, Mrs. John Gilbert, John T. Raymond, Oliver Doud Bryon, Agnes Perry Booth, and William Crane, the permanent cast was recruited from among the less notable. In general, the critics found little to praise about them—"Her leading man must never sing too well, or act too convincingly; her leading lady must never be guilty of a personal comeliness that is too much in evidence," one of them wrote.

Ed Marble, the stage manager, had joined Lotta from California and after her retirement became an interlocutor in a minstrel show. Her comedian was E. A. Locke; young Clement Bainbridge was the leading juvenile; A. D. Bradley, who had met

Lotta when he directed the Woods Dramatic Company in Chicago, was the "heavy"; and two women, Kate Newton and Julia Hanchett, acted the important female parts. Lesser performers were recruited from resident companies. The number of supernumeraries provided by the theater depended upon the importance of the star, and Lotta always insisted that for a show like *Firefly* she be allowed as many soldiers as Edwin Forrest in *Richard III*. Forrest himself insisted on a number no less than that assigned to Edwin Booth in *Macbeth*. At the Walnut Street Theater in Philadelphia, thirty-two "supers" were provided Lotta for *Firefly,* equally divided between the Foreign Legion and the Arabs. They were poorly paid but, like the newsboys, Lotta remembered them at Christmas time.

She had become a yearly favorite during the New Orleans Mardi Gras, summoned there by "Royal Edict XVI, section 3, requiring service of all loyal subjects. . . ." To which the actress replied that "I, Lotta, one of the most diminutive but most loving, tender myself and banjo to service wherever and in whatever capacity his Most Gracious Majesty may direct." Of course, this was press agentry, but Lotta entered into the spirit of the Mardi Gras willingly, secretly pleased to be "summoned" during the most profitable period of the local season. Ben DeBar had bought the Opera House there, outraged because the previous owner had painted out the portrait of Shakespeare over the proscenium arch and substituted his own. DeBar promptly restored the Bard, but in 1875 it was entertainers like Buffalo Bill, Texas Jack Omohondoo, and Lotta who drew the crowds in New Orleans.

This year, 1875, was also the year of the fountain, the great symbolic act in Lotta's life. It set her apart, as a profusion of other charities was to do as she got older and richer, from the ordinary run of actors, whose fortunes were not only less spectacular, but more likely to be spent on personal indulgence. Lotta considered the money which the fountain cost her a small payment against the perquisites of success which San Francisco had made possible.

Yet it was never intended as a monument to herself, but rather as a wholly practical means of supplying water to horses and, for that matter, people. The rough design seems to have been Lotta's own, but the city fathers, who were entrusted with the final execution, added numerous medallions and bas-reliefs, and raised the height from sixteen to twenty-one feet. (The cost also rose—from its original estimate of $6,000 to $10,000.) Cast in Philadelphia, it was shipped in sections to San Francisco and dedicated on September 9. Lotta, who was playing in Cincinnati at the time and did not get to see the fountain until four years later, asked Henry Edwards of the California Stock Company to represent her.

The ceremonies constituted a virtual holiday for the people of San Francisco. Crowds began forming long before the unveiling at Geary, Market and Kearny Streets; the police were unable to keep them back, and two companies from the National Guard were called to keep order. At length, a passage was forced and a number of dignitaries, including Mayor Otis, were escorted to the speaker's platform by the 4th Artillery Band. Edwards made a gracious presentation speech on behalf of Lotta, the Mayor then unveiled the fountain, and Mary Ann's twin sister, Mrs. Vernon, was led forward to receive the first drink. After which—in the *Chronicle's* words—"everybody rushed forward."

What the public saw was a fluted shaft reminiscent of the lighthouse in *Zip*. Over each of the four basins was the head of a griffin, and above these, in heraldic posture, were alternating bears' and seals' rampant. Black tin cups were chained to the stonework. Medallions commemorating such California enterprises as mining, farming, and shipping were affixed to the shaft, while wrought-iron lilies sprouted arabesques. These, in turn, supported a six-sided lantern crowned by a stem bearing three groups of small golden balls. The *Alta California* called it "the most ornate cast iron work ever bronzed," and the *Chronicle,* writing in a more practical spirit, remarked that the location was such that a man could throw a cup of water into any of five or six nearby saloons. Horses, it was facetiously rumored at first, were so startled by the edifice that they customarily gave it wide berth, and could be lured into taking a drink of water only in cases of extreme thirst.

The attendant publicity embarrassed Lotta. Although a small plaque testified to the donor's name, she had never intended it to be called "her" fountain. It belonged to San Francisco. Not until 1879 did she play there again, because—it was claimed—Lotta did not want people to think she was expecting tribute for her generosity.

Possibly there was some truth in this; in any case, this is how San Franciscans explained her absence. But perhaps the major reason was her increasing involvement at this time with Henry E. Abbey, a rising young impresario for whom she became the principal financial backer.

Abbey was just one year older than Lotta, the son of a Connecticut clockmaker who had moved to Akron, Ohio, where he opened a jewelry business in which his son was employed. In those days, theater tickets for advance attractions were frequently sold in jewelry stores, and young Abbey, who earned a commission on each sale, got a taste of the theater that appealed to him. He seems to have been a persuasive salesman—of tickets, if not watches—and after a few years "got tired of fitting wedding rings on young women," as he put it, and struck out on his own.

For a time he was treasurer of the Euclid Avenue Opera House in Cleveland, and from there went to Ellsler's Opera House in Pittsburgh. He knew a money-maker and he knew a flop, and he possessed the sort of sixth sense about actors that later led him to back the American tours of Sarah Bernhardt, Henry Irving, and Lillie Langtry. For a brief time, he had managed the Worrell Sisters. Lotta knew him through her appearances in Cleveland and Pittsburgh, although not, perhaps, as well as Mary Ann, who picked up the nightly receipts from Abbey at the box office. Abbey was not long in discovering that Lotta was a money-maker.

He was a dapper, handsome man, tall, thin, dark-complexioned, with black, closely cropped hair and a slight, black mustache. There was no doubt that Lotta liked Abbey—some said she was in love with him—and he was quick to take advantage of the relationship for Lotta's sake as well as his own. In 1876, the Park Theater, at Twenty-third Street and Broadway, had been auctioned off by its creditors. A relatively small house of 1,000 seats, it had been built for Dion Boucicault two years before and was now dark. With Lotta's money, Abbey proposed to lease it—a splendid new theater for her New York performances.

To manage the Park, Abbey formed a partnership with another entrepreneur named John B. Schoeffel. Resident theater companies were still a strong institution in New York, and Abbey hired John T. Raymond to assemble a cast, which included Agnes Booth and Mrs. Sydney Cowell. Mary Ann, representing Lotta, left it to Abbey to book the plays and take care of general business affairs, but she saw to it that both of the Crabtree boys, at one time or another, were employed in the box office. Lotta reopened the Park on November 27, 1876, in *Musette,* which ran for three weeks, and followed it with a revival of *Little Nell,* with the popular comedian William Crane taking the part of Dick Swiveller. George Odell, writing several decades later, questioned what Lotta's "unrivalled clog dance" had to do with either Little Nell or the Marchioness. "The last scene gave us 'The Grave of Little Nell,' and the 'Apotheosis of the Flight of Innocence' tearfully uniting Little Nell with Little Eva. . . . Had she belonged to the 1920s, Lotta might have been drafted into the Ziegfeld Follies, the Scandals or some such."

Meanwhile, Lotta's relationship with Abbey was said to have taken a romantic turn, and gossip had it that more things bound them together than money. The major obstacle to marriage was Abbey's invalid wife. The actress Anna Pingree insisted that Abbey once told her that "Lotta made a solemn vow that since she could not marry him she would live and die a virgin." There is a sound of post-facto heroics about this, but Lotta seems to have been strongly attached to Abbey, and when, following Mrs.

Abbey's death, he married an actress named Florence Gerard, Lotta was deeply hurt. "The broken romance actually broke the heart of the great Lotta," William Seymour of the old Boston Museum stock company declared later. "She admitted it as a reason for her failure to marry."

The difficulty with this story is that there is no real evidence that Lotta suffered a broken heart; she remained a friend of Abbey's until his death and on one occasion, when he was in low water, restored him to solvency. The Abbey-Lotta "love affair" was very likely a convenient business relationship, but the gossip writers, then as now, needed grist for their mill.

For seven months in the spring and summer of 1876, Lotta, Mary Ann, and brother George had again traveled in Europe. George was a cosmopolitan young man of twenty who, ever since his accident, had been educated in private schools. A photograph of George taken in Paris and inscribed to his "Dear Mother" from "Loving Son" reveals a young man of impeccable elegance wearing a fawn-colored Eton hat with raked brim, a wing collar, and a sporty waistcoat. The trip was another cultural foray for Lotta, who resumed her French studies, poked into art museums, and went to the Comédie Française. The Paris interlude was an extended one: "We had lovely apartments bordering on the Bois de Boulogne," she wrote to a friend in America. Then there was The Hague, Berlin, Stockholm, and an expedition into Norway "as far as the railroads would carry us." In Dieppe, Lotta took up painting, found that she had a flair for it, and was "delighted with the discovery." It was no passing fancy; Lotta painted for the remainder of her life, and quite creditably. At the end, she painted herself, dressed as the Marchioness—over and over.

In Liverpool, after a visit to Crabtree in Cheshire, she, Mary Ann, and George embarked for the return voyage. Would "Miss Lotta" entertain the passengers with a recital? the captain of the *America* asked. She proposed a benefit for sailors' orphans, and passengers jammed the saloon to hear her—there was very little that was theatrical about Lotta at such close quarters, but what there was had to be paid for.

Success never spoiled her, but it provided Mary Ann with the basis for certain social pretensions. Summers, now, the family rented a cottage at Newport. "Doc" Shea, a veterinarian who was still living in 1925, recalled the elegant "turnout" which Lotta and Mary Ann drove along Bellevue Avenue at four in the afternoon in the parade of carriages that all Newport took part in. It was the extent of their participation in the colony's social life; the really prominent families did not entertain them. Yet one of the reasons for summering in Newport was that Mary Ann liked to be around millionaires.

Another reason, no doubt, was its proximity to Fall River, where Lotta had bought into the cotton brokerage house of B. F. Randall. This was not simply a speculation—in return for Lotta's $50,000 investment, her two brothers would be given the benefit of Randall's business experience, although time would demonstrate that this was rather dubious. Randall was to "look after" the Crabtree boys and, according to a clerk in the firm, "teach them the value of a dollar." Meanwhile, through Robert Dunlap, young Louis Livesey, Lotta's "sixth" first cousin, had secured a job in a Fall River hat store. The three boys lived together in a boardinghouse.

During the summer of 1877, Lotta and her mother drove up every weekend from Newport, partly so that Mary Ann might check up on the boys, and also in order to check up on Randall. He was an admirer of Lotta's who never missed seeing her perform in Fall River, and every shipment of cotton that left his warehouse was stamped Z I P in her honor. Had Lotta been superstitious, an incident that occurred about this time might have been considered an omen: playing *Zip* in New York, her hair caught fire from the torch with which she lighted the signal beacon.

Then it was discovered that Randall was holding out part of the profits, the partnership was dissolved, and Lotta sued to recoup her losses. The boys, of course, were pulled out of Fall River, Louis Livesey was given the job in Dunlap's store in New York, and George went on a trip to Argentina with Clement Bainbridge, Lotta's leading juvenile—not so much for George's benefit, it was rumored, as to remove the handsome young actor from Lotta's presence. Not long before this, Mary Ann was reported to have been in Troy, New York, making arrangements for her daughter's appearance when word arrived that Lotta had consented to marry Bainbridge in Albany, where the company was playing. Mary Ann rushed to Albany. There was no marriage; probably none had been intended, but "the madam," as Bainbridge always called her, took no chances. The actor obligingly went with George to South America—it was a long way, and it took forty-eight days to get there.

George had already begun to show both artistic and literary ambitions, and in his log of the trip he sketched the harbor at Buenos Aires and wrote stories and poems. But he missed Livesey; Louis was the only one who knew about a limb being rearranged. "He would make a good doctor," George used to say. On board the liner was a young Englishman named O. E. Huss with whom George struck up an acquaintance; he had money, aspired to be a theatrical producer, and wanted introductions to the profession. Back in New York, George obligingly wrote a "To whom it may concern" letter extolling Huss as "intelligent, sober, honest and industrious, and [I] can safely recommend him to whomever these shall come." The industrious Mr. Huss thereupon presented himself to Miss Lotta Crabtree!

The whole business might have been passed over as a joke, but Huss was both humorless and persistent, and what was worse, he had a habit of feeding doubtful information to the newspapers. At Lake George, where he joined the family for a vacation, he was reported to have "saved Lotta from drowning"—but the item appeared in a Washington dispatch to the *Chicago Inter-Ocean,* and people at Lake George seemed to know nothing about it. Huss, who sensed that affairs of business might be the key to a successful affair of the heart, as far as Lotta was concerned, offered to lease Washington's National Theater for her. None of this strategy succeeded, and eventually he put in circulation a story that he and Lotta were to be married, then denied it at length. One of the few cryptic items found in Lotta's effects at her death was a scrap of paper that read: "Lotta Crabtree is the wife of O. E. Huss. Married lately." The date was July 22, 1883. But the handwriting is not Lotta's. Eventually, Huss returned to England.

When George returned from Argentina, he went into the box office at Abbey's Park with brother Jack, who was listed on Lotta's programs as "manager of the company." The Park was the one real stone in Mary Ann's glittering string of beads. In the six years of the new Park's life—it was demolished by fire in 1882, on the day that Lillie Langtry was to make her American debut—a policy of wholesome comedy filled the house with laughter, and the box office with money. Occasionally, Clara Morris, a discovery of Augustin Daly, but who was managed by Abbey for a time, added a strain of emotional extravagance in such plays as *Camille* and *The Hunchback*. Miss Morris suffered real torments and wept genuine tears. Later, she would carry bottles of medicine with her on stage, and she kept a physician in her dressing room to minister to her during intermissions, which might last forty-five minutes while the audience conversed in hushed tones in the lobby, as though gathered outside a sickroom. But in general, Abbey and Schoeffel booked lighter stuff.

Robson and Crane, a popular comedy team whose plays *Our Boarding House* and *Our Bachelors* ran intermittently at the Park, typified the sort of fare audiences expected to find. They were never embarrassed by risqué situations or suggestive lines. The humorist George Ade later declared that Crane "always proceeded on the theory that theater patrons lived at home with their wives," and as far as the Park was concerned, this was substantially the case. (It thrived so handsomely on this policy that in 1879, Lotta secured another theater for Abbey and

Schoeffel in Boston. This was the old Beethoven Hall on Washington Street, which Abbey remodeled in exactly fifty working
days, keeping only the original four walls. This, too, was re-
named the Park.)

More and more, Lotta was drawn into personal appearances
for charity; demanding as her own schedule might be, she found
it difficult to refuse these requests, when everybody knew her to
be the most generous of stars. In Philadelphia, accompanied by
some local musicians, she entertained at an almshouse. Colored
inmates were brought in after the main show for their own performance. Looking into their dulled faces, Lotta asked the super-
intendent what they would like to hear—and was advised to sing
"Dixie"!

Poor Edwin Adams, debt-ridden, too ill to act—dying, in fact
—was propped on a chair at the Academy of Music in New York
to receive the tributes and proceeds at a huge benefit tendered by
the profession. Lotta romped for him in a burlesque of the third
act of *Othello,* playing Desdemona. The matinee included a little
of everything—Tony Pastor was on hand, along with Harrigan
and Hart, and Bryant's minstrels. Mrs. John Drew and Henry
Crisp did a scene from *The School for Scandal;* Clara Morris
emoted heavily in the fourth act of *Camille.* Abbey was one of
the ushers.

The scene from *Othello,* with the famous E. H. Sothern as the
Moor and W. J. Florence as Iago, had been billed as the main
attraction, but Sothern "refused to be funny," the *Times* man
reported, and Florence was "dead-weightish as Iago." They
"went on and on dully, sullenly," although as Desdemona "Lotta
was prodigious. Had she been seconded by Messrs. Sothern and
Florence, the performance would have been indeed memorable
as the cleverest burlesque on record."

Disappointed in the tragedians, the audience cheered the
soubrette. It was a bitter rebuke for Sothern, and when the benefit was repeated a week later in Philadelphia, he declined the

role, starring this time in a burlesque aptly called *The Crushed Tragedian*. Lotta fell back on the familiar *Nan, the Good for Nothing*. But the testimonials served their purpose; more than $9,300 was netted at the New York performance alone. Two weeks later, Adams was dead.

Lotta did not go abroad in 1877, nor the next year. *La Cigale,* with its circus setting, was added to her repertory, adapted from the French of Meilhac and Halévy by an American dramatist, Olive Logan. She introduced it in New York, October, 1878, at Abbey's Park. Lavishly mounted, it was the only play in which Lotta "wore really smart clothes," one of her cast was to say.

Miss Logan, a rabid feminist and would-be reformer, was doing her best to make a lady of Lotta; she believed the female figure should be fully clothed, and at the time was carrying on a crusade against the English burlesque troupes then cavorting about the country. In a lecture called "The Blond Burlesque Girl," Miss Logan used a tomahawk, scalping knife, and other pulverizing instruments to rip up a blond dummy, filling the stage with tangled yellow hair, fractured tights, sawdust calves, and dyestuff. Thus, she came to her task of adapting *La Cigale* "expressly for Lotta" (as the programs stated) with an unusual regard for propriety, and no doubt something was lost in translation. In any case, the play was never very popular, although it was proof that Lotta's talent could transcend the role of gamin. Audiences agreed, but preferred *Musette* and *Little Nell*. Stubbornly, Lotta kept *La Cigale* alive until her retirement; whatever immortality the play may have today is due to a minor reference to it in Joyce's *Ulysses*.

Earlier that same year, after a long winter season that had begun in New Orleans, and taken them into thirty cities throughout the South and East, Lotta and her mother had gone to San Francisco.

It was July, 1878, and the cool Bay breezes were a relief after the hot trip out. There was no engagement scheduled, and the two women arrived without fanfare. The purpose of the trip was confidential.

Four years previously, before her fling in the cotton business in Fall River, Mary Ann had been induced by a certain E. P. Hutchings to invest $50,000 of Lotta's money in a scheme "which he strongly recommended, but which he knew to be valueless" (according to legal papers later served on Hutchings). The money, which represented the better part of a year's earnings for Lotta, was lost. But then, in the spring of 1878, the fast-talking promoter turned up unexpectedly at the Crabtree apartment in New York, ostensibly for the purpose of making restitution. Not in cash, it appeared, but in the form of a tip on a gold mine in California that could be purchased "for a small amount of money."

Improbable as it may seem, considering the fleecing that Lotta and her mother had already undergone, the idea dazzled them. Mary Ann especially never outgrew the mining-camp mentality in which Lotta had been launched on her career. The fourteen watches, and the satchel full of gold nuggets with which the family had departed California for the first time, left a permanent impression, a scar of temptation that never really healed. Mary Ann had seen gold come out of the ground and flow into her purse literally the same day it was mined. To the end of her life it remained the basic metal. And so it was that she came to buy a mine of her own. There was a sentimental bonus in the fact that it was located in La Porte—once Rabbit Creek—the scene of Lotta's first triumph as a child performer.

From San Francisco, Lotta and Mary Ann journeyed to Sacramento, where they were met by Hutchings and a man named John Thomas, half owner of the "Saw Pit" mine (the other half, it was claimed, belonged to a certain "Judge Shepherd" back east). Together, the party proceeded to La Porte, where they took rooms at the local hotel. Hutchings, however, had not counted on the excitement that swept through the town when it was learned that Lotta Crabtree had arrived; he had no desire to see the scheme ruined if the Crabtrees should discuss the reason for their visit and cautioned them not to discuss the matter with anyone. The low price—$28,000—might encourage interest on the part of some speculator, he warned. Hutchings' advice was followed altogether too faithfully.

Meanwhile, La Porte had girded itself for a mighty reception. From Gibsonville, eight miles away, a brass band was summoned. There were serenades. Lotta was assured by a member of the welcoming committee that the gold thereabouts had imparted the golden glow to her luxuriant hair. While all this was taking place, Hutchings and Thomas sweated out the suspense in their hotel room. The band played again, there was more singing, and then the District Revenue Officer, a General Barnes, made what the local newspaper called "a neat address." The two promoters, when they heard it, quietly relaxed, for the General had inadvertently become an ally, pointing out, as a local booster, that the mines in the vicinity of La Porte had produced over $100,000,-000 worth of ore since the first discovery. Obviously, in Mary Ann's opinion, there was more where that came from. On this note, the following day, Hutchings and Thomas spirited the two women off for an inspection of the mine. It had, they claimed, brought in $27,000 worth of ore during the three months preceding.

Back east, Hutchings took them to see "Judge Shepherd," and in September the deal was concluded. The sum of $28,000 was paid over, the deed delivered. Jack Crabtree was pulled out of the box office at the Park—Cousin Louis Livesey took his place—dispatched to California, and put in charge of his mother's interests there. Mary Ann still had high hopes that her son could be settled into some sort of gainful occupation; at the Park, too, he had made a nuisance of himself with some of the female members of the company.

Actually, almost the first thing Jack did in La Porte was get into a fight with one of the mine operators when he tried to seize a handful of ore. But for once, Jack was right. Whatever might be said of the young man's profligate nature, not to mention his youth—he was then twenty-four—he knew a swindle when he saw one. The "Saw Pit" looked like a gold mine; Chinese coolies worked the diggings, and the sluice boxes rattled with ore. But Jack was not long in discovering that the ore was mostly tailings —the mine had produced not $27,000 worth of gold in three months, but $2,700 (Hutchings had simply added a cipher to the income statement) and had probably cost more than this to bring the gold out of the ground. It was common talk among the local miners that the "Saw Pit" was exhausted.

Jack's first inclination was to hurry back to New York with the bad news; in fact, he spent several days in San Francisco, where he gave an elaborate dinner for his aunt, Mrs. Vernon, and his cousins, the Liveseys and the Fretwells. Mrs. Fretwell remembered him later as a young man of great charm, easygoing, "more like his father than his mother." But it was Mary Ann to whom he was accountable, and she was stunned—as was Lotta—when he finally arrived home with information that the mine was a bust. Hutchings was immediately sought out, but proved elusive, having left his rooms at the Fifth Avenue Hotel. He was traced to the Metropolitan Hotel, was discovered to have left there for the Astor House, and was finally run to earth on the Bowery, having also run out of money. "Judge Shepherd" left no trail at all. The money was lost.

It had always been Mary Ann's hope that a financial coup would relieve her daughter of the incessant traveling; after fifteen years on the road, the luster of success was no longer quite so glittering. A few performances in the major cities would have sufficed, but obviously, such was not to be, and in April, 1879, Lotta set out on the road once more. In Boston, the new Park Theater opened with *La Cigale,* and much ceremony. Within an hour after tickets went on sale, the house was sold out. Mayor Prince attended, and New York critics journeyed up to see this stunning playhouse for themselves, noting that electric stage lighting had been installed, and that the red plush seats were far the most comfortable in Boston. Mr. William Winter of the *Tribune* added the observation that "four elegant private boxes" commanded a "fine view of the audience. . . ." Abbey himself came on stage to take a bow, and Lotta carried off a "wagonload of flowers."

But behind this outward prosperity there were strains. Although the New York Park continued to flourish, Abbey, who was almost always overextended, did not. As collateral for the theater, he had put up real estate in Akron, Ohio, that he had inherited from his father. Interest and principal were to be paid through Lotta's lawyers, but the payments were overdue and it would appear that the attorneys' handling of the matter left something to be desired. "A shocking mess they made of it," Mary Ann noted in her item book. "Never trust money to lawyers again." Like many self-made women, she changed them frequently.

Years later, Lotta would put her business affairs in the hands of Francis Wellman, who, in 1879, was still escorting her around Boston and calling on her at Dunlaps' in New York, in competition with the persistent O. E. Huss. A pencil sketch of Huss, made by brother George, reveals a not unhandsome man with a rather large mustache, a full head of hair, and a prominent nose. In the press, Mary Ann was blamed for standing between them, but this was doubtful. Lotta was fickle, her mother would say later; she liked to have men around her, collected them the way she collected teapots or took up Christian Science or Theosophy. She let Aunt Jane worry about the outcome, as Mary Ann worried over money. In a healthy sense, Lotta was in love with herself; with men she only pretended to be—these were her favorite roles, and kept her young. To marry would be to age.

Helena Modjeska found her tense and high-strung. The two were appearing in Philadelphia. Modjeska, who had recently added *Peg Woffington* to her repertoire, was having trouble with the Irish brogue, as well as the jig she danced in the last act. The

great tragedian's Polish accent was bad enough; added to a
brogue, it was almost unintelligible. Lotta "had a good laugh,"
Modjeska wrote of the incident, then flew backstage to show her
how a jig was done.

Returning to San Francisco in the summer of 1879, she played
in Lucky Baldwin's palatial Academy of Music—the crystal
chandeliers were said to have cost $1,600 each. With Baldwin's
backing, Maguire had developed a strong stock company; he was
also indulging his chronic weakness for grandiose theater, and for
once, Lotta was not exactly the center of attention.

She arrived in the wake of a raging controversy over the most
ambitious of Maguire's projects yet, an Oberammergau type of
spectacle called *The Passion,* written by Salmi Morse. In addition to 80 singing parts, the production called for a chorus of
more than 100, and mob scenes of 400 men, women, and children. Every unemployed actor in San Francisco found work.
With Lotta's backing, Abbey planned to bring *The Passion* to
New York, although it appeared that the Park Theater was not
large enough to hold the full cast, let alone an audience that
could pay them.

But San Francisco was up in arms, divided on whether the play
was the greatest sacrilege of all times, or in the nature of a second
coming. The effect on audiences was overwhelming. Some spectators knelt and prayed throughout whole scenes; others were outraged. William Winter, in his biography of David Belasco, asserted that "ignorant Irish who witnessed it were so distempered
that, on going forth, some of them, from time to time, assaulted
peaceable Jews in the public streets." It was as though they had
chanced to hear first of the Crucifixion nearly two thousand years
after it occurred, Winter added.

James O'Neill, later to become famous as the Count of Monte
Cristo, and even more famous as the father of Eugene, played the
Christos. After a time, according to Belasco, who was Maguire's
secretary and the prompter for the play, O'Neill came to believe
he *was* the Christ. "He gave up smoking. . . . He walked the

streets of the city with the expression of a holy man on his face. Whenever he drew near, a hush prevailed such as one does not often find outside a church." Belasco remarks that he himself "was never without a Bible under my arm" during this time.

Nevertheless, the Board of Aldermen passed an ordinance banning further shows of *The Passion*. Maguire closed it for a time, then reopened the play; the police moved in and arrested the principal performers, fining O'Neill $50 and the others $5. In spite of this, Abbey went ahead with plans to bring the show to New York, securing Booth's theater and, in an effort to put off the authorities, renaming it Booth's Tabernacle.

Added to this excitement in San Francisco was the political turmoil of an election campaign. The Reverend Isaac Smith Kalloch, a crusading minister who had declared his candidacy for mayor, was denouncing corruption in general and the candidate backed by the *Chronicle* in particular. On the afternoon of Lotta's first matinee in *Musette,* a storm of activity broke out in the lobby, and shouts and imprecations flooded into the auditorium. Editor Charles De Young of the *Chronicle* had shot and killed Kalloch in front of his church; mobs had set upon him forthwith, but De Young had managed to get away, and friends had eventually dragged him inside the Academy of Music. Outside, the 10th and 12th Ward Rifles, the French Volunteers, and the Kearny Light Guards were marching up Market Street to restore order, while the "sand lotters" were being egged on by hotheads spoiling for a fight.

Torn with curiosity, some of the audience went out to investigate. Maguire became alarmed; De Young was in danger of being lynched. Word went backstage to keep the show going, and in spite of the din, Lotta persisted with *Musette*. Most of the spectators remained in their seats until the end of the act, by which time De Young had been removed to safety. Only then did Lotta discover her inadvertent role.

Musette was followed by *Little Nell,* with young David Belasco playing Foxy Joe. But the citizens of San Francisco were in no mood for light entertainment. Although they had given her an enormous, triumphant welcome, they did not continue to fill Baldwin's huge theater. Back in New York, Abbey was having his own troubles. Public pressure had compelled him to cancel plans to produce *The Passion,* but Morse, its author, for whom the play had become an obsession, hired the old 5th Regiment Armory. At considerable expense, he improvised a theater, but even this failed when police prevented the sale of tickets. The chapter was closed, tragically, when Salmi Morse drowned himself not long afterward in the East River.

Lotta toured until the late spring of 1880; then, on May 29, she, George, and Mary Ann sailed for England aboard the *S. S. Egypt.* They were accompanied by Clement Bainbridge, who was going on to Switzerland with George. In the Cockburn will case forty-six years later, May 29 was an important date.

More significant, however, was what happened to Jack. He had been dissipating, had lost weight, and was thought to have an incipient case of tuberculosis. Mary Ann was worried. At the same time, mindful of the way in which he had acquitted himself in La Porte, she was convinced that the time was again propitious to launch him on a business career.

The original get-rich-quick scheme with Hutchings should have been a lesson to Mary Ann; yet, having failed to learn the first time, she might be excused—when the gold mine dazzled her—from learning the second time. The stage was now set for the third scheme. It had come to her attention that there was a silver mine, the "Kentucky," for sale in Tombstone, Arizona, at a price of $1,500. Although silver wasn't gold, it was coin of the realm—Schieffelin's original "Tough Nut" mine, which had drawn prospectors to Arizona like a magnet, was reputed to be of such pure ore that you could press a silver dollar into the outcroppings and leave a clear impression of the American eagle. Besides, to lose $1,500, should such prove to be the case, compared with previous losses, would almost be making money. Mary

Ann bought her son an elaborate camping outfit and sent him west. His father had made a similar expedition to the California gold fields twenty-nine years before, although on that occasion Mary Ann had done her best to dissuade him. Times had changed.

4

"Put It in the Safe"

THE CRABTREES returned from Europe early in September, 1880, in time for a fall tour. Jack remained in Tombstone until late the following year. Why he came back was never clear to his family, but it was understood that something had marred his relationship with a man named Bullock, with whom he had formed a partnership in a livery stable. (The Kentucky mine, having produced very little silver, had been sold for a third of its cost.) Mary Ann had put up the money for Jack's share of the livery business—legally, in fact, it was she who was Bullock's partner, although the two never met—but now the partnership was dissolved. The first that she and Lotta knew of this was on a cold December day in Providence, when Jack turned up unexpectedly without an overcoat. He never said much about Tombstone after that; it was a curiously closed chapter in his life.

Henry Abbey had also gone to Europe in 1880, returning with the biggest catch of the Continent, the sensational Sarah Bernhardt. By the time Lotta arrived home, the Divine Sarah was sweeping across the country on a special train that included several coaches for her baggage alone.

Lotta was no Sarah Bernhardt. She traveled light; so light, in fact, that when railroads began to charge theatrical companies for excess baggage, Mary Ann threw away the heavy, brass-cornered trunks and bought rattan hampers. For a good many years, the Combination, Lotta's stock company, had traveled by ordinary sleeper, but in the 1880's Mary Ann leased a private Pullman, and, unlike Bernhardt's, it housed not only the star but the entire company. The men were berthed at one end of the car,

Lotta and her mother at the other; the center lounge was converted at night into a bedroom for the remaining women. During the day, Mary Ann usually stationed herself amidships, where she could keep an eye both fore and aft. All socializing was done in the lounge under her surveillance, and it was an inviolable rule that everyone present must be fully dressed. The men were not permitted to smoke. At night, when the lights had been turned out, Thomas Joyce, the "walking gentleman" of the company and an Irishman with a fine tenor voice, appeared at the doorway to the ladies' section and crooned a lullaby.

The company at this time consisted of about a dozen men and women, in addition to the Crabtrees: Eddie Dunn, the business manager; Lotta's maid; Albert, the steward; and sometimes one of the brothers. An advance man traveled ahead, although on the occasions when Jack filled the job, this was not always the case. Jack, who had a habit of detouring himself to the local race track, sometimes traveled *behind* the company.

All of the actors were screened by Mary Ann for their moral character, and it was generally understood that the company was a poor risk for any actress who might be looking for a husband. Dunn, the business manager, attended to the details of transportation, secured hotel reservations during the longer engagements, hired extras, and paid off the cast at the end of the week. One thing he did not do, however, was pick up the receipts at the box office. This task was handled by Mary Ann after each performance—in case the theater should burn down overnight—and the amount entered in her cash book. For years, she accepted nothing *but* cash, but when Lotta played in one of Abbey's theaters, she consented to take checks. These went into her bag, and might remain undeposited for weeks at a time. This was not carelessness; Abbey was frequently low in funds, and the old lady quietly ascertained the state of his finances before presenting the checks for payment. At one time, in Boston, she carried $20,000 until Abbey could cover his other obligations; it was an aspect of Mary Ann's nature not generally suspected.

Contractual affairs with theaters were also handled by her.

Mrs. Edward Kidder called Mary Ann "the terror of managers,"
and with good reason. Sharing terms at the time were usually
divided sixty per cent for the star (who paid the actors out of this
sum) and forty per cent to the house. But it was not uncommon
for Mary Ann to exact seventy per cent for Lotta, and even
seventy-five. Moreover, Lotta's name must always top the bill—
that is, it should appear before the name of the play, or the name
of the author. (The latter was sometimes omitted altogether.)

But to managers, she was worth it. For three weeks at the
Boston Park during the 1882-83 season, Lotta grossed $9,500,
$9,700 and $10,000. Edwin Booth, who had preceded her, averaged $7,500 a week, a fact duly noted by Mary Ann when she
negotiated with other managers. Year in and year out, Lotta was
the most highly paid actress in the country.

Her popularity increased in spite of—or perhaps because of—a
number of "vile and cheeky imitators," as the *Mirror* called
them. There was "Little Nell, the California Diamond." She,
too, played the banjo. The name rang a bell with audiences, and
one of her plays, *Fidelia, the Fire Fly,* might even have been
confused with Lotta's own *Firefly.* Lotta's success had been too
spectacular to ignore. When seventeen-year-old Minnie Maddern
made her debut at Abbey's Park, in *Fogg's Ferry,* the *New York
Sun* was constrained to point out that "she came forward like a
new Lotta," adding that "she can sing even worse than Lotta
can." Like all the others, Miss Maddern was looking for a short
cut to Lotta's public.

This public was a remarkably heterogeneous group of people,
and not easily deceived. Men came to ogle at the daring cancan,
the diminutive dresses, the military panache, the tiny ankle
thrust out from behind the curtain at the end of the show. ("But
—I don't understand!" an old actress is reported to have exclaimed after watching the audience go wild at this piece of
business.) But men did understand. "Seeing a woman's ankle in
those days was a novelty," the actor John E. Henshaw once commented. "Men would stand on the street corner and wait and

watch for girls to cross the street so they could see them raise their skirts. A rainy day would be a rich harvest." The men who saw Lotta perform were not ordinary men, either. A fashionable first-night audience often included General Dan Sickles, Pierre Lorillard, William Winter, Frederick Coudert, George and Jay Gould, William K. Vanderbilt, and August and Perry Belmont. Lotta was just the thing for the tired businessman of the 1880s.

But their wives saw a frolicking tease who reassuringly turned the tables on the menfolk. In Washington, President Cleveland and his cabinet found Lotta an anodyne for the cares of public office. Southern belles warmed to the banjo playing, and the matrons knew that her private life was utterly moral, however she might behave on stage. Children saw an elflike creature who appeared to be one of them—a twelve-year-old boy in Rochester once asked his father to bring Lotta home so that he could play with her. She appealed to every member of the family.

The plays themselves demanded almost no intellectual concentration, but in this respect they were no different from most of the drama—apart from Shakespeare and the classics—that passed through the nineteenth-century theater. The *New York Herald,* reviewing *Musette* in April, 1881, remarked that the title role "had no more to do with unfolding the story than it has with solving a problem in Euclid." Once playwrights had learned how to build a character around Lotta's eccentricities, the plots were unimportant—claptrap affairs in which all ended happily. Lotta's contribution to this formula was to make sure that virtue was rewarded only after a prolonged bout of mischievous tomfoolery, and Victorian audiences were undoubtedly purged of a good many domestic inhibitions through watching her misbehave.

Henry Abbey, who had introduced both Bernhardt and Lillie Langtry to American theatergoers, dallied with the idea of sending Lotta to England. True, both European stars had succeeded partly on the strength of their scandalous private lives, Mrs.

Langtry having but recently enjoyed a liaison with the Prince of Wales. Nothing comparable could be claimed for Lotta. Huss, the proper Britisher, still squired her around, and he had been joined by a doctor's son with the equally unromantic name of A. Hallergross, but it was clear by this time that Lotta would marry neither of them. On the other hand, there was a certain raciness to her acting that might compensate for her blameless off-stage life. An acquaintance of Abbey's, Harry Jackson, manager of the Opéra Comique, arranged to sponsor her, and it was agreed that Lotta would open in London late in 1883.

She and Mary Ann spent the fall in Paris. The French lessons were resumed, and Lotta went to the Comédie Française a good deal, although she could never quite make out what the actors were saying. She was painting again, too. Finally, she arranged for an adaptation of another Meilhac and Halévy play, *Mam'zelle Nitouche*. In December, the two women crossed the channel, visited Crabtree briefly, and then settled into a West End hotel. "This is my first appearance here . . . and my ways may not hit the taste of your playgoers," she told an interviewer for the *Pall Mall Gazette*. Already, she was feeling apprehensive. Manager Jackson had launched an aggressive publicity campaign; the British public was told of her virtue—pointedly, in view of Mrs. Langtry's reputation—her dazzling talents, and, not least, her wealth. Her coming would be "a revelation to London, which had never seen anything so great from America before."

By the time the curtain went up on *Musette,* on Saturday night, December 22, Jackson's publicity had done its work. The Opéra Comique was jammed. *Musette* had been selected largely because of its English setting, but when Lotta made her appearance on stage, as a child of fourteen in gypsy costume, she was greeted with a cold silence. This was unnerving, but as the act went on, the audience grew restless and noisy. The truth was that they found little about their native country in the play which they recognized, or at any rate, cared to acknowledge. A lecherous baronet who scampered through the countryside after an innocent girl? It was not the morals that bothered them, but the social illogic; a baronet would never chase a gypsy.

Musette baffled the audience. The noted T. P. O'Connor of the *Daily Telegraph* wrote:

[They] could not make head or tail of this "dramatic story" . . . and their vain efforts to follow the thread of the plot and unravel its perplexing mysteries seemed utterly to demoralize them. . . . I was a little late coming in, but already the whole gigantic horrible disaster had come. For almost from the first moment after the curtain had risen, a tremendous—almost like an organized—riot had started. Every word of the play was interrupted, every actor was hissed, and the noise grew in violence as the time went on, until at last it was a hurricane of catcalls, of loud guffaws, of insulting sneers.

Not only was the play bad—O'Connor likened it to "the kind of penny dreadful that has ceased to be read"—but the Opéra Comique had added insult to the affair by replacing its usual two-shilling pit with an "upper circle," for which an extra sixpence was charged. Frequenters of these lower-priced stalls thereupon sent up a chant, "Where's the pit?" Strong exception was also taken to a young actor in the cast named Arthur Dacre, who had recently figured in a divorce action against his wife. To the din from the "upper circle" were added uncomplimentary allusions to Mr. Dacre's behavior in court.

Lotta was stunned; the reception was even worse than her New York debut at Niblo's. Bravely, she struggled through the business of *Musette,* unaware that worse was to come. Well along in the play, she sings a duet with "Billy Bokus" to the tune of a Moody and Sankey hymn, "The Sweet Bye and Bye." Like many of her musical numbers, it was a burlesque, but it outraged a good portion of the "upper circle," who, having already paid sixpence more than they were accustomed to, were in no mood to hear the sacred music of the Salvation Army profaned by an American actress in short skirts. Adding fuel to the flames was the fact that at the very moment Moody and Sankey in person were conducting an evangelistic mission in London's Stepney section; the song seemed a calculated insult.

Pandemonium broke loose. "With the fear of Moody, Sankey, and General Booth before their eyes," the critic Clement Scott wrote, "the righteous audience howled at Lotta and punched one another's heads in the gallery with truly Christian resignation. I never remember such a scene in a theater. Half the people were fretting and fuming about the luckless hymn-tune and the rest were blackening one another's eyes in the name of religion."

When the number ended, Lotta stepped forward, obviously puzzled. "I don't understand it," she addressed the audience, adding in an undertone to those on stage, "I was not prepared for such a reception as this." In the confusion, it was still not clear to her that the calls for an encore were ironical. When she complied, a new storm erupted, a free-for-all broke out in the gallery, and the ushers were compelled to eject the more unruly demonstrators, who marched into the street derisively humming "The Sweet Bye and Bye."

The curtain fell amid hoots of disapproval. But even this was not the end of the demonstration; as baskets of flowers were handed to the stage over the heads of bewildered musicians, the audience began groaning and yelling. A bunch of Parma violets was tossed to Lotta and, after a moment's hesitation, she put them on her head. No one had told her that the American custom of floral tributes was heartily distrusted by the British theatergoer, who assumed that the flowers had been supplied by the actress herself. As the hooting continued, Lotta fled to her dressing room in tears, followed by numbers of the cast, who tried to console her. But they, too, were shaken. A reception backstage, planned for after the play, was canceled.

It was a bitter experience; the following day's notices confirmed the debacle. The *Times,* comparatively gentle, remarked that "it would be a kindness to the public and to Miss Lotta herself to frankly relieve her of the trammels of *Musette* and to allow her to caper about the stage in her own way." The production was "an unfortunate fiasco . . . dull and stupid to the last degree," the *Pall Mall Gazette* thundered in a lead review, lowering the curtain of silence on Lotta, who was not mentioned in its pages again.

Distraught by the calamity, Manager Harry Jackson sought to salvage something from the ruins. He had engaged Lotta for eight months. Attendance was declining badly and *Musette* would have to be jettisoned; moreover, word of the play had gone out to Stepney Green, where the Moody and Sankey revivalists were in no mood to tolerate any more sacrilege on the London stage. Lotta toned down the hymn tune, and rehearsals were begun immediately for *The Old Curiosity Shop*.

This was not the Brougham version, but an adaptation that had been made by Charles Dickens the younger. Two years previously, Lotta had bought the American rights to the play for £2,000. It had never been produced, and Dickens was called in hurriedly to patch up the script. The play opened on January 12, 1884. With Dickens, Lotta was treading on territory even more sacred to Englishmen than the Salvation Army, and manager Jackson, who was taking no chances, posted a number of police constables throughout the theater against the possibility of another riot. He also persuaded Lotta to substitute a mandolin for a banjo, and to play her solos sitting in front of the footlights, thus removing the American tunes from the English context of the play. To give his imprimatur to the whole proceedings, Dickens posted himself conspicuously in a front box, where he could be seen by the audience.

The play started haltingly. Lotta obviously lacked the proper pathos for Little Nell; the danger was not that the audience would riot, but that they would fall asleep. Then, dressed as the Marchioness in rose-pink petticoats, openwork silk stockings, and high-heeled shoes, Lotta pulled a gilt chair downstage, grabbed her mandolin, and began singing. The effect was electric. Even as Nell, during the numerous changes of character, she began to take hold. It was a wild, American interpretation that had very little to do with Dickens, and the mandolin was "amazingly noisy," noted the critic Austin Brereton, who added that nonetheless Lotta's performance was "brilliantly successful and fascinatingly clever." The audience broke into cheers at the end, and Dickens, preening himself, came on stage to take a bow. The more sober members present, however, must have wondered if his father were not by this time turning in his grave.

The reception given *The Old Curiosity Shop* reassured Lotta. The Prince of Wales attended the performance on January 15, which delighted Mary Ann, although perhaps not so much as the news that Lotta was drawing better houses than Henry Irving. Of course, Irving was a London staple, while Lotta was a novelty, although regarded as an imitator of the American Minnie Palmer, who was kicking around in even shorter dresses than Lotta's across the street at the Royal Strand.

This was one of the odd facets of Lotta's engagement in London. Ten years younger, and the cheekiest of all imitators, Miss Palmer had hurried to England in advance of Lotta with a tinkly little play called *My Sweetheart*. She had caught the public's fancy with her antics, and left no doubt that she considered herself the "original" while Lotta was the imitator, capitalizing on her popularity. In the meantime, a British theatrical publication, *Under the Clock,* had launched a prize competition to determine "by public vote . . . which of the two American artistes, Lotta or Minnie Palmer, is the more popular with London audiences."

The contest had a slightly phony ring, even for a theatrical paper, and from the first the Palmer forces accused Jackson of rigging it for Lotta's benefit. If so, the maneuver backfired; by early March, when all the votes were in, Minnie had posted 1,065 to Lotta's 541. Piqued, Lotta set about restoring some of the old Brougham routines, all but eliminating Little Nell to concentrate on the more colorful Marchioness. "Since one had given up all hope of tracing Dickens in the piece, the new alterations might have been regarded as improvements," *Under the Clock* commented wearily. But the public missed Nell and back she went. Business picked up.

With failure behind them, and the younger Dickens to introduce them to London society, Lotta and her mother settled into a flat at 6 Half Moon Street, in the Piccadilly section. London did not know quite what to make of this American eccentric who had created a riot at the Opéra Comique and then redeemed herself, whose off-stage behavior was blameless to a fault, and who moved continually under the protective wing of the tiny little woman in black taffeta who was her mother. Still an innocent who could be overwhelmed in the presence of other celebrities, she might sit through an entire dinner party adding hardly a word to the conversation. The Bancrofts had her to dinner; Lord and Lady Landesborough gave a party; then Henry Labouchere, M.P. and editor of *Truth,* invited half the theatrical people in London to meet her. "I couldn't talk, and I haven't a doubt that Mr. Labouchere thought me stupid," Lotta confessed to an interviewer. Still, as she put it, she was making "barrels of money," and the invitations kept coming.

The Old Curiosity Shop ran through April, and on May 12, she opened in *Mam'zelle Nitouche,* the "comic vaudeville" she had acquired in Paris. It had elegant costumes and dazzling sets, but the plot complications, concerning a young convent-school girl who runs away with the chapel organist and engages in twenty-four hours of rather wild escapades, make the story virtually beyond description. The *London Times* described its humor as "both fresh and abundant," and the play won immediate favor with London audiences, for however much they might resent Lotta trifling with British institutions, they saw nothing wrong about her playing fast and loose with the French. Actually, the play was not as loose as when Lotta saw it in Paris with the incomparable Mme. Judic in the lead role; in Lotta's hands the Gallic naughtiness had largely evaporated.

But the vehicle displayed her in a new light. She sang *opéra bouffe,* rattled the snare drums, and marched around in cavalry boots. There was no end of intrigue. Incongruously, a Japanese song was interpolated in the second act, puzzling audiences considerably. But Lotta had won London to her side; if she *were* an imitator of Minnie Palmer's, she was far more talented.

In September, 1884, Lotta brought *Mam'zelle Nitouche* to Daly's Theater in New York. Still smarting from her treatment at the hands of the London critics, she felt compelled to defend herself to an American public ignorant of the London stage—a public that had heard altogether too much about Lotta's "debacle." "I never dined a single critic," she announced, somewhat smugly. "They all expect it in London. They want huge dinners, about fifty courses, and then they'll condescend to speak favorably of you."

Although this may not have been entirely untrue, it had had little to do with Lotta's own experience, which, after all, had turned out rather favorably. Then, too, John R. Rogers—Minnie Palmer's husband—had spread the word that he had been chiefly responsible for that disastrous opening night, having packed the Opera Comique with Miss Palmer's partisans. This rankled Lotta, because she knew that Rogers was a liar, but to deny the allegation put her in the position of accepting the more damning explanation that she had affronted English theatergoers with a bad play. All in all, it made for a difficult home-coming.

But *Mam'zelle Nitouche* went on as scheduled. The critics were not overwhelmed. "It does not much matter what the piece may be when Lotta is the center of attraction," the *Times* noted. "We look upon her antics in the same spirit as we watch the gambols of a sportive infant. . . ." But the truth was that she was no longer quite so sportive. Alan Dale, a popular drama writer, calling on Lotta at the Dunlaps', found her attired "in the most juvenile manner, in a white muslin dress, with broad blue sash tied in a big bow at the back." Off stage, the getup seemed incongruous. What was worse, Mary Ann did all the talking, and Dale went away with the feeling that although the child prodigy of the American stage was still prodigious, she was no longer a child. (She was, after all, thirty-seven.) Lotta was a bit hefty to be romping in such short skirts; her voice broke occasionally on the high notes. Managers were beginning to apologize for her "hoarseness." A tour, scheduled to begin in October, was postponed when Lotta came down with pneumonia. Unlike Clara Morris, Lotta found herself grounded by illness, and it was not until December that she played again, this time in Brooklyn.

With the Park Theater gone, Lotta made most of her New York appearances at the Grand Opera House, operated by Abbey and Schoeffel. The two men were also running the Park in Boston, but were losing heavily in an effort to produce opera there. Rumor had it that Mary Ann still hoped he would marry Lotta and wanted to do nothing to embarrass him. There is no way of proving her real intentions, but when his creditors threatened to throw him into bankruptcy, her charity took a new turn. With Lotta's money, she bought Abbey and Schoeffel's interest in the Boston Park for $100,000 cash, restoring them both to solvency.

It was a canny investment, for Lotta would live to see the theater assessed at $600,000. But there was also an immediate reward; for the next several years, the Park provided employment for the two Crabtree boys, George as "Business Manager" and Jack as "Proprietor and Manager." Mary Ann may have considered $100,000 a fair price to keep them out of trouble, as this had proved to be no small task.

Many of George's problems could be traced to his maimed leg. No one really expected him to be able to earn a living, although occasionally he took walk-on parts in Lotta's plays where a lame character was called for, or when a crowd scene disguised the limp. A good deal of private tutoring had been lavished on George, and he wanted to write plays for his sister; his notebooks were crammed with dramatic scenes, short stories, and verse— fledgling stuff, but not without feeling. The title of "Business Manager" at the Park was at least partly euphemistic, but it gave him an earned income. At one time, George had courted Minnie

Dunlap, but no marriage ever took place. One of his poems may explain his reluctance to be a rejected suitor:

> I'm a jolly old batch
>   So jolly oh jolly
> I've a key they call latch
>   Jolly so jolly
> I come home at night
> No, not always tight
>   But jolly, yes jolly.
>
> I've no scolding wife
>   Jolly *so* jolly
> I've a free easy life
>   Jolly *so* jolly
> But once in a "weil"
> I can't say I feel
>   So awfully, awfully jolly.
>
> When my friends leave the town
>   Jolly for *them,* jolly
> I have studies called brown
>   Really, not very jolly
> Then I feel that my life
> With a sweet little wife
>   Would be much more jolly.
>
> But pshaw why complain
>   Be jolly, yes jolly
> I'm ugly and lame
>   Anything but jolly
> So if I proposed
> I should only get 'No Sir'
>   And that wouldn't be jolly.

Jack, or Ashworth, was of another stripe. Decked out in silk shirts, and wearing a solitaire that beamed brighter than the lighthouse in *Zip,* he cut a debonair figure in New York and

Boston sporting circles. A private dining room at the Hoffman House rang with gaiety whenever he gave a dinner, which may explain the caliber of his guests: Maurice Barrymore; Steele Mackaye, the playwright and producer; the arctic explorer William H. Gilder; Colonel Tom Orchiltree, the trotting authority; and an international gambler named Billy Deuitsch, who had achieved fame when he broke the bank at Monte Carlo. Younger than most of these men, Jack was hardly in their financial class, but one and all they were delighted to eat at his—or rather, Lotta's—expense. She thought then that Jack was destined to be short-lived, and wanted to make his last days joyful.

And joyful they were, although Jack was to live another thirty-five years. When young Maurice Bernhardt came to the United States to visit his mother, Jack gave him a dinner, preceded by an evening at the old Madison Square Garden, where John L. Sullivan was fighting. Sullivan won his match, and was invited to attend the dinner. Liquor flowed freely. After a couple of hours of eating and drinking, Sullivan was ready to resume fighting and began to look around the room for a partner. Efforts to restrain him failed, his gloves were sent for, and Billy Deuitsch, the gambler, was finally picked to stand up to the champion. Well-oiled by this time, Deuitsch was in no condition to protest, and was soon flat on his back. Sullivan's enthusiasm mounted; he started after some of the other guests, and there was a wild scramble to get away. It was Sullivan's manager who subdued the fighter and got him into a Turkish bath, "turning on the vapor to the full limit," as a newspaper account of the event reported. The guest of honor had by this time safely escaped.

For a man of Jack's convivial nature, New York was just the place. But to Mary Ann, it was a city of temptations, and to keep him away from them as much as possible, before he was installed as manager of the Boston Park, she made him the advance man for the Combination. His job would be to move one date ahead of the show, to see that the theater had proper equipment, that billboards were posted, and that interviews and advertising were arranged for. The work was made to order, since it involved considerable entertaining on an expense account; it also kept Jack away from the girls in the company, and took him in and out of a city before he could get into trouble. At least, that was the idea.

But Jack had a habit of disappearing. "We were never sure whether he was ahead of us or behind us," H. Brooks Harper, one of the actors, recalled. Harper, who sometimes acted as Lotta's business agent, would write ahead to ascertain if Jack had arrived; if not, he himself would go. "I don't remember Jack ever carrying a grip," Harper said. "He just used to stuff clothing in his overcoat pockets."

Both George and Jack moved to Boston in 1886. Managing the Park was hard work, but they seem to have risen to the challenge, although Jack found excuses for frequent trips to New York. Louthicum, his tailor, had no equal in Boston. Then there were engagements to keep at the race track. But the Park prospered; Mary Ann, who set the policy, never dreamed for a moment of putting on grand opera.

In New York, Abbey's Grand Opera House presented Lotta in *Mam'zelle Nitouche* in March, 1885. Then came a new play, *Larks,* written by Mrs. C. A. Doremus. Lotta had met her ten years before in Louisville, where she and Mary Ann were guests of the family. They had remained friends, seeing a good deal of one another in New York—Mrs. Doremus had seen the Crabtrees off to Europe in 1880, and became an important witness in the Cockburn case later.

Larks was a sketchy piece of work, its heroine posing as a boy in order to deceive her uncle. "In this character she worries the life out of the old gentleman, torments many other personages, and enjoys several remarkable adventures," *The Theatre Magazine* noted in reviewing it. The public found it tame. Lotta withdrew the play—one of the very few in which she could not overcome the inanities of the script.

It was followed two years later by *Pawn Ticket 210,* written by

David Belasco in collaboration with Clay Greene, another Californian who, like Belasco, had come to New York a few years
before. Although Belasco was to achieve considerable success as a playwright, no one who saw this made-to-order hackwork
would have guessed it. He and Greene had been promised $5,000
for the play, of which $1,000 was a down payment, but when
Pawn Ticket 210 opened in September, 1887, at McVicker's in
Chicago (on which Lotta now held a $40,000 mortgage), the re-
views were so bad that both authors were prepared to forgo the
balance due. They had come to Chicago for the opening and
were staying at the Palmer House; newspapers were sent up the
next morning, and after digesting the notices, Belasco and
Greene walked downcast into Lotta's room. To their astonishment, both the actress and her mother appeared quite cheerful.
"Don't pay any attention to the criticism," Lotta assured her
visitors. "None of my plays has ever received good notices, but
the public comes. We have a great big success in this piece."
Belasco said nothing about his intention to forgo any further
payment on the play.

Pawn Ticket 210 was almost a parody of the kind of play that
had made Lotta famous. As a small child, "Mag" (Lotta) has
been pawned by her mother to "Uncle Harris" for some needed
money. She is to be redeemed in ten years, and in the meantime
the old Jew—altogether a caricature—keeps Mag in his pawn
shop, along with the watches, rings, and a few banjos, which the
child strums from time to time to amuse herself. Uncle Harris
grows very fond of the waif and intends to adopt her when the
redemption period has passed, but Mag is mysteriously claimed
by a businessman in the nick of time. Installed in his home, she
becomes the instrument by which a crooked deal is foiled and (to
no one's great surprise) is reunited with her mother. Uncle Harris, in a bloody last act, is murdered by thugs. "Spectators of this
amazing medley might well have divined its purpose," William
Winter complained; but audiences ate it up, and *Pawn Ticket
210* remained Lotta's chief reliance during the 1887-88 season.

Nevertheless, there were disturbing intimations of a change in taste. The Dickens vogue was fading, and Lotta dropped *Little Nell* for the first time in twenty years. Mary Ann, perched in a house box, discerned that those who came to see their favorite were the old people and the very young—the newsboys. Unfortunately, the latter were not, as a rule, paying customers. In Chicago, during a return engagement of *Pawn Ticket 210,* one hundred fifty free seats were set aside for them. At the end of the first act, the boys presented Lotta with a bouquet in which a gold pen and pen holder were nestled; Lotta stuck the pen in her hair and went on playing. Then a local theatrical journal revealed that the company's business manager had supplied $25 to buy the flowers and pen.

More and more, such tributes became managed. During one season, the *Nashville Herald* recruited its entire staff to march in a body from the printing plant to the Vendome Theater behind the Vendome's silver band. "The most striking spectacle, perhaps, ever seen in any city in the United States," the *Herald* said, describing the procession. Reporters, clerks, pressmen, stereotypers, and one hundred sixty newsboys, all eating peanuts and bearing torches, shot off Bengal lights and Roman candles as "green, blue and yellow fire lit up the city." But Lotta knew too well that the *Herald* was touting itself and that she was merely the instrument.

Two years before Lotta opened in *Pawn Ticket 210* Mary Ann built a summer "cottage" on Lake Hopatcong, in northern New Jersey. "Cottage" was perhaps not quite the right term for an eighteen-room mansion with a wine cellar, an English butler, and a French maid, and it was much too accessible to the summer homes sprinkled throughout the area to afford seclusion. The area was being developed by the hotel magnate, William Breslin, along with Robert Dunlap, as a colony for millionaires called "Breslin Park." This suited Mary Ann to a T. She planned everything, including the furnishings, which were ornate and expensive. A huge fireplace graced the front hall, and about the first thing visitors saw upon entering was a huge oil painting of Lotta. But the actress did not see the house until after it was finished, and then she was rather alarmed to discover that Mary Ann had left out the parlor.

"Attol Tryst" was a present from mother to daughter—constructed, of course, with Lotta's money. Architecturally, the style was an odd combination of Queen Anne and Swiss chalet, built on the split-level pattern down a steep, heavily wooded hill. Massive foundations of gray stone were surmounted by red-shingled walls and sweeping verandahs that were as wide and deep as those of the Hotel Breslin itself. There was a billiard room, a music room, and a library filled with teapots, which were Lotta's collecting craze at the moment. She kept a banjo in the music room, and played pool and smoked in the billiard room. A steam yacht named *Lotta,* as well as a sailboat, roamed the lake; Jack, who traveled down from Boston to sail, boasted to his passengers that he knew every rock in Hapatcong, and usually proved it by jamming the boat into a rock or two before the cruise was over.

Guests were fascinated with Attol Tryst—"Attol is Lotta spelled backwards," Mary Ann never failed to explain—but they were never quite sure what to do with themselves when they weren't eating or being shown about the grounds. Without a parlor, being entertained was difficult, at least for the women; men might be lured into the billiard room. Possibly this was Mary Ann's way of keeping the men and the women apart. She was proud of Attol Tryst, and in 1893 she sent for Crabtree. It was one of two sights she wanted him to see before he died. The other was the Columbian Exposition in Chicago.

Attol Tryst was the first really ostentatious gesture in Lotta's life, and she must have sensed that it was a prelude to retirement. There were constant references in the newspapers to her wealth, variously estimated at between half a million and a million dollars. But the papers were wrong. The total was nearly two million. The income was piling up. Dunlap's friend, John Jacob Astor, proposed buying the northeast corner of Seventh Avenue and 118th Street in Manhattan, which, he assured them, would someday be a high-class residential neighborhood. Lotta bought it for $200,000. A lot more went into bonds, and the bonds were usually stashed in a safe at Attol Tryst. Once, during a dinner party, the serving-maid asked Mary Ann what she should do with some leftover chicken. The old lady, who had been talking of other things, paused and looked up. "Do with it?" she declared loudly, to the considerable surprise of the guests. "Why, put it in the safe."

According to Helen Leslie, Lotta was seldom allowed as much as a dollar in "spending money" at any one time. She expected to be treated as a child "who has never done things like other women," as her mother explained, and when Mary Ann was not around, Lotta was continually having to fall back on her business manager for small change. Her major purchases were always charged, but Mary Ann also saw to it that most of them were returned to the stores. Miss Leslie, who joined the company in 1888 as a leading juvenile, accompanied Lotta to Marshall Field's during one of Mary Ann's infrequent absences. "You will take her to purchase the few things needed to complete her costume for *La Cigale*," the old lady had directed. "Mr. Dunn will advance money for the purchase and you will keep an *exact* account of what you spend."

But in the dress goods department, the star went on a spending spree. "She bought not yards, but things by the bolt or reel. She never asked the price," Miss Leslie recalled. She was terrified at what might happen when Mary Ann found out. When she did, everything was sent back to Marshall Field's.

It is difficult to believe that Lotta was the complete child in money matters that her mother made her out. Quite possibly, she enjoyed playing Mary Ann's game. The old lady had always handled her affairs, and Lotta was quite content to let her go on doing so. Investments were made in her name, theaters purchased, relatives assisted. Her cousin, Annie Fretwell, was given $3,500 with which to buy a house in San Francisco—quite an adequate sum for those days. The money was Lotta's but the advice that went with it was Mary Ann's. "Now make the best bargain you can, and if you can't make a bargain buy a house as Mrs. Hopkin's daughter has done and rent it."

To Mabella Baker, another member of the company, Mary Ann once declared, "Never buy a thing the first time you see it. Look it over, then go home and think about it, and if you still want it the next day, then go back and buy it."

Helen Leslie's first meeting with this remarkable woman occurred at the Hotel Brunswick, in Boston, where she had been sent by an actors' agent for an interview. The actress, then in her twenties, heart aflutter, entered the room to find Lotta's mother sitting in an armchair staring out a window—"a tidy old lady, dressed in black taffeta." Nothing was said. "She did not turn her head or look my way, but continued her occupation. But—what was it? Clicking sounds—like heaps of coins being lifted and jingled in her lap; and that is exactly what she was engaged in doing. This continued for a quarter of an hour."

Yet there were contradictions in Mary Ann's nature. The bag which she lugged everywhere might hold more than a thousand dollars in cash, and many times that amount in jewelry; and although Albert, the steward, was given a gun with which to protect the valuables of the company, Mary Ann went unarmed. The jewels, incidentally, were genuine, used for *La Cigale* when costume jewelry would have served. One piece was Bolton Hulme's $15,000 locket, a huge moonstone relief of Lotta's face rimmed with diamonds. Another was the Grand Duke Alexis's bracelet. In Chicago, when the Empress Eugénie's jewels were sold to raise money for this former consort of Napoleon III, Mary Ann paid $13,000 for a bracelet with a ten-carat black diamond. She was assured that she had gotten a bargain, and perhaps she did. But, as with all the other jewelry, it is doubtful if Lotta ever wore the bracelet off stage.

Of all the company, Lotta dressed the simplest. It was almost a point of honor. She had spent her entire life changing costumes, and when she stepped off stage, she wanted to return to the real Lotta. And although she seldom fraternized with her cast, emergencies sometimes broke down the barriers. Once, playing a number of small Georgia cities, they were all stranded in Jessup when Lotta's Pullman was mistakenly hauled through to Macon without them. They were due in Waycross that night, and Eddie Dunn was frantically dispatched for a consultation with the stationmaster.

Dunn traveled in a cutaway, striped trousers, gray spats and topper; he also carried a cane. All of this apparently impressed the stationmaster, who finally produced an old hog car. Dunn went off to the nearest farmhouse, bought a load of hay, and had it carted over to the railroad tracks, whereupon Negroes lined the car with hay and the actors piled in. A derelict locomotive clanged into view, making "uncanny sounds of pain," and finally rattled the company off to Waycross to meet the Macon local, while Lotta, laughing and joking, entertained everyone with tales of her pioneer days in California.

There were times, in the South, too, when lunch stops were made at odd, wayside crossings, and then the company would descend on families that catered to travelers, waiting outside the cabin while chickens were caught and cooked. Except on such occasions, Lotta and her mother dined by themselves, often in their hotel room, or in Lotta's suite in the Pullman. When Mary Ann was away, Lotta ate alone, but the old lady had given orders that she was to be accompanied by a member of the cast (female) if she ventured on the street. In Kansas City, Lotta led her escort, Mabella Baker, to a fortuneteller. When she came out, Miss Baker saw that Lotta was visibly upset; apparently, the "fortune" had been unfavorable. Then the actress burst out laughing. "Mabella, she didn't know what I did for a living. She didn't even know who I was!"

Lotta did not employ contracts with her actors, proud that her word was better than anything that might be put on paper. And in spite of her mother's economies, she was considered generous. One perquisite Lotta insisted on providing was a carriage to transport the cast to and from hotels; Mary Ann regarded this as an extravagance, but Lotta argued that to have the company riding around in public conveyances was bad publicity. The old lady offered to compromise: the women would ride in carriages, while the men would use streetcars. And this is the way it was settled.

Mary Ann might run the business end of things, but Lotta took charge of the plays, directing them herself, with a sure instinct, aware that they were silly and unimportant—and very profitable. In this respect, the 1890-91 season was to cap her career. In Washington, President Harrison came to see Lotta not once but twice; to make room for extra seats, the orchestra was moved under the stage. In all of the larger cities she was feted by leading citizens, General Robert E. Lee Jr. doing the honors in Richmond, and no less than three millionaires—John Flood, John Mackay, and "Lucky" Baldwin—turning out to welcome her to Denver. Mary Ann was flattered, but it is doubtful if they meant as much to Lotta as the bewhiskered miners who came to cheer her during the one-night stands. It was the western half of the itinerary she had looked forward to, booking visits to places she had not played in decades.

At Virginia City, Nevada, an old-fashioned barouche with open top stood waiting for her at the little wooden railroad station. Lotta and her mother had barely seated themselves when suddenly, with a shout, a band of miners appeared, unhitched the horses, seized the shafts, and puffed up the hill at a lively clip. The escort grew as others surrounded them—"hard-boiled men of visage but soft as mush under their red flannel shirts," an eyewitness noted. The theater was in the rear of a barroom, where an audience almost entirely male sat on packing boxes and upended barrels as Lotta cavorted for their entertainment. She was not exactly the child they remembered, and neither were they the young men who had idolized her thirty-five years earlier, but Lotta pushed back the clock. Everyone was young again.

Lotta cast aside her regular bill and performed a medley of songs and dances from the past—minstrel numbers, breakdowns, ballads. The rattle of bar service brought back the melodeon days, and Lotta threw herself into each number with a frenzy. The banjo was hauled out for the first time on the tour, and her fingers became raw as the miners called for their old favorites. Then there was a hail of coins and nuggets—everything had to be "just as it was" when the Comstock Lode was making millionaires out of Irish immigrants. Helen Leslie writes:

"It was Lotta, their baby, their beloved child of camp trail or mine that they were welcoming back to their hearts. To watch her skip, scramble, slide on her tummy when she went after the coins and nuggets was a liberal education in activity and humorous gesture."

When the performance finally ended, and Lotta had changed into street clothes, the miners hoisted her on their shoulders and marched, singing and weeping, to the hotel. Mary Ann herself grew sentimental. But there must have been a sense of foreboding—how fitting it would be to end one's career in the style that had launched it.

In other ways, the tour was not so sentimental. San Francisco no longer displayed the "brave wickedness and splendid folly" that editor Frank Soulé had discovered there forty years before; commerce, not mining, was king. Gone were the melodeons, except for the "Belly Union," which had deteriorated into a dive. The famous California Theater stock company had disbanded, and "Lucky" Baldwin's theater was closed much of the time, although it opened for Lotta's return. But Maguire had left the city, having drifted off to New York. All told, he had built eleven theaters in the West, but he belonged to a more flamboyant era, and in the end the West turned its back on him. He died, forgotten and almost destitute, in 1896.

One other old friend was missing. Two years before, Mart Taylor, now more than sixty years old, had written a letter to the *San Francisco Morning Call:*

I am now very sick, and have been so for a long time. I am money-less, an inmate of the County Hospital of Suisan, as above stated. I am among strangers; was taken worse while negotiating an entertainment, and here I am,

Yours, completely tired out.

The editor of the *Call* added that "somebody who knows both Lotta and her unfortunate first manager would do a good turn by forwarding the actress poor Taylor's sorrowful brief." There is no indication that this was ever done, and Lotta did not learn of Taylor's misfortune until after his death.

But the fountain still splashed away in the center of the city, and the whole company went down for a drink of water before leaving for a tour of the Middle West. Then came a final lap through the East. With four weeks remaining—they had reached Wilmington, Delaware, in mid-May—the tour encountered an unexpected, and fateful, turning. George Boniface, Jr., who played Lotta's "villains" for several seasons, had asked for his release so that he might accept an offer to tour Australia. Reluctantly, Lotta let him go and a utility actor named Parker took over the part. Near the end of the second act of *Musette,* Lotta, to annoy the villain, leans her whole weight against his shoulder. He pushes her away, and she repeats the business with his other shoulder. Finally, with her back to him, she falls against his chest. On this occasion, the actor buckled and Lotta collapsed full force on the floor.

A howl of laughter went up from the audience, who assumed the prat fall to be part of the show. Lotta hobbled off stage in pain. She was helped to her dressing room as the cast gathered outside in alarm. It was obvious to Mary Ann that Lotta was in no condition to continue, and Jack, who had joined the company for the last few weeks of the tour, stepped before the curtain to announce the end of the performance. A doctor was called; sedatives were administered until Lotta's personal physician, Dr. Whytal, could be summoned by telegraph from New York. He gave a bleak diagnosis: a vertebra had been fractured.

The season was over—one of the most successful in twenty-seven years on the road, netting Lotta almost $87,000. (An equivalent sum today would be at least $200,000—and it was tax free.) There was a long recuperation at Attol Tryst, and in the fall of 1892 she started out once more, but after six weeks of agony the tour was canceled. Lotta never acted again.

"I do not look back to the wandering life I led for so many years with a bit of regret," she would say much later, yet she welcomed the end, glad to be free of the relentless grind of travel, of living out of trunks—or rather, rattan hampers. Even after her injury had completely mended, she resisted all inducements to make a farewell tour. Lotta was not going to compete with Bernhardt. And unlike the Divine Sarah, she didn't need the money.

At forty-five she was the richest actress in America. Her nearest counterpart among male actors was Joe Jefferson, who had made a fortune playing *Rip Van Winkle.* Shortly before his own retirement in 1904, Jefferson proposed that he and Lotta team up and tour the country together in *The Rivals;* their combined wealth would overpower audiences everywhere. Correspondence, and a good deal of lighthearted speculation about casting the play followed, but nothing came of it.

Lotta knew that the era that had fashioned her was on the way out. She had spanned a single theatric phase, a time of extravaganza and minstrelsy, of the child actor. By the 1890s, the appeal of such dramas was flickering out. Drawing-room comedies were coming into fashion, with their marital complications and what passed at the time for sophisticated dialogue. Mary Ann did not approve of them—it was all right to be daring in a child's part, but an adult should mind his morals, even on the stage. Then, too, there were the new "realistic" plays; in Steele Mackaye's *Money Mad* a replica of the Clark Street Bridge in Chicago swung fifty feet into the auditorium to allow passage of a sixty-foot-long steamboat. In such company, *Pawn Ticket 210* seemed contrived, and *Musette* hopelessly vapid.

Lotta had triumphed in such vehicles because she knew that

audiences came to see her, not the play. "No play was the thing in Lotta's case; *she* was the play," Miss Leslie once observed. An actress? The critics might deny her the claim, but what did it matter? She triumphed on her own terms. And it was not all dazzle and entertainment. ". . . there was not one of [her contemporaries] that spoke dialogue of the everyday life more intelligently or more naturally," the critic Alfred Ayres contended. "She sang a little song, danced a little dance, strummed a little banjo," a reviewer might complain, yet this hardly explained her popularity. Lotta was *sui generis.* A contemporary writer tried once to put into words what it was that had held a whole generation in thrall: "The secret of her charm was as hidden as the scent of the rose; it was there—somewhere. . . ."

There was a sense of fulfillment about Lotta's retirement. Almost all of the plays that had been written specifically for her, from *Hearts Ease* on, had used the theme of the waif separated from her rightful parent. Sometimes she lived in a mining camp, sometimes, as in *Zip,* in a lighthouse; eventually in a pawn shop. But mother and child were always reunited; the "happy ending" was not marriage, but wealth and mother's comfort. The real-life parallel was striking. Mary Ann was getting old, and to go on playing without her was unthinkable.

5

⊙⊙⊙⊙

Attol Tryst

IN SEPTEMBER, 1891, George Crabtree died suddenly while en
route from Liverpool to New York on the *S. S. City of Rome* and
was buried at sea. Just thirty-five years old, he was the last close
link with the elder Crabtree, whom he had been visiting prior to
his death. In Mary Ann's item book, the event was duly noted
in a two-line entry; unwritten was the sense of loss that pervaded
Lotta and her mother at his passing—George had been the lame
duck, the young man of unfulfilled promise, given to self-con-
tempt, mysterious disappearances, and lonely retreats into drink.
A shadow had darkened his life that he could not seem to escape.
"He left nothing but an empty bottle," an actor said of him, but
this was not quite true. There were unproduced plays, unpublished stories, sketches and drawings. . . . Lotta treasured them
until she died.

With Mary Ann, she retired to Attol Tryst and Jack assumed
George's position as Business Manager of the Park in Boston.
Two years before, the theater had been completely remodeled
and could boast, among other advantages, the finest dressing
rooms in the city. A visiting star, however, did not always get
the star's accommodations, for Jack had fixed up two rooms for
himself, reserving them—to put it bluntly—for the entertainment of lady friends at such times as might suit their conveni-
ence. One of these friends was a girl named Annie Harris, who
modeled fur coats at R. H. White's department store on Washington Street across from the theater. Jack met her in 1892, during a run of the play *Venus*—a coincidence which he looked

236

upon as a favorable omen—and courted her for the next seven years, although courtship is perhaps too mild a term. Jack "was a pretty wild fellow," Charles Howard, the hard-bitten drama critic of the *Boston Globe,* recalled. Howard knew the Crabtrees well and was fond of Lotta, although he could never stand her brand of cigars.

Perhaps it was Lotta's smoking, and the generally low esteem in which members of the theatrical profession were held by women of refinement, that created a minor scandal in 1893 when Mrs. Augusta Kidder proposed her name for membership in Sorosis. An exclusive New York women's organization dedicated to "literary, artistic, and philanthropic pursuits," Sorosis took itself very seriously indeed. A single negative vote could exclude a nominee, and the voting was conducted solemnly by dropping little white or black balls into the ballot box.

On this June day, the meeting was held at Sherry's on Fifth Avenue. After the ladies had dined and conducted their routine business, they passed on to the real purpose of the occasion—making Lotta Crabtree a member; indeed, she would be the most famous of them all, and quite possibly the wealthiest. Mary Ann and her daughter had come into the city and were staying at the Plaza nearby, waiting to be notified. But instead of a summons of welcome to appear before the assembled group, a reporter from *The New York Times* turned up late that afternoon with the news that of the 217 votes cast, seven of them were negative. Lotta had been blackballed! The outcome, he assured the two women, had almost torn Sorosis apart; half the members present had walked out in protest after a near free-for-all on the floor. Many had threatened to resign, the meeting ending in wild confusion.

The whole affair made good copy in the *Times,* and public sympathy redounded to Lotta, who remained an unruffled and amused bystander. But Mary Ann was indignant—"For fifteen years it has been the dream of my life to have my daughter a

member of that society," she declared. Lotta not good enough for
the Sorosis ladies? Ridiculous!

For Lotta, the incident left no scars, but Sorosis was never
quite the same again. (The club was later merged into the General Federation of Women's Clubs.) The affair, too, was a pre-
view of what life in retirement might be like if one got involved
in female good works. In her later years, Lotta was shoehorned
by her friends into a few pet societies, but she seldom attended
meetings. It was not necessary to gabble and pass resolutions in
order to be philanthropic; the thing to do was to give the money.
Lotta gave it.

At Attol Tryst, Lotta and Mary Ann spent the remaining
summer months of 1893 in what they jokingly called "seclusion."
But the house was a tomb without guests, and Lotta too restless.
She was painting now; friends came and went, and if they stayed
long enough, they had their portrait done and ready to take with
them at the end of the visit. Rachel Booth, an actress, and her
husband, the comedian Jimmy Powers, had come down from
New York, and Mary Ann did her best to persuade the clever
Miss Booth to take over Lotta's roles in some of her plays; she
would even see to the backing. But Rachel Booth, who had just
made a hit in Charles Hoyt's *The Tin Soldier,* had no wish to be
another Lotta and declined, flattered to know that Mrs. Crabtree
gave no other actress the opportunity. Not until 1919, when
Mary Pickford saw movie possibilities in them, did anyone consider reviving the old Lotta hits; but by this time, both the
period and the plays were thoroughly dead, and nothing came of
the idea.

Lotta had conceived of Attol Tryst as a place to entertain her
old friends from the theater. Mary Ann saw it as a chance to rub
shoulders with the summering millionaires. With the exception
of "Kil Kare Castle"—an imposing fortress built by the patent
medicine king, Colonel George G. Green—it was the most elaborate of all the homes in Breslin Park but even so, life at Attol

Tryst was not very exciting, except when Jack turned up with two or three lady friends during the absence of his mother and sister. Society at Lake Hopatcong was given to dinner parties and dances at the Hotel Breslin, a mammoth establishment which boasted corridors ten feet wide. Residents of the colony were a settled, married group whose behavior was notably without scandal. At Attol Tryst, lady visitors would discover a preponderance of their own kind, a circumstance which sometimes led them to cut short their stay, not always wisely. Mrs. Kidder tells of the time when one handsome young belle read a pretended telegram calling her to New York that evening.

Lotta, realizing the situation, expressed cool regret, saying, "I will drive you to the train when I go to meet the gentlemen due tonight," naming several distinguished men who were expected. The visitor began to temporize, but Lotta was adamant at the affront, and although the young woman stammered, "I-I—might arrange somehow to stay," she was taken to the station just in time to meet the handsome male delegation.

Some of the handsome males, it should be added, would have been better uninvited. Two New York City brokers, "young men of stately appearance," a newspaper account described them, supplied male companionship on frequent occasions, at Mary Ann's invitation. As time went on, they gained her confidence; and of course, they had a proposition, ill-fated, as events proved, and Mary Ann lost $30,000 when the firm failed.

Crabtree himself visited his family at Attol Tryst in the fall of 1893. He had not been in good health, but perked up noticeably, took in the Columbian Exposition, and even made a trip to San Francisco. He was seventy-five now, a man whom age had made sober and respectable. He had advanced to the degree of "mark master" in his local Masonic lodge. For all his faults, Mary Ann had never for a moment considered abandoning her husband; it was simply not done, and at the end they traveled across the country in a harmony that had seldom existed in the old touring

days. In late December, she and Lotta put him on the ship for
Liverpool. He died three days after reaching home.

"Write and tell us when you first heard Mr. Crabtree was ill,
when he was buried and all the particulars of everything you can
remember," Mary Ann wrote her husband's brother, John Henry
Crabtree, when a cable was received with news of his death. "It
was a great shock to us as he had improved so and looked so
well," Lotta said in a letter to Mrs. Doremus, disclaiming that
her father had been "half forgotten to us." Perhaps both mother
and daughter felt a trifle guilty. They were reassured when John
Henry Crabtree sent an obituary notice from the paper at
Altrincham. Crabtree had been given the full rites of the Masonic lodge and interred "amid every manifestation of respect on
the part of a large number of friends," including the cochairman
of the Local Board. Oddly enough, in the newspaper account of
the funeral, no mention whatever was made of Lotta.

Obscurity in her own country was not to overtake Lotta for
some time; her wealth saw to that. At forty-seven, the imaginary
child had grown into a woman of property. Mary Ann taught
Lotta the fundamentals of investing, keeping accounts, the management of her own business affairs—this in anticipation of the
old lady's slackening powers. She was seventy-five, "old-looking"
(but would live another ten years). Perhaps, she reasoned, with a
sounder grasp of the handling of money, Lotta would not be
tempted to give so much of it away. Charity bred its own insist-
ent demands upon Lotta—that and the ubiquitous promoter.
Attol Tryst was one way of keeping it all at arm's length. Lotta
was not a speculator, and Mary Ann would learn her final lesson
at the hands of her niece's husband, Edwin Fretwell, in San Francisco. In the meantime, there was Abbey. Overextended again,
Abbey needed $30,000 in a hurry.

This was in August, 1895. Lotta, Mary Ann, and brother Jack
had returned shortly before from a grand tour of Europe and
Africa that had lasted ten months. They had gone to England

first to settle Crabtree's affairs, and to endow John Henry Crabtree with a pension of £4 a month, every payment to be acknowledged promptly. From Cheshire, the party went to London, and from there to the Continent. Jack was in his glory, performing the same role he had filled as advance man for the Combination; that is, he made hotel arrangements (at the best places), entertained himself at the gambling casinos, and was frequently missing when the time came to move on. It was by far the most extensive trip the Crabtrees had ever made, ending with a trip up the Nile.

They had barely returned home when Abbey appeared. Like Maguire before him, he had sunk a fortune in grand opera, and his creditors were pressing him. Lotta had never forgotten his loyalty; she had even forgiven him for not marrying her—if she had ever really thought he would. He offered her a mortgage as security for the loan, and Abbey was once more made solvent.

But Lotta had stepped in at the brink of a disaster that the money simply postponed. The following May, the floundering producer announced that he had failed. Everything was gone. The whole Abbey empire of opera houses, theaters, acting companies, and traveling stars collapsed to the tune of $300,000. A shock went through the theater world that this could happen to a man as "successful" as Henry Abbey. It was followed a few weeks later by the news that he had taken suddenly ill and died. In her item book, Mary Ann noted the failure but not the death.

During the trip to Europe, Lotta had suffered intermittently from what was politely known as a "female" difficulty, and upon returning, she had gone almost at once into Dr. Walker Gill Wylie's private sanatorium in New York for examination and treatment; a tumor was removed, and with it the uterus. The newspapers, which were given none of the medical details, reported Lotta hovering near death, but the operation was not dangerous and she recovered quickly enough, the center of attention for Dr. Wylie's staff. Mary Ann had taken a room at the sanatorium to be near her daughter, and was outraged on a couple of occasions when the nurses mistook her for a patient.

Again, there was convalescence at Attol Tryst, broken by occasional visits from the Doremuses or the Dunlaps, or an all-day tallyho ride to Dover with Colonel and Mrs. Green. Sometimes she watched the live pigeon shoots on the lake, or invited the summer residents to a "recital" by Miss Virginia Vaughan, who read Oriental poetry. But one suspects the guests were equally intrigued with the collection of Oriental art objects with which Mary Ann had filled the downstairs hallway and music room, or the grandfather clock, made to Lotta's specifications, in the form of one of the towers of Notre Dame.

Alone, she played the music of Chaminade on the grand piano —a far cry from minstrelsy. You had to surprise her to listen; Lotta never performed, even for guests. "One morning many years ago, at a time when I chanced to be at Lake Hopatcong," George W. Floyd, her onetime manager, wrote in 1906, "I surprised Lotta about daylight at the piano."

She was idly fingering the keys and did not hear my step, and in one of her momentary pauses she enthusiastically hugged herself and exclaimed with childlike delight in the discovery of a tremendous fact: "Oh, I'm so crafty!" The idea of associating craftiness with the open-minded and always honest Lotta appealed to me as so colossal a joke that I could not refrain from betraying her to our friends . . . when we were seated at breakfast.

Jack had brought his steam-and-naphtha launch, the *1492*, all the way from Boston, had declared himself "master" of the vessel, and during the summers ferried guests across the lake from the landing, where they had arrived by carriage from the railroad at Dover. The *1492* was a gaudy craft elegantly trimmed with polished brass and gleaming ebony woodwork, "one of the most novel and complete crafts to be found on the lake," the local newspaper called it.

One guest, a stranger to the townspeople, stayed the whole

summer of 1897, and this, indeed, was matter for speculation. A livery man who carted supplies to Attol Tryst would remember many years later that the guest "appeared to be an Englishman— tall, light complexioned, with sandy hair and sandy, sideboard whiskers [and was] very friendly with Lotta."

There was talk about the visitor because he stayed so long; some thought he was a British army officer. If so, it is unlikely that he was a cavalryman; Lotta's new team of horses ran away with him one day and bolted through a fence. The stranger departed soon afterward. The town, which had little enough to gossip about, made the most of the incident.

Sixty-eight years later, a few old-timers still remembered Lotta as a woman who was not afraid to defy convention. Mrs. Georgianna Cook Beatty was the local dressmaker during the 1890's; in an interview with William Parker in 1965, this bedridden old lady, then ninety-four years old, related with a sparkle how Lotta always insisted on having her dresses "shorter than anyone else." Mrs. Beatty shortened them every year, and by the end of the century they had risen sixteen inches from the floor, to the consternation of the staid female members of the colony, who threw up their hands. But the men simply threw furtive glances at Lotta's ankle—the one reminder of her theatrical fame that she flaunted.

Mrs. Beatty also recalled that Mary Ann wore the same set of black buttons for twenty-seven years, changing them from dress to dress as she got older. She had paid $50 for the buttons to wear to a funeral and could not bring herself to throw them away. Eventually, she was buried in them.

After 1902, when Mary Ann had begun to fail, the Crabtrees spent less and less time at Attol Tryst, and it was later rented out. The apartment over Dunlap's store on Fifth Avenue was also given up, and a smaller flat was rented on West Fifty-ninth Street, just off Broadway, primarily for Mary Ann. However, Jack and his wife, the former Annie Harris, could be found here at times, although nominally they lived in Roxbury, Massachusetts, and occasionally Lotta stayed with them. It was a strange relationship because no one was ever certain that Jack and Annie had bothered with the formalities of a legal marriage.

The uncertainty dated back to 1899. Jack had known Annie then for seven years, and his devotion was such that Annie's parents were beginning to wonder when he would make her a decent woman. Minnie Dunlap, who described Annie as an "adventuress," understood that they were married, but that Jack had not dared tell his mother. Annie's brother, it was reported, had appeared with a pistol at Jack's room in the International Hotel in Boston, found Annie present, and herded the couple, at gunpoint, into a cab. They were driven to a Roman Catholic rectory, dispensation was hurriedly arranged for Jack, and he and Annie were married by the parish priest. Mary Ann, sharing many of the prejudices of her time, was decidedly anti-Catholic, and it was this aspect of the marriage, rather than his mother's disapproval of Annie, that Jack feared. He later insisted that they had been married by a justice of the peace, an explanation which satisfied the old lady completely, and no more questions were asked.

Whatever the real truth, Annie became a member of the family. Perhaps at last, Mary Ann thought, her son would "settle down." Lotta, who had long ago learned to swallow her disappointments, accepted Annie charitably, but without illusions; spiritually, the two were poles apart. Yet Lotta's heart went out to this woman who might yet salvage something of Jack. Gifts were exchanged on all proper occasions, and every letter that Lotta wrote to Annie began "Dear Sister—". Strangely affectionate in tone, the correspondence continued for years, until Lotta's rupture with her brother in 1911. For all practical purposes, she supported them, although the "allowance" of $12,000 a year was never enough. Grace Kramer, a friend of Lotta's, once asked her why she didn't cut him off. Lotta thought about this for a moment, obviously not for the first time. "Grace, would you take away the crutch from a man you had made a cripple?" she replied.

There was another Annie—her cousin, Annie Fretwell—with whom lifelong relations were undergoing a strain. In 1902, during a visit to San Francisco, Mary Ann had entrusted almost $200,000 to Edwin Fretwell, Annie's husband, as an investment in the bank of which he was president. The stock had been placed in a safe-deposit box under Fretwell's care. Now, in May of the following year, the Crabtrees returned to San Francisco to discover the stock certificates missing. "You should have seen their [the Fretwells'] faces when we opened up the box!" Mary Ann noted in her item book. The upshot was a lawsuit in which Lotta recovered the stock, plus interest. And she was done with Annie Fretwell, although Annie was not done with Lotta.

For the next two years, much of Lotta's time was spent taking care of Mary Ann in the apartment on West Fifty-ninth Street. There were interludes at West Chop, Massachusetts, where she painted, or trips to Lakeville, Connecticut, to an inn managed by the daughter of Julia Dean Hayne. With the Dunlaps, she went to the theater, but Mary Ann seldom ventured out anymore; at eighty-five, she looked ten years older. Lotta, approaching sixty, might have passed for forty. There was a reciprocal irony in this: Mary Ann had given up her youth so that Lotta might keep hers forever. When she died, on April 11, 1905, something inside Lotta shattered. For the first time, she began to show her real age.

An unexpected sequel to the old lady's death was the discovery that she had never bothered to make a will. Mary Ann had handled millions of dollars, but everything had been banked in Lotta's name. At any rate, both Lotta and Jack searched the safes, bank vaults, and even her black bag for a last will and testament without success. What they did find, in Mary Ann's apartment, was $70,000 in cash, $20,000 of it hidden in a granite coffeepot.

6

Life Without Mary Ann

SIX WEEKS after Mary Ann's death, Lotta booked passage on the *Bremen* for London, only to find that being abroad and alone was unbearable. She had made the mistake of trying to take her mother with her: "I stay in my room until eleven reading and talking to my darling's photo," she wrote Annie and Jack from the *Bremen*.

But London was gloomy and cold. Within a month, she was back home, wisely having decided to get over her grief by keeping as busy as possible. The apartment at 128 West Fifty-ninth Street seemed tomblike, filled with echoes from the past, and Lotta, who could not bear to live there, moved to a hotel. Jack came down from Boston frequently; he was running through his inheritance even faster than Lotta had expected. Sometimes he brought Annie along and the three went shopping, although social visits were awkward; Lotta's friends found it difficult to accept Annie Crabtree. There were slights, which Annie herself sensed, and after a time the visits stopped.

The Park, in Boston, which had been leased, was no longer managed by Jack. As usual, he was at loose ends, but the trips to New York were not without purpose. He proposed that Lotta set up a racing stable. Lotta had always loved horses, and there was something improbable about the idea that appealed to her, no matter how much it might shock her friends. Jack would manage everything; if there was one thing he knew, it was horses. Lotta's interest in racing was as much a concession to Jack as an attempt to replace her own sense of loss with the activity once filled by the

stage. This in itself would have been sufficient reason, and probably no one was more surprised than Lotta when the enterprise
at first proved to be financially rewarding.

With Jack in charge, everything was conceived on a grand
scale. The stables, located on a farm in Atlantic, Massachusetts,
were equipped with the best of everything, including a trainer,
Tom W. Murphy, who was known as "the wizard." Meanwhile,
Jack and Annie moved onto a seventy-acre estate at Squantum,
overlooking Quincy Bay. Here, a large clapboard house with
broad piazzas squatted on the highest land of the peninsula and
commanded a spectacular view of the water and the savin-cov-
ered hills that ran down to the shore. Jack liked privacy and
installed a sign at the entrance, "Beware of the Bull," although
it was common knowledge that no bull was on the premises. Jack
also paid his respects to his family tree: the street fronting the
house was named "Livesey," the two roads into the property,
"Crabtree" and "Sonoma." The house at Squantum was actually
owned by Lotta, and at times she stayed there with Jack and Annie.

Things moved quickly. By 1906, Jack had acquired Roberta,
The Outlaw, Nut Boy, Sonoma Girl, Lady Thistle, and My Star.
He had a weakness for the big purses, and interestingly enough,
the horses often won. Nut Boy, which one racing paper called the
best double-gaited horse in the country, could claim eight wins
out of nine starts, for purses that totaled more than $19,000.
Sonoma Girl, for which Lotta paid $26,000, had begun badly
with three straight losses in 1907, then found her stride and took
a $10,000 purse at Detroit, followed by a $5,000 win in Cleveland, two more in Columbus for a total of $15,000, and finished
the season in Lexington, Kentucky, by winning the $5,000 Tran-
sylvania Stake.

Eventually, Lotta was to own twenty trotters, and to earn a
reputation as "Queen of the Turf." But she was hardly queenly
in manner: people at Readville or Mystic Park were curious
about the tiny woman who strode through the paddock in inde-
cently short skirts and bobbed hair, giving words of encourage-

ment to the horses before post time. If they had seen her arrive, they also marveled at the sight of a woman driving her own automobile, an early-model touring car which she had named "Red Rose." Sometimes the horses ran faster than her car, Lotta used to say; but she insisted on being modern at all costs (and the cost was considerable), even though "nice women" did not often drive these gasoline monsters.

For the next four years, Lotta's silks appeared in the major trotting events from New England to Kentucky. Occupied increasingly with her own business affairs, which she handled personally, Lotta herself did not follow the circuit outside of New England. "I have no secretary, but read and answer all my own correspondence," she boasted to an interviewer. "My mother taught me business. It was not easy, but she kept at it until she made me learn."

Perhaps she learned too well. Jack, with characteristic extravagance, pursued a course that began to eat up the profits, having surrounded himself with aides-de-camp, hangers-on, and even a valet, while Lotta was doing her own donkeywork to save the cost of a secretary. And she was beginning to discover that racing, even when the horses won, could be an expensive way to make money. Jennie Scott, sired by the famous Peter the Great, had been added to the string, the costliest acquisition yet. New trainers were brought on from Illinois. The stable grew as Jack traveled about the country while Annie stayed behind at Squantum. A newcomer was a bay mare that Lotta decided to name after herself, only to discover that a "Lotta" was already in the field, pre-empting the choice. (Actresses were a favorite source of names for race horses, among them "Lillian Russell.") The mare, therefore, was reluctantly called "Lotta Crabtree," which struck its owner as somewhat ironic, considering that her own fame had been so studiously built up without a surname. But she won her share of races, and long after the stable had been sold, Lotta kept the mare at Squantum, no doubt out of sentiment; it lived to be thirty-four years old.

In 1909, Lotta bought the Hotel Brewster in Boston for $500,-
000 cash. Just around the corner from the Park Theater, on
lower Boylston Street, it was convenient to the theater district
and became a favorite stopping place for actors and actresses as
word went around that special rates were given to members of
the profession. Sometimes Lotta met her guests at the railroad
station in "Red Rose"; she put flowers in their rooms and supplied the dining tables with milk, butter, and eggs from the
farm. Best of all, she taught the bellboys how to call out an
actor's name so that it sounded important. The Brewster became
known for its unusual hospitality. Where else could you be attended by a celebrated entertainer in retirement, the owner of a
racing stable, and a millionaire, all in one person?

Lotta lived at the Brewster, whenever she was in Boston, for
the remainder of her life. She never tried to manage the hotel,
and the men she hired had a hard time pleasing her, and
came and went like birds of passage. In 1910, Jack was put in
charge, and this proved to be a mistake. Through the miasma of
recrimination that surrounded the artesian well incident, it is
difficult to determine just how deliberately Jack set out to deceive his sister. He did propose to sink a well, through the basement floor, to obviate the necessity of buying water from the city;
giving Jack the benefit of the doubt, this may have been done in
good faith. But when the well proved to be dry, Jack tapped the
service main and supplied it with city water; it was a stupid
move, and when Lotta discovered that she had paid for a useless
well, she was furious.

The stable, too, had begun to lose money. To a great extent,
Lotta's heart went out of racing when her favorite, My Star,
slipped on the ice and had to be put down. In 1910, after winning a $10,000 purse at Buffalo, Sonoma Girl had an accident at
Poughkeepsie when another horse ran into her; the experience
left her permanently shy, and her days of glory were over. By the
following year, after the artesian well episode, Lotta had had
enough. It was the end of a long, trusting, and yet unhappy

relationship. The stable was sold, and Jack and Annie moved out of the house at Squantum.

Once, a friend asked Lotta how much her family had cost her. Thinking of Louis Livesey, the Fretwells, a father pensioned off in England, and Jack, she put the figure at about a million dollars. It was an unpleasant subject. "Money!" she burst out a moment later. "I've had it all and there's nothing to it."

Money was to be Lotta's consuming passion until her death; but unlike Mary Ann, she would be ruled not by getting it so much as giving it away. Benevolence became almost a compulsion with her. With Minnie Maddern Fiske, she spent hours discussing her wealth—and Mrs. Fiske, who had not fared well in retirement, was envious. Money went to the New England Anti-vivisection Society for a life membership. Money went to the Audubon Society and the ASPCA. Occasionally, a check went to Mrs. Fiske; Minnie was one of the few old friends with whom she could be intimate, and the two women gadded about in a Boston that would boast of Lotta as the second largest individual tax-payer in the city.

In 1911, Lotta leased the Brewster to John Lane, retaining a suite of rooms for herself and an additional room at the end of one corridor for storage of her theatrical mementos. Relieved of the overall supervision of the hotel, and rid of Jack, she returned energetically to her painting—at Squantum, in good weather, sometimes at East Gloucester or Rockport, where an artists' colony had grown up. The professionals looked upon Lotta as an amateur, but they didn't criticize her painting so much as her failure to buy more of their own canvases. Lotta was incredibly persistent at her art, and in 1912 she sailed for Paris to study at the Académie Colorossi, in the Latin Quarter, where both Edna Wallace Hopper and Wilson Mizener had taken residence (separately), giving the place a theatrical imprimatur. It was an atmosphere that made Lotta feel right at home, although Miss Hopper proved to be not quite her cup of tea.

These were years of renewed purpose in Lotta's life. She was free to travel, free to work for the causes she believed in, free to speak her mind. Her charities proliferated, and although some of them might verge on the eccentric, they whirled around a core of goodness. It was the fountain all over again. Lotta was easily influenced. A New York friend, Mrs. Curtis Freshel, persuaded her to join the Millennium Society; the apocalyptic title disguised a group of female vegetarians, and for several years Lotta dutifully went without meat. Better, she insisted, than going to meetings!

But she was too shrewd to suppose that vegetarianism would bring about the millennium, and her real interests were turned militantly elsewhere. The pink banquet hall at the Brewster became the scene of a reception for the actress Mary Shaw, who was promoting the newly formed Players Equal Suffrage League. Billie Burke, Margaret Anglin, and Jane Cowl came, and Lotta was elected vice-president. She had met the dazzling Miss Burke the year before when she was acting with John Drew at the Hollis Street Theater, seeing herself "reincarnated as I was in my younger days." Backstage, after the play, an animated exchange followed without the young actress realizing with whom she was speaking, for Lotta had been introduced as Miss Crabtree. Miss Burke was both puzzled and amused. When her visitor turned and walked out the stage door, Billie turned to her manager, Victor De Kiraly. "What a dear old lady," she said. "Who was she?"

Mayor John "Honey Fitz" Fitzgerald came to her tea dances, run for the benefit of the unemployed. But after 1914, these causes lost some of their urgency as the fighting in Europe threatened to involve the United States. There was no doubt as to where Lotta stood on the issue; she hated "this fiendish war" and was passionately opposed to supplying the Allied powers with arms. Lotta knew nothing of politics; she spoke as a humanitarian. No munitions maker, large or small, was immune to her scolding. Letters to the newspapers denounced the Colt Manufacturing Company, Winchester Arms, Du Pont, and Bethlehem Steel. One especially barbarous weapon that drew her fire was the manufacture of four million "aerial arrows" to be shot out of cannon. Lotta urged her readers to support a bill then pending in Congress that would have prohibited all trade in munitions between the United States and Europe.

War was another reason why women should have the vote. "How many deaths of brave men, how many widows, how many orphans shall [the United States] be responsible for? How many wounded and crippled soldiers, how much pain and anguish will be chargeable to our account?" she argued. Like most Americans, she supported the Government once we were in the war, but she never regarded it as anything other than the work of bungling men, and her patriotism was really pity for the victims.

In the fall of 1915, Lotta was invited to the Panama-Pacific Exposition in San Francisco. November 6 had been set aside as "Lotta Crabtree Day"; there would be ceremonies at the fountain, and Lotta was expected to address the throng. The idea for this return engagement had been that of Fremont Older, editor of the *San Francisco Call,* and although she demurred at first, when it became evident that her appearance was regarded as virtually an affair of honor for the city, Lotta agreed to make the trip. A speech several pages long, written and memorized, gave tribute to her adopted city; but it also set forth Lotta's views on vivisection, charity, and—not least—the debt she owed to Mary Ann Crabtree. "What I am, what I have been, and what I was, I owe entirely to her. . . . My mother was the most wonderful woman that ever lived—and I want the world to know it."

She started for the Coast with William Morse and a companion, Mrs. Margaret Kilham, a painter whom she knew from Gloucester. When the party arrived, the whole city was enjoying a carnival mood, and Lotta plunged into the spirit of the Exposition with a buoyancy that belied her sixty-eight years and the exhausting effects of the journey. She suffered through ceremonies at Exposition Hall; she tramped through dozens of exhibits. When she learned that a horse named Peter Scott was entered in the harness races, she hurried over to the track. Lotta had raised Peter Scott as a colt in Atlantic—and now she saw him win a $10,000 purse!

On the evening of November 6, William Crocker, the banker, and his wife called at the St. Francis Hotel to escort Lotta to the fountain. Dressed in a yellow gown that shimmered with queenly radiance, she stepped into a stagecoach pulled by four white horses, while five police officers, who had known Lotta years before, presented themselves as an honor guard. Outriders dressed as placer miners went ahead as the coach moved off toward the fountain behind a brass band.

The entire area around Geary, Market, and Kearny Streets was roped off, the streetcars had stopped running, and thousands of San Franciscans, most of whom had only heard of Lotta, milled about, waiting to see what she looked like. When the coach pulled up to the platform in front of the fountain, the official Exposition Choir of three hundred fifty voices burst into the *Hallelujah Chorus;* they, too, were dressed in yellow and the platform was banked with hundreds of yellow chrysanthemums. It was a scene Maguire might have staged in one of his more grandiose periods.

The singing ended. Lotta waved her arms and threw kisses, waiting for the storm of cheers to die down so that she could begin the talk she had been rehearsing right up to this moment. "Dear friends—" she began and then, overcome with feeling, realized that she had very little to say. People had not come here to hear a lecture by a cranky old woman! She abandoned her talk and began to improvise. For a few minutes she spoke of her happiness at being there, but then she could not go on, and began weeping. Thousands of voices set up the cry, "LOTTA! LOTTA! LOTTA!" Then silence swept over the square and finally everyone wept with her. It was the largest audience Lotta ever faced, and the last.

At the St. Francis Hotel, a few days later, as Lotta stepped off the elevator into the lobby, a dark-haired woman about thirty-five years old approached her. Supposing at first that she was an admirer, Lotta politely acknowledged the greeting and continued on. But she was not to get away so easily. The woman followed her, drew abreast—there was something she wanted to tell Lotta; it was important. She had come all the way from San Gabriel to see her.

Hard-luck stories were nothing new to Lotta, if such it was. Following her usual custom, she instructed the woman to put her request in writing and have the note delivered to her room. In due time, if anything could be done, she would hear from her.

The note, when it came, was disturbing. In all probability William Morse saw it; in any case, it was not answered. The name Carlotta Cockburn meant nothing to Lotta.

The remaining years of her life were spent painting, giving her money away, and growing old. She lived for the first two of these activities and dreaded the third. Occasional well-meaning requests only reminded her of the inexorable passage of time. In October, 1917, John Barrymore wrote asking her to take part in a "gorgeous pageant of the stage" as part of a bazaar at Grand Central Palace in New York for war relief. "At the very end of the pageant, we want to have you appear among us all as the beloved Queen of the American stage in whichever of your most famous characters you would select." She was tempted, but found it impossible to pick up such a tangled thread, and declined. "It seems like a dream to me that I was ever on the stage," she had told a newspaper interviewer, but evidence that the dream had been real was locked in the memento room, a jumble of costumes and play-scripts and all the things she had saved from her travels in Europe.

Emma Donovan, a pleasant, efficient spinster, had been hired as secretary-companion. She lived at the Brewster, handling Lotta's correspondence and screening the applications for money, which poured in from all sources. But the money did not pour out to every supplicant. Lotta's charity was highly personal.

Forty wounded American soldiers were undergoing treatment at Parker Hill Hospital and Lotta sent them each $50. Cash was what they needed; the knitted mufflers and wristlets would be supplied by the Red Cross. "She wanted to do big things with her money," Jim McHugh, the Brewster's manager, explained. Her income at this time ran to as much as $42,000 a month. Lotta's gifts were usually passed out $1,000 or more at a time, and most of them went for animals. She could be very single-minded about this; a $2,000 contribution to a rest farm for horses was just twice the amount given to a rest home for aged couples in Roxbury. In 1921, when Emma Donovan told her that the Animal Rescue League was holding a Christmas dinner for horses, Lotta thought for a time that the horses were to be given some kind of special feed. She would have approved.

The consuming worry of her last years was the disposal of this wealth after her death. It became an obsession. Her will was written and rewritten, and codicils were added, until General Edwards simplified the problem in 1921. The story had gone round that Edwards had been removed from his command in France because of a too humane concern for the welfare of his troops, and nothing could have pleased Lotta more. This, and his flattering attentions—the General's box at Braves Field was always at her disposal—made Lotta vulnerable. As the executor of her will, he, in turn, was prepared to defend her idiosyncracies, including the fountains that Lotta wanted to have erected all over the country. These might be the childish fancy of an eccentric old woman, but it was her money and that was how she wanted to be remembered.

Lotta's brother Jack died in 1920, while living in the South. Lotta saw him last in 1918, shortly after the death of his wife, Annie, when he used the Brewster as the staging area for a hunting trip he planned to make in North Carolina. Emma Donovan recalled that for several days Jack brought a variety of weapons and camping equipment into the lobby, where they remained until his departure, baffling the hotel guests no end. Lotta had never cut him out of her will; her final act of kindness toward

Jack was to bury him in the family plot in Woodlawn Cemetery, the Bronx.

One other matter remained in reckoning up her accounts— how to memoralize Mary Ann. Actually, Lotta wanted to saint her. The nearest she could come to this was a stained-glass window that was commissioned in Europe at a cost of $20,000, shipped to New York, and offered to a "church on the East Side" —records do not specify which one. It was refused, possibly because its donor had been an actress, possibly because there was no record that Mary Ann had ever attended that church, or any other. In disgust, Lotta kept the window in a warehouse, where it remained long after her death, unclaimed until the storage company offered it free to any church that would take it. Mary Ann's window, a triptych of angels, with Lotta's name on a plaque at the bottom, today is one of the delights and curiosities at St. Stephen's Church in Chicago, where, as a theatrically commissioned work of art, it is not entirely out of place. The comedian George Gobel, once an altar boy at St. Stephen's, is enshrined in another window nearby.

Lotta traveled a great deal in her last years, trying to get away from old age. With Mrs. Maria Bryant, a close friend at this time, she went back to Lake Hopatcong, but the millionaires were almost all gone, and Attol Tryst had been sold—she would never live there after Mary Ann's death. Lotta and Mrs. Bryant stayed with the family of the liveryman who had hustled her baggage over to Mt. Arlington each summer from Dover. The summer house at Squantum was gradually surrendered to the weeds and the elements; the furniture gathered dust and the farm buildings fell apart, but it remained in Lotta's possession until she died. Gloucester saw her more often, a gifted amateur who spent her days at the shore painting, then changed into antiquated garments, dined alone at the hotel, and spent her evenings smoking on the terrace. A small solo exhibition of her work was held in Boston in 1922.

Mrs. Bryant's journal, from 1920 on, gives a detailed picture of this autumn period. She writes of watching the North Scituate moonrise with Lotta, of visiting Mae Howard's stables and fussing over a blind lap dog, of sweltering through the heat of a Fourth of July afternoon at Braves Field, of walking all the way from Twenty-ninth to Forty-fifth Streets in New York shopping for antiques. But by 1924, arteriosclerosis had set in and Lotta left the Brewster less and less. Sometimes Mr. Morse took her driving. A man named Hind, a contractor who worked for Lotta at the Brewster, and who had become quite fond of her, sat in her room as she talked of the old days in the theater. Actresses didn't know how to make people laugh anymore, she used to say. Everything was too sophisticated. She was not too ill to reminisce, would remember the time she slapped "Ashworth's" face once when he took her horse and carriage without asking . . . the time she had thrown a pitcher of ice water at her father's head. "He thought he was the star instead of me," she laughed. Lotta hated the idea of death. She sent for Dr. Daniel Emery Chase almost daily, knowing there was not much that could be done for her; what she really wanted to do was discuss the Bacon-Shakespeare controversy, and he obliged.

On September 2, 1924, Lotta's condition grew suddenly worse, and Dr. Chase moved her to a sanatorium in Melrose. She remained exactly one day, and returned to the Brewster. Fifty years before, Mary Ann had stood vigil outside her door in hotels all over the country while Lotta slept. Now, sensing that the end was near, everyone at the Brewster walked quietly. On Wednesday, September 24, Mrs. Bryant paid a visit "and took her some of our wild flowers we gathered in the woods. She asked me to bring 'Tod' [Mrs. Bryant's baby] in, so I told her I would give him a nice bath and come in Friday A.M."

It was the last time Mrs. Bryant saw her. The following day, word came from Emma Donovan that Lotta had died. She had not wanted a church funeral, and arrangements were made to ship the body directly to Woodlawn Cemetery. Lotta was interred on September 28, a Sunday. On the same day, on behalf of the acting profession, William Crane—once Dick Swiveller to Lotta's Little Nell—placed a wreath at the base of Lotta's fountain.

Not many attended the burial: Mr. Morse, Miss Donovan, Mrs. Bryant, a theatrical costumer, the actor Will Rising, some friends from the Millennium Society. Mrs. Freshel, who met the train bringing Lotta's casket from Boston, recalled her surprise when the door of the baggage car was opened. A handsome police dog was tied to the handle of the box. "The baggage man could not have known what he had done by chancing to fasten the leash to Lotta's casket, but it was a kindness for which she would have been grateful."

At the graveside, an Episcopal minister read the brief committal service. Lotta was buried next to Mary Ann.

Book Four

THE COCKBURN CASE

1

Mrs. Logie Takes a Roomer

LOTTA WAS DEAD. But the fight for Lotta's money was very much alive. Ida May Blankenberg, decisively beaten back in her raid on the "beautiful fortune," had served four months in jail and returned to Tulsa. Now, in December, 1926, a year and a half later, it was Carlotta Cockburn's turn. The intervening months had been used intensively by both sides, largely in digging up evidence and securing witnesses. Perhaps a more prompt trial would have simplified matters without changing the outcome, but this is hindsight; in August, 1925, Judge Chase, was just beginning to unwrap Jack Crabtree's Tombstone past, and the more he worked the more there was to unwrap.

The issues in the Cockburn case were paternity and legitimacy. If Carlotta could prove that she was the daughter of Jack Crabtree, and as such Lotta's heir at law, she would have the right to contest the will before a jury. Judge Chase shuddered at the prospect; she might inherit the entire estate. Mrs. Cockburn's lawyers, of course, used the long hiatus to good advantage. That cry in the California newspapers—"I need my mother's help now more than I ever did"—failed to produce Annie Leopold Crabtree, but it did flush out a good many people who remembered Annie as a young woman. One of these was Darius Rickard, a former cashier in a Seattle horse parlor who had worked for Jack Argyle, the bank-roll man whom Annie had married long after Jack had left her.

Rickard knew that both Annie and her husband were dead, but that a brother, Henry Leopold, half owner of a small gear manufacturing company, lived in San Francisco. He telephoned Leopold, the two made an appointment, and, scenting money somewhere in the case, offered their services to Mrs. Cockburn's West Coast attorneys. Mr. Robert Lewis also answered the advertisement, as did a Mrs. Hutchinson. Within a short time several Tombstone pioneers living in California agreed to appear as witnesses for Mrs. Cockburn.

Working out of Tucson, attorney James Wright combed the mining towns of southern Arizona to produce another set of oldtimers who remembered Jack Crabtree: as the brother of Lotta, he was a conspicuous figure in Tombstone. But there was one character sought by both parties who proved elusive: this was the remarkable Samantha Kate Taylor Logie, onetime proprietor of the San Jose House in Tombstone. The search for Kate Logie had begun in the spring of 1925; by the following August, the Pinkerton Detective Agency in Los Angeles had traced her to suburban Glendale, where she lived alone in a small house on Everett Street. Judge Chase instructed the Pinkertons to investigate Mrs. Logie and not to spare the expense—

What followed, according to the Pinkerton accounts, was one of the strangest episodes in the annals of private espionage. But then, the subject herself was a very strange woman. Outwardly, Kate Logie resembled scores of elderly widows who had settled in and around Los Angeles in the early 1920s, living comfortably, if frugally, in vine-covered bungalows on palm-lined streets. She was a stout woman who wore "switches" and false teeth, Operative E.L.B. noted when she first called on her. A sign in the front window advertised a room for rent and the young woman's arrival created no suspicion. When E.L.B. returned the following day with her husband, Operative A.X.—the two were, in fact, married—Mrs. Logie rented them the room with no questions asked. It was understood that A.X., who "traveled," would reside there only intermittently, while E.L.B. remained with Mrs. Logie.

It is not possible to describe E.L.B. or A.X. In the Pinkerton files they exist simply as initials. From internal evidence, how-ever, it appears that they were both reasonably young—probably in their thirties—and disarmingly respectable. To Mrs. Logie, E.L.B. became as much companion as roomer—"Dearie this and dearie that," as the operative wrote her superiors in the daily reports that were gotten up after the old lady went to bed. For the next twelve weeks, E.L.B. shadowed every move the old lady made. She eavesdropped on conversations, snooped around her bedroom, observed the mail that came into the house, met Mrs. Logie's friends, and, in general, acted more like a paid com-panion than a paying roomer.

The Pinkertons, as a result of their investigations in Ari-zona, knew a good deal about the old lady, and it was believed that she knew quite a bit about the birth of Carlotta Crabtree. The problem was to get Kate Logie to talk about her life as Kate Taylor. One could hardly blame her. Now an active member of the Methodist Church, where she taught a Bible class, she was also known to the good people of Glendale as a dedicated tem-perance worker, albeit something of a busybody. It was the good opinion of these people that Mrs. Logie was determined to keep.

During the 1880s, she had run "the sportingest boardinghouse in Tombstone," as one oldtimer had put it, and seems to have entered into the spirit of the town with considerable relish. When compared with the out-and-out bawdyhouses which flour-ished elsewhere in town, the San Jose House was a respectable establishment, although as a centrally located hostelry, it became a convenient first-aid station for victims of gunplay in the streets. Not a few of these men were hauled into the lounge of the San Jose until medical help arrived. The private *Journal* of George Whitwell Parsons records these incidents matter-of-factly. "Today the monotony was broken by the shooting of Charles Storms by Luke Short," he wrote on February 25, 1881. "Both gamblers, L.S. running game at Oriental. Storms probably aggressor, though very drunk. Shot through heart." Storms gasped out his life on a sofa in the San Jose House, "game to the last," Parsons remarks.

It was this lurid chapter in her past that Glendale knew nothing about. Already, on two occasions before E.L.B. arrived, she had been the target of intrigue. Mrs. Cockburn herself had turned up early in the summer wanting to know if she was the "Samantha Taylor" who had once been a dancer in Tombstone's Bird Cage Theater. Frightened to death, the old lady had denied it, and sent Mrs. Cockburn away empty-handed. Soon afterward, an investigator hired by Mrs. Cockburn's attorneys had been planted in the house to gain her confidence. This ruse had failed too. "That Dan Rose, to sneak in my house, pretending to be a story writer . . . I got wise to him. He was spying on me but I surely got rid of him quick," she confided to E.L.B. later.

Although Kate Logie was a "foxy old woman," in E.L.B.'s words—and, one might add, with good reason—she never became suspicious of what was going on. "God sent me a nice Christian woman," she remarked; and it was natural that she came to confide in her. She had sinned, but all this was a closed chapter. "Twenty or more years ago, the Lord talked to her," E.L.B. reported, "and told her that her mission in life from that day on was to bring lost souls back to the straight road which leads to God and salvation."

Like Saul on the road to Damascus, Kate Taylor Logie reversed her course. She became an evangelist. A small printed booklet, which included more than a dozen testimonials garnered from years of revival preaching, gave proof. "A sermon from Sister Logie would convince all that God has called one woman to preach the Gospel," the editor of *The Evangelist,* in Statesboro, Georgia, had declared after hearing her. A Denver pastor was somewhat more restrained: "The Lord did a great work in her own soul"—seemingly, after the Tombstone days, both a necessity and an accomplishment. The old lady was disturbingly vague about Mr. Logie, but it was after his death that she had hit the sawdust trail. Once, she returned to Tombstone for a series of revival meetings, and carried out her new role with astonishing credibility. A testimonial to her visit by the minister of the local Methodist church described her as having "stirred the people of Tombstone as they have never been before." Considering that the friskier inhabitants of the town remembered her in another connection, E.L.B. pointed out, this was saying quite a bit.

For seven years, she had served as pastor of a mission in Cripple Creek, Colorado. Then, from 1915 to 1920, she had been the House Mother of the W.C.T.U. in San Diego. After moving to Glendale, she "took in" two homeless girls, sending them from house to house to sell doughnuts to members of the church until the girls, tiring of this, had moved out. It was after they had left that she decided to rent out the spare room.

On September 1, E.L.B. noted in her report: "Today she admitted her rebellious life at Tombstone." Nothing came of this immediately, however, since, on the following day, the Lord sent Mrs. Logie another roomer. Mr. Duffy was a carpenter working on a local construction job, a man in his sixties who minded his own business and could be counted on to pay his rent in advance. Kate Logie asked him if he was a Christian and saved. Mr. Duffy simply laughed and said he was too old to be saved. A few nights later a stone came crashing through the old man's window. Mr. Duffy leaped out of bed in astonishment, to be reassured by his landlady that it was probably the work of a drunk. Such people had it in for her because of her activities with the W.C.T.U. As both Mr. Duffy and E.L.B. were to discover, from time to time the old lady fastened her switches on, straightened her false teeth, and descended on the slums of Los Angeles, where she took part in street Gospel meetings among the down-and-out. These meetings appeared to consist chiefly of admonishing them not to drink.

Shortly after the rock-throwing episode, which was a jolt to them all, Kate Logie confided to "Dearie" that she was writing a book about the early days of Tombstone. A few trips to the ice cream parlor and the author was persuaded to show her the manuscript, which, unhappily, took its heroine only as far as the stagecoach ride into Tombstone. E.L.B.'s primary mission, from this day on, was to get Kate Logie to finish the story. She offered to help with the writing, while A.X., who stopped there from time to time, and who was also made privy to the "book," promised to show it to a "scenario writer" whom he knew in Hollywood. Mrs. Logie never doubted that he was telling the truth.

"Bessie Stein in Tombstone" (for such was its title) proved to be a puzzling collection of reminiscences; the persons involved in the life of Samantha Elizabeth Hale—her maiden name—were disguised by pseudonyms, Samantha herself being known as "Bessie Stein." One of E.L.B.'s major tasks, therefore, was to uncover the real names of the characters and, more important, to locate Jack Crabtree among the dramatis personae—if, indeed, he was one of them.

The story had a racy, authentic quality which made it hard to believe that its author was the pious, or at least pseudopious, old lady who preached on street corners. She came from a good family in San Jose, California, and had gone to Tombstone to visit a girlhood friend who had moved there with her husband. Bessie's beau, a young man named "Bush," gave her a going-away present—"a little ivoryhandled sixshooter" and a box of cartridges. Bessie called it her "loud speaker," and somehow it went with the black derby hat "pierced through the front with a long silver dart" and the gray mohair skirt and long basque trimmed with black satin and abalone buttons. Debarking at Maricopa, Bessie boarded the stage for Tucson and Tombstone; among the passengers were several men and a young girl, Carrie Hanson. "It was a hell of a country," one of the men said of Tombstone. "All the men were rogues and thieves, all the women were bad, every bush had a thorn, and the whole country ought to sink or be burned up."

With "Dearie's" help, the book began to take shape. It was

revealed that by the time she arrived in Tombstone, her friend had moved away and she herself lived for a while with Carrie Hanson. Then she met Ed Schieffelin (with Carrie, the only two characters in the book who were not disguised); Schieffelin had sold his interest in the Tough Nut mine for $250,000 and was a comparatively wealthy man. Even so, he hung around town in a red flannel shirt and corduroy pants. "Bessie" attracted him; he invited her to ride horseback with him. "Unbraid your hair and let it flow over the horse's hips," he pleaded—Schieffelin's own hair, black as jet, reached to his shoulders.

Samantha Hale—"Bessie"—was still, in her own words, a "rose bud," not fully "tuned up" with life in Tombstone. An Italian saloon keeper had offered her $50 a night to sing in his establishment, but she refused. Schieffelin was impressed with her; what the town needed, he said, was a comfortable hotel and a sensible young woman to run it. He would put up the money if Bessie agreed to manage the place. This done, a Chinese cook was hired and Carrie Hanson brought in to help out.

Thus did San Jose House come into existence. It served as a convenient spot for the people of the demimonde to meet their betters. No doubt it had its share of assignations. Gamblers such as "Napa Nick" Nichols and "Gummy Kid" Willetts took their ease in the lounge, and Storms died there. House rules were few, and generally overlooked. "Bessie Stein" ruled with a free and easy hand, but she seems to have made the hotel pay. When Ed Bush followed her to Tombstone and proposed marriage, she refused him, although not before she had deeded him a piece of land adjacent to the hotel for his livery stable. "Bush," as Kate Logie admitted later, was Ed Bullock.

Under the prodding of E.L.B. and A.X., Kate Logie spun out her story. Then, late in September, the old lady was thrown into a fright by a visit from Carrie Hanson, the "wild flower" who had worked for her at the San Jose House. It was almost as if Carrie had discovered that she was a character in Kate Logie's "book."

After leaving the San Jose House, Carrie Hanson had become "Paul Bond's woman," but all this was in the past. Now she was a Mrs. Warnekros who lived in Los Angeles and rode around in a chauffeured limousine. Mrs. Logie was visibly upset by this call— the two old sports of Tombstone had long avoided one another. But this was an emergency; Mrs. Warnekros had been tracked down by a detective representing the Cockburn side. Although she had told him nothing, there was the danger that he would get to Mrs. Logie, and the "wild flower" wanted to be sure that the other woman kept silent. The net effect of this visit was that Mrs. Logie, in a mood of discretion, put aside the book.

For more than a week, she refused to talk about Tombstone. Shaken by the appearance of Carrie Hanson Warnekros, Mrs. Logie was also reminded of her community standing; on October 2, she was elected vice-president of the local W.T.C.U. Two days later, a Sunday, she addressed the Bible class at the Methodist church and in the evening, with E.L.B., went to the Angelus Temple at Echo Park. The following morning, a woman "claiming to be from out of town" rented a stall in Mrs. Logie's garage. It was suspected that she might be another spy. "Sister, we must be on the lookout," Kate Logie warned E.L.B.

Life with Mrs. Logie was not without its lighter moments, as the following extracts from E.L.B.'s daily reports indicate.

I bought a pint of ice cream this evening and as soon as she saw it she said a prayer, "O God, bless these nice people who bought ice cream." [September 9]

When I entered the house I found Mrs. Logie trying to make love to old man Duffy. . . . [September 10]

She showed me various pieces of ore that according to her were excavated in the early days of Tombstone. Mrs. Logie keeps these ores as relics, under lock and key, afraid that someone will steal them. [September 11]

She claims she gets so near to God when she teaches the Bible that she feels a reaction all over. [September 13]

A new branch store of the Piggley Wiggley opened in Glendale. The management gave away thousands of packages as souvenirs, one to each customer, and Mrs. Logie made several trips trying to get as many packages as possible. [October 10]

A bond salesman called today, Mr. Johnson. While in her company he requested Mrs. Logie to let him hear some of her whistling and she whistled some of the old time songs and many times she repeated, "There's going to be a hot time in the old town tonight." She explained this song was the hit of Tombstone in '79. . . . [October 20]

Meanwhile, Mr. Duffy had moved out—the old lady's incessant attempts to read the Bible to him at certain times, and make love at others, had become too much. And what with the recollection of Mrs. Warnekros's sudden visit fresh in her mind, it was not easy ot get back to work on the book. E.L.B. cajoled her, holding forth the prospect of publication, with attendant profits that would ease Kate Logie's financial situation. For several days, she discreetly urged the old lady to get back to work, putting aside her fears. None of this had any effect. Then, the operative struck deftly at the old lady's most vulnerable chink—God Himself. "I suggested to her how uplifting it is to hear testimonials in our church of people who had done wrong, who are not afraid to tell everybody what they did," she reported to her office.

This was too much for Kate Logie. "Tears came to her eyes, but it was just for a second or so. Then she smiled and said, 'Yes, you are a good woman, sister.' " In a long, rambling account she at last began to name names. One incident was recalled vividly:

A straw wagon, composed of several people, stopped at the San Jose House. It was quite dark and Ed Bullock, being told I was leaving for a return visit to California, had the wagon stop to make a call. He wanted me to join him with the party and I insisted for him to stay in the house with me. Ed Bullock then told me he had to return to the wagon and proceed because among the party was Mrs.

Jack Crabtree, who was going to have a newborn and he did not care to have her in such condition in the wagon. This was the first time I heard that Jack Crabtree was going to become a father.

If anything, E.L.B. had done her work too well; Mrs. Logie had not only confirmed Mrs. Cockburn's own story, but, having unburdened herself, she added that "having spoken to God during the night," it was her "Christian duty" to acquaint Mrs. Cockburn with the facts in her possession.

When reported to the Los Angeles bureau of the Pinkerton Agency, this threat brought about a hastily called strategy council. It was decided that Operative Schooley should call on Mrs. Logie, identify himself as a representative of the Crabtree Estate, and endeavor to dissuade her from contacting the claimant. The attempt failed, Schooley being "unable to get her to see her Christian duty plain enough" to hold off, as he reported to the Boston office. The old lady, determined to go ahead, decided to telegraph Mrs. Cockburn, inviting her to Glendale. A.X., who was present at the time, offered to send the telegram himself. He was going to Los Angeles and could drop it off at Western Union.

An agent almost never permits his conscience to determine a course of action. Thus, when A.X. did send the wire to Mrs. Cockburn—"COME AT ONCE IMPORTANT TO YOU"—it was not in the spirit of fair play but on the orders of his superiors, who assumed that Mrs. Logie would persist in her efforts to reach the claimant, and that it was important for A.X. and E.L.B. to retain her confidence. Moreover, one of them would be present during Mrs. Cockburn's visit and could, in a sense, "control the situation," as Schooley explained. "Under other conditions we might easily find ourselves in no position to learn what transpires."

The scheme was not notably successful. Mrs. Cockburn, who arrived the following day, accompanied by her husband, lost no time in getting an affidavit from Kate Logie. In a night message, in cipher, to the Pinkerton office in Boston, Schooley passed on E.L.B.'s report:

LOGIE TOLD CLAIMANT THAT FEW DAYS PREVIOUS TO BIRTH BULLOCK TOLD HER ABOUT MRS. JACK'S EXPECTED MOTHERHOOD LOGIE MAKES POSITIVE STATEMENT JOHN A. IS CLAIMANT'S FATHER

The only remaining hope was to destroy the old lady's credibility, possibly through contradictions appearing in her "book" about Tombstone; with E.L.B.'s encouragement, the manuscript was finished on November 8 and turned over to A.X. under the pretext of being shown to a scenario writer. Copies were sent to the Chase office in Boston and the original returned to its author three days later. To Judge Chase's dismay, the Pinkertons, at considerable cost to their client, had documented the case for the opposition. There might be some value in knowing just which cards Mrs. Cockburn held, but it was slight consolation. Chase had the colorful details, but Mrs. Cockburn had the affidavit.

The two Pinkerton operatives left Kate Logie's house for good on November 15. A few days previously, Mr. Duffy, the carpenter, had unexpectedly returned to take his old room. "Mrs. Logie recited another prayer, thanking God for leading Mr. Duffy back to the house where God is a daily visitor," E.L.B. wrote in one of her last reports. The good people of Glendale remained ignorant of the redoubtable old lady's past to the end.

2

"Those Confounded Shootings"

WHEN JUDGE PREST stepped into the gloomy old Suffolk County Probate Court one morning in December, 1926, the curtain was set to go up on the second act of a drama in which, for once, Jack and not Lotta Crabtree was to be the central character. On the big oak counsels' tables in front of the bench lay a pile of typewritten depositions, and from behind the tables could be seen the familiar faces of attorneys who had appeared before Judge Prest as co-counsel in *Blankenberg vs. Crabtree,* but who now confronted each other as adversaries.

Mrs. Cockburn, a sedate woman of forty-five who wore a pink hat, sat with her lawyers, Sherman Whipple and the florid Jim Hoy. "She had a sad dignity," Baldwin recalled. "She never smiled, yet she showed a calm, intelligent interest throughout the trial. The old-timers of Tombstone, almost to a man, were on her side."

Next to Chase at the defense table were Frank Stewart, Baldwin, and, for good measure, General Edwards. The front row of the spectators' seats was occupied by a picturesque collection of witnesses, most of them in their seventies or eighties; all told, seventy-three were heard during the trial, a majority for the plaintiff.

Forty-nine of these men and women testified by deposition, in Tucson, Los Angeles, or Hannibal, Missouri, their answers stenographically transcribed, bound into thick volumes, and, eventually read to Judge Prest in a solemn monotone for days on end by Chase and Baldwin, on one side, and Jim Hoy or

Whipple on the other. The Judge was known to doze off at times, especially when court reconvened after lunch, which he customarily took at the Union Club. When this happened, counsel might call one of the "live" witnesses—there were twenty-four on hand at one time or another—to brighten the proceedings.

They were a bizarre and colorful lot. Two were retired actors who had played with Lotta. Four were ex-gamblers. One was an Episcopal priest, the author of a book of meditations on St. Luke. The doctor who had delivered Carlotta was one of the Western deponents, as was Wyatt Earp, former U.S. Marshal in Tombstone. Another was a Mary Jane Durwood, who had married "Buckskin" Frank Leslie three months after he had killed her first husband in an argument.

Mrs. Doremus, the Ouija-Board woman, was among those who testified for the defense, along with Thomas Lollis, a drawling, backwoodsman from the Great Smokies; Louis Livesey, the fanatic-eyed cousin, now farming in Vermont; and his sisters, Sophia Livesey and the roving Mrs. Fretwell, who had come up from Mexico City for the Blankenberg case and had been traveling—at the Estate's expense—ever since. Finally, there appeared one John Calvin Jones, a hearty white-haired old Indian fighter who had spent the greater part of ten years chasing the Apache chief Geronimo through the mesas of southern Arizona.

Scores of exhibits were unloaded in the courtroom as the trial proceeded—maps of Tombstone, old playbills, deeds to a silver mine, tax records, letters, mortgages, death certificates, photographs. . . . From these, and the testimony of witnesses, virtually every relevant fact concerning Jack Crabtree's memorable stay in Tombstone was dredged out of a pool that had lain stagnant for forty-five years. When the waters settled, Tombstone was restored to its first flush of silver-scrambling, gun-shooting grandeur, and Jack's own role in the affairs of the town lay floating ingloriously on the surface.

Hoy's strategy was plain. "Not only was [Lotta] not capable of making a will," he told the court, "but there is a question of undue influence [General Edwards's], of mental incompetency. . . ." Could a woman who talked about leaving half her fortune to building drinking fountains for horses and dogs be considered competent?

Chase took up the defense in an oblique way: he would counter Hoy's and Whipple's grand strategy with apparent trivialities. "We had to suppress any sympathy for Mrs. Cockburn as a person and to take advantage of every triviality against her," Baldwin recalled. "Lotta's will was a public-spirited will, and we knew that it expressed her wish to give her wealth to the public from whom it had come. Therefore, Mrs. Cockburn must not break the will. She must not prove her kinship and consequent right to contest it. We must deny her legitimacy and, if possible, prove her to be another man's bastard."

As the trial proceeded, the trivialities were to be telling ripostes to Mrs. Cockburn's claim: the date that George Crabtree was carried up Mt. Blanc on the back of a guide; the time that Jack threw his camping outfit into the Hudson River; the year Geronimo surrendered; the fact that Mrs. Cockburn's given name was Carlotta and not Charlotte; finally, Tombstone's reputation for outlawry in the 1880s. In their bizarre, seemingly disconnected way, Chase hoped they would exonerate Jack as the father of Mrs. Cockburn.

The claimant relied on dates. It was vital to show that Jack and Annie met in San Francisco *before* going to Tombstone; that the year was probably 1879, although no later than the summer of 1880—early enough to conceive a child born in March, 1881. To this, she would add the testimony of numerous witnesses who had known Jack and Annie as "husband and wife," and Carlotta as their child. Whether or not there had been a ceremonial marriage was not decisive; even if Arizona in 1881 did not legalize common-law marriages, living together as husband and wife was some evidence that a legal marriage existed.

Jim Hoy opened the case for Mrs. Cockburn by sketching her early life. If sympathy could sway justice, he would make the most of it. His usual blunt and bullying manner softened when he spoke of the infant Carlotta, then rang with contempt as he described the father's desertion six months after her birth. When the child was little more than a year old, her mother went to Tucson, leaving her with Mrs. "Buckskin" Frank Leslie, now Mrs. Mary Durwood. Mrs. Leslie was probably not the most suitable person in Tombstone to raise an abandoned child. A short time before, she had been Mrs. Mike Killeen, but this arrangement had come to an end when Leslie shot and killed Killeen during an argument, of which she was the principal cause. Three months later, after Leslie had been acquitted of murder on a plea of self-defense, he married her. A tough cowboy, he was accustomed to notching his revolver every time he shot somebody—he was to kill two men and one woman in his nine years in Tombstone—but in any case his new wife had no intention of keeping the baby, whose first name she did not even know. When Annie failed to return for it, she made a rather startling decision: she traced Bullock to Tucson, where he had gone after selling the livery stable, and turned the infant over to him.

Was this strange? Not at all, Hoy insisted. Bullock had been Jack's partner and would know how to reach him; he did, in fact, write Jack, although without success. Forty years old at the time, and unmarried, Bullock began to bring up another man's child. In 1884, Bullock legally adopted her, giving her his name. By this time, he had a ranch near Tucson, and it was here that Carlotta spent the next four years of her life.

But as the child grew older, there was the matter of schooling. When Carlotta was five, she was sent to live with Mrs. Jessie McVeigh, Bullock's sister in Hannibal, Missouri. So that there would be no mistake as to parentage, should anyone in Hannibal ask questions, Mrs. McVeigh sewed name tags in little Carlotta's clothes. The tags all read "Carlotta Crabtree."

Carlotta remained with the McVeighs for six years, attending the public school, playing with the McVeigh children, wondering why people pointed her out as the "niece of Lotta Crabtree"; at that time, the name meant nothing to her. Sometimes McVeigh Harrison, Mr. McVeigh's nephew—a tall, good-looking boy who was a few years older than Carlotta—read stories to her in the parlor. Then Mrs. McVeigh became ill, and Carlotta was sent back to Arizona. For a time, she lived on the ranch until Bullock, concerned that she was not in school, placed her in the Sisters of St. Joseph Orphanage in Tucson. She had ceased to be Carlotta Crabtree and was Lottie Bullock again.

Before sending her to the orphanage, Uncle Ed had revealed something of great importance to Carlotta. On a shelf in his kitchen at the ranch there was a black metal box; he pulled it down, unlocked it, and showed the girl a sheaf of documents: her adoption papers; two letters from Crabtree (one to Bullock, the other to a man named Cowell); and the note given to her mother by Dr. Gibberson when the baby was born. Someday, he told her, she might need them.

But of course, they hadn't meant much to her at the time. After a year in the orphanage, she went to the Sisters of Mercy Sewing School, later lived with a Mrs. Macauley, then a Mrs. Burroughs—doing kitchen work in both houses for her board—until she moved in with a Mrs. Russell. Here she remained until she married at twenty-one. She never saw her mother. It was after Bullock had died in 1905 that she had gone back to Tucson to claim the black metal box. The ranch had long been sold, and the box was about all that he had left her.

It is almost impossible to refute facts; and there were certain facts in Mrs. Cockburn's story that gave no quarter. Dr. Gibberson's note. The letters from Jack. The sworn testimony that Jack and Annie had lived together as husband and wife and that a baby had been born to them in a cabin on Fourth Street. Kate Logie's deposition on behalf of Carlotta. The problem for Chase was how to refute the implications based on these facts. It would not be easy.

Early in the case, he stumbled on a failing that was common to almost all of Mrs. Cockburn's witnesses: they had an understandable and seemingly harmless desire to restore Tombstone to its infamous days of outlawry. If some of this was exaggeration, so much the better. The witnesses were old, and they were garrulous. Chase let them talk on.

He had a reason for this—or rather, two reasons. In the first place, he wanted to demolish the idea that newlyweds—assuming that Jack and Annie *were* married in San Francisco—would pick a town as lawless and immoral as Tombstone for their wedding journey. But more importantly, Chase was determined to show that if there *wasn't* a ceremonial marriage, a common-law reputation didn't mean anything in Tombstone—or at least, not very much. The law judged these matters by applying community standards. Where half the population lived in sin, where gambling was wide open and shootings common, there were no real standards by which to measure a couple's intention to live together as man and wife. It was a subtle distinction, but it might keep Mrs. Cockburn from proving her legitimacy. Without this, she was no heir at law. Thus, the worse Tombstone could be painted, the better for the Estate.

In this respect, the old-timers were remarkably obliging. Most of this testimony was taken by deposition. In Tucson, where the witnesses were still close to the scene, their statements bore some resemblance to fact—"If a man and woman said, 'We are Mister and Missus,' they were, that is all there was to it, and no man dared run into a bullet as a consequence of suggestion that such might not be the case," a local justice of the peace explained. The depositions taken in Tucson were chiefly concerned with Jack's presence there and his general reputation, which was considered good. He was "very dressy, neat-looking, and had a kind of a swing as if he owned Tombstone itself," a Mrs. Hutchinson testified. Annie was described as "tall and rather inclined to hold

herself forward; very graceful in her movement . . . very nice-
looking; dark hair, blue eyes, and she wore her hair combed back
and rolled low in the back of the neck."

The show moved on. Among the deponents was Mrs. Logie—
for the claimant. Questioned in Los Angeles by Chase, she still
had no notion that he had planted two Pinkerton agents in her
house. Her deposition was favorable to Mrs. Cockburn. But
many of the other witnesses drew a longer bow; frail and elderly
they might be, but their memories were resilient beyond Chase's
fondest hopes—and to Jim Hoy's growing alarm. Robert Lewis, a
mining engineer, recalled that gambling was so readily accepted
that the professionals lived in the best lodging houses, including
the San Jose. As Lewis rambled on, Judge Chase drew him a
little deeper into the trap. Lewis had also known Annie Leopold
Crabtree—perhaps too well.

Q. You knew all the fast women in town?

A. A good many.

Q. There were a good many of them?

A. I could say that I knew them all; one or two might have
come in without my knowing it, but I was a pretty lively youngster and I got around a lot.

Deeds showed that although Jack was far from "owning
Tombstone itself," he had purchased (in Mary Ann's name) a
small silver mine, fourteen lots on Fourth Street, and a half
interest in Bullock's livery stable. Improbable as it might seem—
and no doubt owing to the scarcity of labor—the cabin that he
and Annie lived in he had built himself. Then the baby came,
delivered by Dr. Gibberson. Not long afterward, the doctor had
left Tombstone with the wife of a local judge, Littleton Price.
Price pursued the couple to San Francisco, saw them living con-

tentedly with Price's young child, and changed his mind about shooting Gibberson. As a result, the doctor was alive to testify.

Hoy called him to identify Exhibit Number 34, written on the letterhead of an apothecary in Tombstone: "Mrs. Crabtree delivered of a girl baby Mar. 19, 1881, by Dr. N. S. Gibberson." Chase demanded that the doctor corroborate the note with records from his Tombstone practice, but the witness declared that everything he owned had burned up in 1884, when an exploding keg of whisky had set fire to the town. And on this point, history bore him out.

Gibberson had had his hands full in Tombstone; he was constantly being called out to minister to men who had been shot. Sometimes he even saw the shooting. Following the famous gun fight between the Earp brothers and Doc Holliday on one side, and the Clanton and McLowery brothers on the other, Gibberson testified he had attended the dying seventeen-year-old Billy Clanton, whose last words, he told the court, were, "Doc, if I could only get my teeth into that son of a bitch's throat, I'd die happy."

"Tombstone was a pretty tough community—about as tough as anything could be," he added cheerfully. Chase was delighted.

Gibberson's deposition was followed by the celebrated Wyatt Earp himself. At seventy-seven, the former lawman was an erect, vigorous six-footer with a crushing handclasp and cold blue eyes. He proved to be one of Hoy's best witnesses. Earp, having stood for law and order in Tombstone, was not ready to concede that it deserved its reputation. It is quite probable that Hoy, who had begun to see which way the wind was blowing, had suggested to his witness that the more lurid aspects of Tombstone be soft-pedaled. Earp tried, but the temptation to color "the seed of fact with a marvelous hue," as Chase later remarked, was too much. In spinning out his Tombstone career, Earp enumerated various killings, among them the following, involving a man who was twitted for wearing a checked shirt:

"And he says, 'The next man that kids me about this shirt I am going to kill him.' The next man he met was his partner, the man he was rooming with, and of course he said to Bradshaw—we called him Brad—he said, 'Where did you get that shirt?' and he jerked his gun out and killed him."

"Any more?" Chase asked.

"That is three," Earp replied. "That is Killeen, the Marshal, and McIntyre. The next man killed was Storms, and he was killed by Luke Short. That is four. That is all I can recollect outside of the trouble I had with the Clanton and McLowery boys."

"Tell us whether it was good or bad or whether it was a lawless outpost," Judge Chase asked politely.

"I called it good," Earp said.*

* Forty-five years after the events, Earp's memory played him false. In one three-month period alone, the *Tombstone Epitaph* reported four holdups and robberies, five shootings, and eight killings.

3

◎◎◎◎

Trivialities

THE PLAINTIFF'S CASE, as we have noted, rested principally on the argument that Jack had met Annie Leopold, in California, either in 1879 or the early part of 1880, and that he had probably married her before they went to Tombstone, where in any case they lived together as man and wife.

But had he? The defense had two witnesses who would testify to having seen Jack in New York at the end of May, 1880, and another, Louis Livesey, who had been with him in June—just about ten months before Carlotta was born. Allowing for a reasonable margin of error, the question boiled down to whether Jack could have been in California—assuming he *did* go there—or even in Tombstone, by July. It was a simple matter of arithmetic, Chase argued; Jack had denied paternity because he could count to nine.

Finally, among the documents dredged up from Tombstone was a deed (Exhibit Number 27) from J. J. Stanton to Mary Ann Crabtree for the purchase of the Kentucky mine. For the Estate, this was an important discovery. According to Judge Chase's reasoning, it proved that the object of Jack's trip west was not matrimony but money. Furthermore, the date—October 16, 1880 —was the earliest written evidence of his presence in Arizona. Mary Ann was going through another of her speculative periods; Tombstone was the place and 1880 was the time. Much of this background could not be introduced into the trial, but it did help establish a motive for Jack's going to Arizona.

The first witness who testified to seeing Jack Crabtree in New York in the late spring of 1880 was the playwright-translator Mrs. Elizabeth Doremus. On May 29, Mary Ann, Lotta, and George sailed aboard the *S.S. Egypt* for Liverpool. They planned to be gone all summer. Mrs. Doremus was at the dock to see them off. Jack had arrived during her visit with a large bouquet of flowers and, of course, she had talked with him.

Clement Bainbridge followed her on the stand. At seventy-nine he was a fine-looking old actor who had played Lieutenant Frank Elden—"Very Brave and Very Susceptible," according to the program—in *Bob*. He had accompanied the Crabtrees on the first leg of the trip, and he recalled Jack's presence at the ship. Bainbridge immediately came under attack by Hoy. Could he be confusing Jack with brother George?

Not at all, Bainbridge replied. George had been busy seeing to the baggage; Jack, in typical *bon voyage* fashion, was busy seeing his family off. Besides, George had sailed with them. Had the actor made other trips abroad about this time? Hoy asked pointedly, trying to test the witness's memory for dates. Several. . . . Then how could he be certain that this was the occasion on which he had gone with the Crabtrees?

Bainbridge grew flustered. All he could do was insist that his memory was right. It was Frank Stewart, interrogating the old man on redirect, who drew forth a telling incident; Bainbridge recalled that it was during the 1880 voyage that George accompanied him to Switzerland.

"Do you remember in connection with that trip any particular experience you and George had at Mt. Blanc?"

Bainbridge picked up. "Yes, very decidedly, very distinctly."

"First let me ask you whether George had any physical infirmities or defect."

"He had a cork leg."

"What was the experience at Mt. Blanc?"

"Briefly or at length?" Bainbridge inquired politely.

"Briefly," Stewart suggested. "Did you climb it?"

"Yes."

"Did anybody go with you?"

"George was carried on the shoulders of guides and porters twelve thousand feet to Grand Mulet." There was a pause. The old actor's eyes gleamed proudly, the courtroom became hushed. "Bainbridge went to the top," he added.

Stewart excused the witness.

It now remained to date Jack's arrival back east, thus closing the chapter on Tombstone. Chase's purpose was to show that, once the Kentucky mine had been sold—for a third of its purchase price—Jack had no real reason for remaining in Arizona, and that he could not have intended to settle down with Annie Leopold as his wife, common-law or otherwise. Edward Kidder was called to the stand. Eighty years old, Kidder was the author of *Niagara,* one of Lotta's less successful plays. He had managed the actress during the season of 1881-82 and was with the company in Providence in December, 1881, when Jack turned up suddenly at the Nickerson Hotel, where they were all staying. "He arrived without an overcoat on a very cold winter day," Kidder recalled, "rushed up the steps, and asked for his sister and mother." The manager had a premonition about this, and was not happy to see Jack; a short time later, Mary Ann sent for him. Jack would be joining the company, she said. Kidder objected, but "Lotta pleaded, and so I agreed to put him on the gallery door to sell tickets for $25 a week."

Kidder could hardly be accused of partiality toward Jack; three years later, when Lotta was in England, Kidder asked her to read a play he had written. She wrote back suggesting that he show it to Jack first. "She wanted me to read it to him," Kidder told the court, "but he never heard but one act. He went to sleep."

One of the revelations of "Bessie Stein in Tombstone" concerned Bullock's pursuit of Kate Logie to Arizona, and his showing up at the San Jose House with Jack and the pregnant Annie.

Chase reasoned that Bullock had been living with Annie Leopold and that Mrs. Cockburn was Bullock's bastard child, legally adopted, which made him a rather devious, or at least reluctant, parent. It had all been a ruse to keep Mrs. Jessie McVeigh from suspecting the truth when she took the child into her home.

"May it please your Honor," he argued, "which one of these two men acted more as a father ought to act toward this child? Was it Crabtree, who disclaimed the responsibility for the mother or for her child, or was it Bullock, who gave it his name and adopted it legally and nurtured it and gave it some education and notice?"

Bullock had been either a sinner or a saint, and Chase would do his best to make him out the former. In this he had the unwitting help of a man whose profession it was to distinguish between the two. Father McVeigh Harrison was a nephew by marriage of Jessie McVeigh, and he had known Carlotta when she was growing up in Hannibal. In his middle forties, he was a man of learning, a member of the Order of the Holy Cross of the Episcopal Church, the author of a two-volume work of daily meditations and a devotional book on St. Luke.

Father Harrison had not seen Carlotta since childhood. Now there was a courtroom reunion between the gentle priest and the dignified Mrs. Cockburn. He had been called by the plaintiff to establish the fact that Carlotta had been brought to Hannibal because her parents had abandoned her, that the father had been Bullock's partner; that out of regard for her brother, Mrs. McVeigh had agreed to let the girl grow up in the family—obviously, a vastly different construction of the facts from that proposed by lawyer for the Estate.

But it soon became apparent, on cross-examination, that Father Harrison had never completely accepted this explanation. Perhaps he regretted that he was sworn to tell the truth, for under Chase's prodding he admitted that Bullock didn't like to talk about the adoption of Carlotta.

"Didn't he want to discuss it?"

"No, sir; not with me at least."

"Did he tell you why?"

"Because it was repulsive to him—I mean, he showed it. I don't think he used the word 'repulsive.' The impression he made upon me was that it made him indignant."

"Now did he tell you that it was before the baby was born that Mr. Crabtree went away?" Judge Chase asked.

"I am not sure whether it was a little before the birth or a little after. I asked him only what I had to about it."

THE COURT: I am just wondering why you used that phrase, "only what you had to ask."

"I wasn't told and nobody asked me," Father Harrison said to Judge Prest, "but I wanted to be sure that my aunt had not had for her protégée an illegitimate child."

CHASE: By your Uncle Ed?

"Particularly," the priest said emphatically.

Father Harrison stepped down. His testimony was not exactly what Jim Hoy had expected.

There was one other triviality which Chase pointed out to the court in this connection. Although called "Lotta" or "Lottie," the child's adoption papers gave her name as Carlotta. Now "Lotta," Chase insisted, was not the diminutive of Carlotta at all, but of Charlotte, which was Lotta Crabtree's Christian name. "Jack would never have made this mistake in naming a child," he concluded; "Bullock might have."

The last witness for the claimant was Mrs. Cockburn herself. When she took the stand to be sworn, it was apparent that she was no Ida May Blankenberg. A tall woman, with evenly gray hair caught back in a bun, she had a quiet manner and a sincerity that could not help but evoke sympathy. Maybe she wasn't Jack's daughter, but she had good reason to suppose she might be. The papers in Uncle Ed's black metal box were not easily explained away.

Much of Mrs. Cockburn's testimony was a review of her pillar-to-post existence while growing up. There was Uncle Ed's *Agua*

Caliente ranch at first, then Hannibal. Mrs. McVeigh she had called "Mama." Then Tucson again, and when Bullock discovered the name tags that his sister had sewn in her clothes, he was displeased. "He said he had bought and paid for the name of Bullock for me. I was Jack Crabtree's daughter, but he had deserted me, and now that I was adopted, my name was Bullock." The orphanage followed, and the sewing school until, a year later, at Christmas, Uncle Ed took her out. Now she was old enough to do kitchen work and began the trek from Mrs. Macauley to Mrs. Burroughs, and then to the Russells. At twenty-one, she married, and the trek began again. Her husband was a boilermaker and worked for the railroads. From Tucson they moved to Tiborn, California, then back to Lordsburg, New Mexico, to Tucumcari, Alamogordo, San Gabriel. . . . When Bullock died, Carlotta came back to bury him; and she salvaged the black metal box—it was about the only thing she got from the estate. The claimant had treasured these papers for sixteen years.

On cross-examination, Chase wanted to know why she had waited so long to establish her paternity. "Did you ever see Lotta Crabtree?" he asked.

"I saw her when she was in San Francisco in 1915."

"Did you actually try to reach her?"

"Yes, I went to the St. Francis Hotel. I called her room."

"Did you speak to her?"

"No."

"Did you get some word that she might be coming down?"

"The bellboy told me she came down on the elevator."

"Did you see her?"

"She said she was very busy and that she didn't have time to talk to me then but she would see me at a later date, and she told me to go to the desk and write out my request and she would make an appointment with me."

Mrs. Cockburn's testimony fitted in with the details of Lotta's visit, even to a description of a gentleman companion who resembled attorney Morse. Perhaps most of this could have been learned from back issues of the newspapers, yet the claimant, who was a convincing witness, did not have the manner of a perjurer. She had gone away from Lotta empty-handed; now she had come to court for her just due.

4

〇〇〇〇

"The Last of the Crabtrees"

TWO IMPORTANT witnesses for the defense, and a surprise witness
for the claimant, remained to be heard. Louis Livesey would
corroborate the date of Jack Crabtree's departure for the West,
and Tom Lollis, a mountaineer from the Great Smokies, had
been called to describe Jack's deathbed confession. Raymond
Baldwin arranged for their appearance by visiting them in advance of the trial—Livesey again at his farm in Vermont, and
Lollis in his cabin in North Carolina.

All that summer, Baldwin had known that Annie Fretwell had
had long visits with the Liveseys in Vermont, where she was
staying. There was something ominous about Mrs. Fretwell's actions; she was a dominating individual, and Baldwin began to
wonder if she had tried to induce her brother to break the will.

The contrast between brother and sister was striking. In his
bucolic surroundings, Livesey was virtually an ascetic. He lived
frugally, dressed simply, and gave the impression of complete
honesty. Not so Mrs. Fretwell. Her silk dresses—in black, gray,
mauve, and brown—were of identical cut, suggesting the Victorian age without sacrifice of current fashion. Hats and gloves
matched each costume. "On the whole, she was a pretty impressive person," Baldwin recalled. "That helped us when she was
testifying in court. And it helped her get expense money from
the Estate—over $4,000 in all."

How much she might have influenced her brother, or even his
wife, was a cause of some anxiety. On the morning of October 16,
1926, Baldwin set out for Vermont by car, taking his wife Joan,
an English girl whom he had met while serving with the Air

Force during the war. After reaching Burlington, where they planned to spend the night, the two went to a movie. When the lights went up, there, a few rows in front of them, was Mrs. Livesey. Yet there was something strikingly different about her—it took Baldwin a few moments to realize what it was. She had bobbed her hair!

"Somebody has been putting ideas into her head," he remarked to his wife. The two left the theater before Mrs. Livesey saw them.

The next morning, Mrs. Livesey greeted her callers pleasantly, yet she seemed withdrawn and careful, not as Baldwin remembered her from his first visit a year and a half before. After a few minutes' conversation with her, he and Louis Livesey, at Livesey's suggestion, retired to a bench outside the house. Arrangements were made for the witness to come to Boston; then Baldwin again broached the question of his having been left out of the will. Livesey bridled—it was easy to see that the matter had previously been discussed to the point where it aroused deep emotions. He paused, collected himself, and then said simply, "I'll never contest. And I won't take a cent for not contesting." Then he added quietly: "I hate to tell you this. I was a little more than a boy at the time, but I was Lotta's business manager, with a power of attorney. I took some of her bonds that I had no right to, and gambled in the market. I lost. I could never pay her back. Lotta owed me nothing—less than nothing. I could never take a cent of hers."

Livesey was an effective witness. He arrived in court with his own attorney, Harrison Barrett, who had been retained to file the waiver of claim. His slim figure erect, his head held high, his dark eyes intent, he testified like a man dedicated, a true believer facing a tribunal of the Inquisition. Jim Hoy's bullying manner failed to rattle him. He *had* accompanied Jack Crabtree to the train shed in Jersey City in 1880; the exact date had been forgotten, but it was probably early fall.

"We went to the Erie Railroad in Jersey City, at that time

called Fabona," Livesey testified. "We went to the train shed and I saw Ashworth on the train, and I got on the car myself."

"How did you go over to Jersey City from New York?" Chase asked.

"We left the foot of Chambers Street by ferry. Ashworth had quite a bundle. I can describe it best as an immigrant's bundle—mattress, blankets, and several cooking utensils—like a man going out west to rough it."

"Did anything happen on the trip over on the ferry boat?"

Livesey hesitated a moment. "Yes. He threw the bundle into the river."

"When was this?"

"In the fall of 1880."

On the basis of Livesey's testimony, it was pretty hard to see how Jack could have reached Tombstone in time to have fathered Carlotta.

And finally, Lollis. In many ways the most colorful witness of all, he was a gaunt, slow-voiced mountain man with a good deal of natural dignity. It was at his cabin in the Deep Creek section north of Bryson City, North Carolina, that Jack had died, on January 29, 1920. Lollis was the last man to talk with Jack, and he had come to Boston only after considerable urging by Baldwin.

Jack had gone to the Great Smokies early in 1919, shortly after Annie's death. He had assembled a pack of hunting dogs and was camping out "on one of the finest trout streams in the state," he wrote attorney Morse. Not surprisingly, Jack was in debt and had taken a job hauling lumber "over the mountains to the R. R. I get $8 per cord. . . . I have two mules to a wagon and two teams. I have an ox team to haul the logs to the wagon. I will have everything paid except for $45 by the 4th of Sept." In his spare time he shot wildcats.

And then Jack came to the real business at hand. He had come across a "mica mine" for sale near Bryson City. Developed properly, there was money there, even though it might not be gold. If Morse could form a little syndicate . . . it would not take much to bond the mine, perhaps a few thousand dollars. "I feel certain that it is going to be a turning point in my career, as it's been a long, long time coming," he added. Jack was then sixty-five years old.

It was his last attempt to strike it rich. That fall, he became too ill to haul lumber and, at Lollis's invitation, moved in with him. Lollis had thirteen children (although not all of them lived at home), and one more person to worry about made little difference. Jack brought along a horse and fourteen dogs. Shortly before he died, he drew a will bequeathing Lotta $150 and leaving everything else to Lollis. Actually, Jack didn't have $150, and "everything else" proved to be the horse and dogs, and a trunk filled with personal papers.

"I talked with him about his future," Lollis wrote Lotta after making arrangements to ship the body to New York, "and he said it was all a joke, that everything was taken care of." Along with the letter went a bill in the amount of $240 for feeding the dogs. The trunk remained in Lollis's possession, and it was to examine its contents, and meet this unique benefactor, that Baldwin made a visit to North Carolina in March, 1925.

"At Asheville I hired a drive-yourself Model T Ford and motored over to Bryson City. There I was told that Tom Lollis lived out at the end of Deep Creek Road. It was cold, and the road, wet and muddy, climbed tortuously along the east side of the foothills, with sharp turns, crude bridges, and occasional washouts. After about an hour's drive, the road ran straight into the creek. There was a cabin on the left, bare of paint, sketchy of foundation, and unadorned by window curtains. I climbed the bank and knocked.

"A pleasant-looking woman came to the door. She was Mrs. Lollis. From nowhere came a little girl of nine, two small boys, and two older girls—perhaps fourteen and sixteen. Mr. Lollis was out, but would be back shortly. I was invited into the front room, which contained a stone fireplace, a bench, table, and cot. On the left, steep stairs led to the floor above. A door in the back wall opened to the kitchen; one on the right, beyond the fireplace, to a downstairs bedroom.

"Mrs. Lollis and I sat on the bench by the table. The children stood around silent—or almost silent; I kept hearing an occasional spitting noise behind me, and when I could do so without embarrassment, I turned and saw that the eldest girl was chewing tobacco.

"Soon Lollis came in, with two grown sons, and I was asked to stay for supper. And while Mrs. Lollis and the girls prepared the meal, I walked with Lollis to another cabin, where his married son lay suffering from a kick in the head by a mule. The lantern hanging near the bed showed the ugly indentation in his skull. The boy's wife stood by, silent, a baby in her arms, a two-year-old at her feet. She was obviously pregnant.

"Supper, before which Lollis said grace, was rabbit stew. When it was over, Lollis pulled out his pipe, pulled the bench up to the fire, and we got down to business.

"Jack Crabtree, he told me, had come to the mountains and lived in a hut some two miles up in the hills. He had frequently passed the Lollis cabin on his way—on horseback—to get supplies. Always he stopped to talk. One day, late in the fall, it was obvious to the Lollises that Crabtree was a sick man, and Mrs. Lollis had insisted that he spend the night. He brought his dogs over, put his horse in the barn, stayed two months, and died there.

"When Jack drew his deathbed will, Lollis was surprised to discover himself a beneficiary. It was at this point that he asked the man if he had a family; Jack had told him no, that he had been married only once, to Annie Harris of Boston, and that he had no children, never had had any . . . his wife had died the year before he came to North Carolina.

"I next examined the papers in Crabtree's trunk. They added little to what we already knew. Among a stack of photographs was a picture of Lotta's fountain. By now it had grown late, and Mrs. Lollis insisted that I stay overnight. How many children slept on the floor I don't know, but they gave me the downstairs bedroom to myself.

"In the morning, Lollis had already broken the thin sheet of ice on the surface of the tub under the pump outside the kitchen door. I washed and went into the kitchen to breakfast. Lollis said grace. They gave me the only egg in the house, and we all had bread and coffee.

"After arranging for Lollis to come to Boston when needed as a witness, I pushed off, stopping at Bryson City to send the injured son some groceries charged to my expense account, and returned to Asheville and to Boston.

"When the time finally came for Lollis to testify, we wrote him, sending the money for his traveling expenses. One morning, a telephone call came to the office from the clerk at a hotel near South Station. After some fumbling noises, Lollis got on the line. When I told him to come right up to the office—it was only a few blocks away—Tom Lollis replied: 'No, Mr. Baldwin, the good Lord has got me this far; but if you want me to go any further, you'll have to fetch me.'

"I found him in the least expensive room in the place. Our greeting was warm: we sat on the bed and chatted for a moment, then Lollis opened his paper suitcase and took out three big red apples, one, he said, for me and one for each of my partners.

"I could not help seeing that the suitcase contained nothing else—except the well-picked carcass of a roast chicken.

" 'Didn't you eat in the diner?' I asked.

" 'No,' he replied. 'I didn't know how safe it was; but I knew anything that Mrs. Lollis cooked would be good.' As I tried starting him toward the door, he held back and said in a low voice: 'Mr. Baldwin, do you think it's all right? I didn't bring a gun.' "

Andrew Thomas Lollis was fifty-eight or fifty-nine years old, he wasn't quite sure which, he told the court. His testimony was straightforward and obviously truthful, and its importance concerned Jack's deathbed statement about having been married only once and never having had children. Interestingly enough, he had offered to adopt one of Lollis's boys, Fred, who was then fifteen. "I said I reckoned not; I couldn't let my boys go."

"You didn't have enough?" Chase asked with some amusement.

"He said, 'I'll make a smart man of him, I will educate him,' " Lollis continued. "I said, 'Doctor'—I called him Doctor—I said, 'Have you got no children?' and he said, 'None.' "

"Will you tell his Honor why you called him Doctor?" Chase suggested.

"Well, one day one of my boys was sick and he passed along and gave him a dose of medicine. The boy seemed to revive, and from that time I called him Doctor. He seemed to like children; but he said, 'No, I never had children; never raised any and never had any.' "

When cross-examination started, Lollis's eyes began to twinkle. He bided his time, answered carefully, and avoided every trap. Hoy asked him, accusingly, if he had talked with Baldwin. He said he had. If a question was misleading or ambiguous, Lollis asked to have it restated. In a vain attempt to shake him, Hoy showed the witness a snapshot which had been found among the papers in Crabtree's trunk. It revealed a man holding up a dead wildcat. Hoy asked Lollis if that was a good likeness; the witness studied the photograph and said it was.

"I mean, did Crabtree look like the man in this picture?"

Lollis sat quietly; then, with a smile: "Well, I didn't mean the cat."

Chase rested for the defense, feeling confident that he had a good case. But at this point, Hoy called an unannounced witness who was to throw open the whole question of dates. In cross-examining Livesey, Hoy had tried to get him to admit that he might have been wrong in his recollection of Jack's departure for the West, that the year was 1879 rather than 1880. Livesey refused to concede this. Now, to Hoy and Whipple's delight, the new witness, John Calvin Jones, testified that he had met Crabtree and Bullock together in *1879,* just outside of Tombstone.

Jones had excellent credentials. He was a seventy-six-year-old former Indian fighter and buffalo hunter who, as a young man, had fought under General Nelson A. Miles, and had been with Buffalo Bill Cody when the latter was a hunter for Horace Greeley on his western trip. Tall and wiry, with a weather-beaten face, white hair and mustache, he lived in retirement on a ranch in Arizona. "I never want to live where I can't hear the coyotes howl," he said to the court in his opening statement.

Jones had been an Indian scout for the Army all through the 1870s and 1880s, and one of his frequent duties was to seek out good horses for the cavalry. It was such a mission, in the fall of 1879, that brought him to Tombstone. Bullock's horses had not "measured up," and he had made no purchases, but he remembered distinctly meeting Jack Crabtree. When he next came to Tombstone in July, 1880, Bullock and Crabtree had built a livery stable next to the San Jose House, and Crabtree rode around in a buggy with a woman who he said was his wife. It was damaging testimony, and General Edwards, who sat at counsel's table, began to fidget nervously.

Chase rose to cross-examine the old Indian fighter with an air of nonchalance. Among other things, he was stalling for time. Jones had been sprung on the defense so unexpectedly that Chase had not had a chance to prepare himself. And so, in what appeared to be a series of irrelevant questions, he led the witness through a good part of his Indian-fighting career, much of which had been spent trying to capture Geronimo, a subject to which Jones warmed up with very little prodding.

Geronimo, the Apache chief, has since become something of a hero in American history, but until his final surrender he was a source of trouble throughout southern Arizona. The problem for the Army was to get him to go on the Apache reservation. All of this Jones described at some length. When court adjourned for the day, thanks to Chase's tactics, he had not finished testifying.

Judge Chase used the break to do a bit of homework. The next morning, he was ready with more questions.

"When was Geronimo captured?" he asked the witness casually.

"Well, he never was captured; he finally came in and gave up."

"When was that?"

Jones hesitated. "If I remember right, '87 or '88."

"Was that when he gave himself up?"

"That was when the last bunch of them came in and gave up, sometime in '88, I am sure."

"Was he ever captured before that?" Chase added.

"No, Geronimo was never captured," Jones replied wistfully.

"You were after him, weren't you?"

"Yes. He was after me, too."

"He was never captured before he came in and gave himself up?"

"No, sir; that is one thing, he never was captured."

"That is all," Chase concluded, smiling softly. Then he added: "Sir, you are a tribute to the climate of Arizona." Although John Calvin Jones could not know it, he had materially damaged his own testimony. General Edwards, who was in on the secret, felt better.

The remaining testimony was in the nature of a mending operation, each side putting on witnesses to repair holes in the fabric of their respective cases made by minor sniping shots of their adversaries. When the evidence had been closed at last, Chase began his argument. Bowing diffidently to Judge Prest, he touched his fingers to his stubby mustache, arranged his papers, and started speaking.

His voice, at first almost inaudible, took on strength as he warmed up, and occasionally, when he came to a point which called for righteous indignation, it became almost a roar. He spoke of the "stale claim . . . which had been deliberately suppressed, lying in the black box of the claimant for almost half a century." He characterized Bullock as a "horseman who had run away from home when he was thirteen years old" and Annie Leopold as "a saloon keeper's daughter from San Francisco."

Over Hoy's objections, Chase proceeded to describe Tombstone. "It was a mining camp," he said, "the like of which probably has never been seen before or since in this country. The law of the land there was the law of the six-shooter. No man dared to inquire of his neighbor who he was; no questions were asked because no man dared to ask questions. It was a place where men were shot for a jest at their comrade's shirt. I say, if your Honor please, that this testimony shows clearly that there was no law and order in that place, and I claim and assert sincerely that this is of the greatest consequence in this case. . . ."

Why? Because no man, not even Crabtree, would take his bride there on a "nuptial flight" from California. "On the face of it," Chase went on, warming up to his argument, "I submit it seems just a bit improper. Why in the world should this young man with a new wife fly to Tombstone? Why didn't he take her to New York? Why didn't he go to Paris, to Switzerland, to London?"

A common-law marriage? He had pretty well demolished that, he claimed, by demonstrating what kind of place Tombstone was. "A reputation that is acquired as husband and wife in Dedham, Massachusetts, is one thing," he argued; in Tombstone, it had no relevance. Chase described Jack's letter to Bullock as "a miserable piece of paper that has been kept and treasured as worth millions all these years," and the notation of Carlotta's birth as a "wretched grimy slip of paper . . . obtained before Dr. Gibberson ran away with Price's wife, with Price after him with a pistol."

The argument was taken down in full by the court stenogra-

pher, but the transcript cannot give the hush in the old courtoom
as he spoke, or the way the spectators sat forward on their chairs,
or the expressions on the faces of Mrs. Cockburn and her counsel.
It consumed the better part of two days. Much of it was concerned with the law of evidence, technicalities, refutation of the
claimant's witnesses. Judge Chase even succeeded in diverting
sympathy from Mrs. Cockburn to Jack, the alleged transgressor.
"And there he was, old, forlorn, living on an allowance from his
sister, while surrounded by Lollis's children and fourteen
dogs."

Finally, there were the dates. Chase asked the court who would
be more likely to have a better recollection of events that had
happened forty-five years before—actors or adventurers? "Memory
is part of an actor's stock in trade," he contended. By comparison,
Western settlers were notorious for their elastic imaginations
and convenient memories. Now he uncovered a final, telling triviality. Reminding the court that the claimant's vital date
was provided by John Calvin Jones, and that the year in question was 1879, he suddenly launched into a discourse on
Geronimo. The Apache chief had not surrendered to General
Miles in 1888, or to anyone else, as Jones had testified. Yet if
anyone ought to remember when Geronimo had surrendered, he
declared with considerable passion, it should be the man who
had pursued him through the mesas of Arizona for ten years. In
fact, his memory had played him false. Geronimo gave up *in
1886!* Could Jones's memory be relied on as to the year Jack was
seen in Tombstone? After all, that was a relatively minor incident in his life; Geronimo's surrender must have been a major
event.

Hoy made his closing statement on the following day, arguing
long and loudly that Jack Crabtree, not Ed Bullock, was the
father of Carlotta and making a good deal of the fact that "the
house that Jack built," as he described the cabin that was later
sold for $50, was situated in "a respectable part of town." This,

he contended, proved that Jack was "domiciled" in Tombstone and thereby subject to the state's legitimation statute. It was, Hoy said, an acknowledgment that Annie was his wife, whether common-law or otherwise. "The wickedness of Tombstone and the number of men who were shot to death there could not undo that marriage," he argued, reminding Judge Prest that no less an authority than Wyatt Earp had testified that "Tombstone was not half as bad as Los Angeles."

But for the most part, Hoy covered familiar ground. He insisted that Jack had come to Tombstone from California with Annie Leopold; that he had introduced her as his wife and, after the child was born, referred to it as his baby; that he intended to stay in Tombstone by virtue of his partnership with Bullock; and that he implicitly acknowledged his paternity in later correspondence with Bullock.

Mrs. Cockburn herself, he reminded the court, had been told that she was Crabtree's daughter and that Bullock had adopted her because her mother and father had deserted her; she had been known as Lottie Crabtree while living in Hannibal and had come into possession of the letters and papers concerning her birth when Bullock died. Why else would he have saved these documents? "We ask your Honor to find that Carlotta Cockburn is the last of the Crabtrees," Hoy concluded, at the end of a long, persuasive argument. As such, she should be allowed to establish her right to Lotta's fortune.

The case was closed at four o'clock, Thursday, December 23—two days before Christmas.

5

Final Judgments

JUDGE PREST did not oblige the adversaries in the case of *Cock-burn vs. Crabtree* with a decision in time for Christmas. It was not until March 30, 1927, that he broke the silence that had left everyone in suspense for three months. By this time, Mrs. Fretwell had returned to Mexico City, Louis Livesey was back in Vermont, Sophia Livesey was again taking care of the post office in Belvedere, California, and Cousin Sarah Ann Crabtree had gone to visit friends in Canada.

The decision, which the Judge delivered with a certain histrionic flair suitable to the nature of the case, took up the better part of the morning. Once more the principals were assembled in the Suffolk County Probate Court. To the dismay of the defense, Judge Prest began by agreeing with a substantial part of Mrs. Cockburn's argument. "I find that for a time Jack lived with Annie, the claimant's mother, in the cabin, and that the claimant was born there on March 19, 1881. I find that for a time Annie did the housework and Jack did the chores, that he got the doctor for her in childbirth, and that after the birth of the child Jack continued to live there for some time. . . ."

But as he droned on, the drift of his decision began to change; it became evident that Carlotta Cockburn wasn't going to get the money anyway. Judge Prest decided the case on three sets of three somewhat loosely related points: (1) Tombstone being the Sodom and Gomorrah of the West, Jack and Annie's conduct did not prove a common-law relationship; (2) Bainbridge and Livesey were right about seeing Jack in New York in the late

300

spring and in the fall, respectively, of 1880; and (3) John Calvin Jones was wrong about meeting him in Tombstone in 1879. Of course, the Judge didn't put his decision in these terms. He spoke of lack of matrimonial intent, the legitimation statute, the law of domicile, and the vital date. This last factor clinched matters for Judge Prest. "But Jones as a scout, though having chased Geronimo for years, was mistaken as to the year when he surrendered to General Miles. Yet the claimant saw fit to rely wholly on the memory of this witness as to the vital date of 1879. . . ."

"I have often thought that the ghost of Geronimo, as much as any other factor, won our case," Baldwin said later.

The decision—technically, a "memorandum"—ended on an inspiring note. "And Lotta M. Crabtree was the last of this Crabtree family, and her testament is her monument."

On appeal, Mrs. Cockburn seized upon this phrase as an indication of prejudice. Judge Prest had been awed by the provisions of the will to the detriment of the real issues. Yet, in its long and careful drafting, the will *was* a monument—and in this sense it complemented that earlier monument, the fountain. General Edwards was to become a Sorcerer's Apprentice!

From a literal reading, it appeared that water was to flow "for dogs, cats, horses and humans" all over the country. The General once calculated that if he were to invest the income from this trust in drinking fountains, he could eventually slake the thirst of the animal population of every city, and most of the incorporated towns, in the United States!

But before this problem could be tackled, the administrators faced a more immediate crisis. Three days after Judge Prest's decision, warnings of another attack on the will were sounded. On the morning of April 2, Baldwin ran into Harrison Barrett on Tremont Street. Barrett was the Boston attorney whom Louis Livesey had employed to represent him in filing a waiver of claim. Now he looked stricken. "Have you heard the news?" he asked. "Louis Livesey has killed his wife with an axe."

Baldwin returned to his office and told Judge Chase. They were both stunned. What had happened to Livesey? The violent act seemed out of character for a man who had gone to such lengths to renounce any part of the Crabtree fortune. Baldwin called Barrett and asked him to find out when the killing had taken place. Had any message been received, prior to the murder, from Mexico City? he asked.

A few days later, Barrett called back. "Mrs. Livesey was killed the night of March 30," he said. "That was the day Judge Prest decided the Cockburn case. That morning, Mrs. Livesey received a special-delivery letter from Annie Fretwell enclosing a check for $100. How did you know?"

Mrs. Fretwell's strategy had failed. Livesey not only refused to collaborate in her scheme to contest the will once more, but, in a rage of conscience, killed his wife for attempting to persuade him. Largely through Chase's intercession, this tragic figure was committed to an institution for the criminally insane. Mrs. Fretwell brought suit on April 27, less than a month after Judge Prest's decision.

Her counsel was a firm of the highest standing, with great experience in litigation. In the meantime, Mrs. Cockburn herself had appealed to the Massachusetts Supreme Judicial Court. Until the appeal was decided, Mrs. Fretwell would have to wait.

More than a year went by before Mrs. Cockburn's appeal was denied. Then on August 25, 1928, Judge Prest dismissed Mrs. Fretwell's petition to "enter her appearance," reminding her that she had spent $4,381 of the Estate's funds as a cooperating witness against the previous claimants. Although she had been *in terrorem,* and legally could have been denied her annuity of $1,000 a year, General Edwards and the administrators took a compassionate view and fixed an agreement that let her keep it. But she did not live to enjoy the legacy; a short time after her brother's death in the institution, Mrs. Fretwell died.

And so it was that, on November 27, 1928, more than four years after Lotta's death, General Edwards was appointed sole executor of her will. It was a moment of glory for the man who, eight years before, had come to call on Lotta at the Brewster, stayed for tea, saw "the most beautiful ankle in the world," and came away with $2,000,000, the income to provide for Massachusetts veterans of World War I. He would see that the money was wisely spent. And the Massachusetts Legislature obligingly passed a bill declaring all of Lotta's Boston property tax free for the 10-year duration of the Trust.

The difference between the evidence in a case and the actual facts does not always come to light during a trial. There is a celebrated example in legal annals of a case in Malta where the judge before whom an alleged murderer was to be tried happened to look out his window one morning while shaving and saw one man stab another. A defendant was soon brought before him charged with the murder, although it was not the man he had seen do the stabbing. Yet, as the only qualified British judge in Malta, he presided at the trial, ruled on the admissibility of the evidence against the accused, and charged the jury. The wrong man was found guilty and hanged. When the facts were later disclosed, there was a furor; the judge stoutly defended his actions on the ground that he had administered the law impartially on the evidence introduced in court.

In the Cockburn case, neither the judge, nor any of the attorneys on either side, were aware of it, but the fact was that in 1880 the only practical way of getting from New York to Tombstone was through San Francisco! Transcontinental trains, with Pullmans, ran from Jersey City to Chicago, and from there to San Francisco. Taking the Southern Pacific, one proceeded to Los Angeles; a line from that city was extended to Tucson in March of 1880, while the last seventy miles to Tombstone were made by stage. To have gone directly from Chicago to Arizona, Jack Crabtree would have had to detrain at Albuquerque, New Mexico, and travel several hundred miles by stagecoach through country infested by hostile Apaches. (Geronimo had not yet been subdued.) And it was highly unlikely that he elected this route.

Baldwin and Chase were discussing this peculiar oversight on the part of the claimant's attorneys one day long after the trial. "Did it ever occur to you *why* Jack dumped his camping outfit into the Hudson River?" Baldwin asked the older man.

The Judge's eyes twinkled and he permitted himself a faint smile. "Yes, it did, and I was hoping Jim Hoy wouldn't ask himself the same question. If Jack were heading straight for Arizona, as we claimed, he would have kept all that stuff. What did Livesey call it—an immigrant's bundle? But since he was going to California, he wouldn't need it. And he didn't—he got rid of it." But as the Judge added, it wasn't up to the defense to help out the plaintiff's case.

It is true that such reasoning did not put Jack in Tombstone in 1879, but it did suggest that he might have met Annie Leopold in California and taken her with him to Tombstone, as so many witnesses for Mrs. Cockburn testified to be their understanding. And in any case, Jack was in Tombstone in plenty of time to become the father of Annie's child. This was discovered some years later.

In 1934, there came to light the *Journal* of George W. Parsons, one of the early developers of Tombstone real estate. In later years he moved to Los Angeles and became a successful promoter in that city, but in the early '80s he was a young man just starting out to make his own killing. He arrived in Tombstone in August, 1880. And the very first entry in his *Journal* was a reference to Jack Crabtree: "Price and a Mr. Crabtree visited me this afternoon late"!

Until the *Journal* was published, the earliest acceptable date of Jack's presence in Tombstone was October 16, 1880, as recorded on the deed to the Kentucky mine. Now it was obvious that he had been there sometime before; if it was July, and even if he had met Annie Leopold in Tombstone rather than California, Judge Chase's "matter of arithmetic" fell apart.

One more disturbing bit of evidence was to pop into the sight lines of the rearview mirror, this time as late as 1951. That year, the University of New Mexico Press published a book by Douglas Martin, then the head of the Journalism Department at the University of Arizona. *Tombstone's Epitaph* consists of selections from the newspaper of that name during the height of the town's notoriety. It is a complete record; the hangings and shootings are here, the whisky barrel explosion that burned up Dr. Gibberson's records, the Clanton-Earp feud, the frontier justice.

But other things are here too; Tombstone had its outlaws but it also had its culture. There were schools. There was a public library. People *did* get married. The Bird Cage Theater was not the only source of entertainment, and saloons were not the only public gathering places. The files of the *Epitaph* reveal a fairly stable middle class in residence right from the first. There were church socials and Sunday-school picnics. And who supplied the free transportation so that the youngsters of the Methodist Sunday School could make their annual outings to Granite Springs?

Edmund Bullock, Crabtree's partner and Carlotta Cockburn's "Uncle Ed" Bullock, shows up favorably in the *Epitaph* as a man who would harness up his best horses for the children of the Methodist Church; who was never known to be in trouble; and who, in 1884, adopted a waif that nobody else wanted. It is true that he gave her his name, but even this might have been an act of kindness.

But this was hindsight. By 1934, the Crabtree Trusts were well-established charities. Long before this, of course, the trustees had solved the problem of the drinking fountains. Few cities wanted them—the horse was very much in decline—although as a symbol of its affection for Lotta, Boston accepted a small fountain on the banks of the Charles River, near Boston University. It is inaccessible to horses; and dogs, for the most part, are indifferent to it. But there it stands, a tribute to a good woman.

Since it was well within the trustees' discretion to interpret this provision of the will in broad, public-interest terms, they decided that the income from the $300,000 Dumb Animal Fund should be wholly channeled to young graduates of the Massachusetts Agricultural College, already a major beneficiary of the Lotta Agricultural Fund. Had not Lotta spoken of "the intelligent and active promotion of agricultural pursuits"?

By this time, too, Lotta's money had begun to reward those who had looked after it so devotedly. In 1928, upon the resignation of Judge William Cushing Wait, Judge Chase was appointed one of the three trustees and served until his death in 1948. In 1940 Judge Prest himself was made a trustee. At an annual salary of $5,000, he helped parcel out the gifts to destitute actors, discharged convicts, worthy young farmers, war veterans and girls pursuing an education in music. He had by this time retired from the bench and bought a fine old house in Lancaster, Massachusetts, which he fixed over to his taste. His library contained shelves from floor to ceiling, and he ordered from Goodspeed's in Boston enough yards of books to fill them. To be chosen at Mr. Goodspeed's discretion, they were to be bound predominantly in blue. Chase remarked afterward that Judge Prest was very pleased with the quality of the books chosen by Goodspeed, as well as his eye for color. Judge Prest died in 1945.

Today, all of Lotta's charities are administered from an office in the Crabtree Building on Washington Street, in downtown Boston, where the trustees meet regularly to manage the estate and pass on requests for grants. Routine work is handled, under their supervision, by Miss Lucy G. Perriello and her assistant, Mrs. Harriet L. Rodgers, two dedicated ladies who work at times behind locked doors; for although Lotta's stocks and bonds have, under the prudent eyes of the trustees, substantially increased in value, the Crabtree Building finds itself in a neighborhood of increasingly undesirable elements. There have been substantial thefts from other offices in the building. On the street level, beneath the Crabtree offices, the former Park Theater grinds out Grade B movies.

But eighty-nine years ago, the building was something to be proud of. Henry Abbey had just opened his new Park Theater in it, built in exactly fifty days, with Lotta's money. The play was *La Cigale,* Lotta the star, and William Winter, the *New York Tribune's* critic, had journeyed from New York to see the opening, on April 14, 1879. "A brilliant inauguration for a handsome new theater," he wrote. Hundreds were turned away.

After Lotta's death, costumes from *La Cigale* were found in the cluttered "memento room" in the Brewster. Along with scores of other items, General Edwards decided to auction them off. The occasion was well advertised, and on January 18, 1929, long before the doors opened at ten o'clock, a crowd gathered in front of Lowenstein's Auction Rooms on Boylston Street—curiosity seekers, collectors of memorabilia, bargain hunters, a few old-timers who had seen Lotta perform. At the signal, they pushed their way in. General Edwards, acting as master of ceremonies, with Miss Donovan at his side, held up a gold horseshoe tied with a pink ribbon. "This is a shoe from Sonoma Girl," he began. "I'm going to open the sale with it, just to bring good luck." It brought $10.

Auctioneer Lowenstein took over and began chanting the bids on the remainder of the items. There were silver loving cups, chairs, vases, swords, medals. . . . There was an old-fashioned talking machine on which Lotta had learned French; it went for $6. A rusty typewriter was next, then came the piles of costumes —the gay blue uniform from *Firefly* with its gilt piping, the gypsy dress from *Musette,* Little Nell's peaked cap. When the theatrical costumes had been disposed of, the auctioneer turned to Lotta's own paintings and finally to some odds and ends that hardly seemed worth bothering with.

One of these was an old bustle. Someone called out fifty cents. Then a dollar. Up went the bids. . . . A young man got it for $18.

Out in San Francisco, the fountain was settling into its role as one of those curious landmarks that seem to endure for no good reason. But by the late 1920s, it had become weather-beaten.

"The trade winds fill its crevices with dust, and the sea fog makes the dust stick," a newspaper reporter complained. The pigeons, too, did not help. With the aid of the California Historical Society, a savings and loan association set about refurbishing the fountain. Chrome water bubblers replaced the original bronze spigots. Sandblasting cleaned the hidden ormolu detail. By this time, the fountain had grown to thirty-six feet—more than twice the height of Lotta's original design. It would keep her name alive long after most of San Francisco's glorious theatrical past had been forgotten.

Like the fountain, Lotta's "beautiful fortune" still flows. Fame meant little to her, and in any case it faded. Money meant a great deal, and her generosity, through her testamentary trusts, has made her—at least in the legal sense—immortal.

APPENDIX A

Chronology

1847
NOV. 7

Charlotte (Lotta) Mignon Crabtree born, New York City, to Mary Ann Livesey Crabtree and John Ashworth Crabtree.

1851

John A. Crabtree joins gold rush to California.

1853

Mary Ann Crabtree and Lotta arrive in San Francisco, early winter, and join Crabtree in Grass Valley late spring.

1854
Summer

John Ashworth Crabtree, Jr., is born, Grass Valley.

Fall

The Crabtrees move to Rabbit Creek (later La Porte), California.

1855
Summer

Lotta gives first public performance. She and Mary Ann join Mart Taylor troupe for a tour of the mining towns.

1856

George Crabtree born, Rabbit Creek. The Crabtrees move to San Francisco.

Mary Ann and Lotta tour the Valley of the Moon. Lotta makes her legitimate debut in *Loan of a Lover* at Petaluma.

In San Francisco, she performs in the rear of Michael Cohen's Auction Store.

NOV. 20

She makes her first appearance in a major playhouse in a song and dance act at the American Theater.

1857

Lotta and Mary Ann tour with Taylor's company through the Sacramento Valley in the spring. In San Francisco, Lotta performs at the Gaieties Theater on the Long Wharf.

1858

Lotta and her mother tour the San Joaquin Valley throughout the autumn.

1859–60

Tom Maguire hires Lotta for his variety bills at the Opera House and Eureka Theater. She begins entertaining at the Bella Union and the San Francisco melodeons.

1861

Lotta tours with Jake Wallace and his minstrels through the Washoe country. In San Francisco, she resumes her career with the melodeons and becomes a favorite at The Willows amusement park.

1862–63

Lotta is the darling at benefits for the fire companies and rifle brigades. She becomes a friend of the visiting Adah Isaacs Menken.

1864
APR.

She takes her farewell benefit at Maguire's Opera House. The Crabtrees sail for New York.

JUNE 1

Lotta's New York debut at Niblo's Saloon is not a success.

AUG.–DEC.

Lotta is a hit in *The Seven Daughters of Satan* at McVicker's Theater in Chicago. She joins the Woods Stock Company and remains in the city until the end of the year.

1865

>She tours the East and Midwest under the management of B. F. Whitman in *The Seven Daughters of Satan, La Petite Fadette,* and other plays.

1866

JAN. 22–FEB. 10

>Lotta opens the year at Willard's Howard Atheneum in Boston, in a repertory which included *Uncle Tom's Cabin, Jenny Leatherlungs,* and *Trapping a Tartar.* An extensive tour of the eastern and southern states follows.

DEC.

>First appearance in New Orleans, at the St. Charles Theater. She plays *Andy Blake, Nan, the Good for Nothing,* and *Ireland As It Was.*

1867

>John Brougham writes *Little Nell and the Marchioness* for Lotta.

SEPT.

>After several road presentations, the play has its New York premiere at Wallack's Theater.

OCT.–DEC.

>Lotta tours with *Little Nell, Pet of the Petticoats,* and other plays.

1868

JAN.

>She returns to New York and does *Little Nell* at the Broadway Theater.

MARCH

>With Lotta as Topsy, *Uncle Tom's Cabin* is the first legitimate play to be produced at the new Pike's Opera House in New York.

JUNE 10

>Crabtree is arrested for stealing Lotta's money, and is released when he makes restitution.

AUG. 10

>*Firefly,* an adaptation of Ouida's *Under Two Flags,* is written for Lotta by Edmund Falconer and introduced at Wallack's.

1869

MARCH

>George Crabtree is crippled while trying to hop a freight train in Buffalo.

JULY 12 — Lotta opens a week's engagement at Brigham Young's theater in Salt Lake City.

AUG. 1–SEPT. 10 — She returns to San Francisco for the first time since her farewell in 1864. With the California Stock Company, she plays *Little Nell, Ticket of Leave Man,* and *Firefly.*

1870

JAN. — Lotta stars in new Falconer play, *Hearts Ease,* in Philadelphia.

MAY 31 — A monster benefit for Col. T. Allston Brown at the Academy of Music in New York includes Lotta in a scene from *Nan, the Good for Nothing.*

JUNE 1 — The Crabtrees sail for a summer in Europe.

1871

JAN. 25 — Lotta is baptized, and confirmed as a member of the Episcopal Church, at the St. Charles Hotel, New Orleans.

AUG. 14 — After a prolonged tour, she takes over Booth's Theater in New York for four weeks of repertory.

1872

JAN. 1 — Lotta is made an honorary member of the Lotta Baseball Club, in New Orleans. She meets the Grand Duke Alexis of Russia, and is rewarded with a diamond bracelet.

APR. 8 — She returns to San Francisco for a three-week engagement at the Metropolitan Theater.

OCT.–DEC. — Crabtree, Mary Ann, George, and Lotta travel to England, where Crabtree henceforth makes his home. George is placed in a boarding school at Bowden, Cheshire.

1873

JAN.–APR. — Mary Ann and Lotta tour the Continent as sightseers. Lotta studies in Paris.

1874

MARCH 30 *Zip; or Point Lynde Light,* written for Lotta by Frederic Marsden, opens at Booth's Theater.

OCT. 10 *Musette,* another Marsden play, is a huge success at its premiere at the Walnut Street Theater, Philadelphia.

1875

SEPT. 9 Lotta's Fountain is given to the city of San Francisco.

1876

She backs Henry E. Abbey in acquiring the Park Theater in New York.

She, Mary Ann, and George spend the spring and summer in Europe.

NOV. 27 The renovated Park is inaugurated with Lotta's performance in *Musette,* followed by *Little Nell.* Sometime during the year, she buys a $50,000 interest in a Fall River cotton brokerage firm. Jack and George Crabtree are given jobs in the company.

1877

Between road tours, Mary Ann and Lotta take a "cottage" at Newport, Rhode Island, which they will occupy for several summers.

OCT. 12 Lotta plays Desdemona in the third act of *Othello,* at a benefit for Edwin Adams, at the Academy of Music, New York.

1878

JULY Mary Ann and Lotta visit La Porte (formerly Rabbit Creek), California, where Mary Ann buys a gold mine.

OCT. 26 *La Cigale,* a French play adapted by Olive Logan, is added to Lotta's repertory, and opens at the Park in New York. Lotta tours for the remainder of the season.

1879

APR. 14   Henry E. Abbey opens a Park Theater in
               Boston, with Lotta in *La Cigale.*

AUG.   Lotta plays in San Francisco at the Baldwin
               Academy of Music.

1880

MAY 29   Lotta, Mary Ann, George Crabtree, and Clement
               Bainbridge sail for England. George and Bain-
               bridge proceed to Switzerland, where they climb
               Mt. Blanc.

JUNE–AUG.   Sometime during this period, Jack Crabtree
               travels to Tombstone, Arizona, to make his
               fortune.

SEPT. 6   The Crabtrees and Bainbridge return from
               Europe.

OCT.–DEC.   Lotta tours Canada and the East. Mary Ann buys
               a half interest in a livery stable in Tombstone.
               Bob, another play by Frederic Marsden, is
               produced for the first time at the Chestnut Street
               Theater in Philadelphia.

1881

OCT. 24   Lotta is reported to be engaged to Mr. A.
               Hallergross, a Philadelphia lawyer.

DEC.   Jack Crabtree returns from Tombstone.

1882

               Lotta is on the road most of the year. Henry E.
               Abbey takes over the Grand Opera House in
               New York, and Lotta plays there in *Zip.*

1883

JULY 14   O. Edwin Huss, a wealthy young Englishman,
               is rumored to have married Lotta.

NOV.   Mary Ann and Lotta go to Paris.

DEC. 22   Lotta opens at the Opéra Comique, London, in
               Musette. The performance is a fiasco.

1884

  JAN.–MAY
The Old Curiosity Shop, by Charles Dickens, Jr., successfully replaces *Musette* at the Opera Comique. A French farce, *Mam'zelle Nitouche,* concludes Lotta's London engagement.

  JUNE
She and Mary Ann return to New York.

  SEPT.–DEC.
Sometime during the fall season, Lotta bought the Park Theater in Boston from Henry E. Abbey for $100,000.

1885

Lotta opens the season at the New York Grand Opera House, New York, in *Mam'zelle Nitouche,* her mainstay for the remainder of the year.

Mary Ann builds "Attol Tryst," on Lake Hopatcong, Mt. Arlington, New Jersey.

1887

David Belasco and Clay Greene write *Pawn Ticket 210,* which Lotta introduces at Mc-Vicker's Theater in Chicago.

1890–91

  SEPT.–MAY
Lotta's last full season of touring. She revisits San Francisco and the West, is injured by a fall in Wilmington, cancels last weeks of tour, and retires to "Attol Tryst."

  SEPT. 27
George Crabtree dies at sea.

1892

Lotta attempts a comeback, but is unable to continue and leaves the stage for good.

1893

She divides her time between "Attol Tryst" and New York City.

1894

  JAN. 4
Lotta's father dies in Altrincham, England.

AUG.	Lotta, Mary Ann, and Jack Crabtree begin tour of Europe and Africa.

1895

JULY	They return from abroad.
	Lotta is operated on, New York.

1899

	Jack Crabtree marries(?) Annie Harris, of Boston.
	Lotta and her mother take up winter residence on West Fifty-ninth Street, New York.

1905

APR. 11	Mary Ann Crabtree dies at the age of 85.
FALL	Lotta underwrites racing stable managed by Jack Crabtree at Atlantic, Massachusetts.

1909

MAR. 27	She buys the Brewster Hotel in Boston, and moves into it.

1910   Racing stable is sold.

1912

	She studies painting at the Académie Colorossi in Paris; returns to Boston in the fall.

1915

NOV. 6–10	Visits San Francisco for "Lotta Crabtree Day" at the Panama-Pacific Exposition.

1916

MAR. 28	Lotta is elected vice-president of the Massachusetts SPCA.

1920

JAN. 29	Jack Crabtree dies in North Carolina.

1921–23

	Lotta spends her summers at Gloucester painting. Holds exhibit in Boston.

1924

SEPT. 25	Lotta dies at the Hotel Brewster. She is buried in Woodlawn Cemetery, New York.

APPENDIX B

Lotta's Plays

LOTTA appeared in scores of plays and skits during her thirty-seven years on the stage. The following list, by no means complete, is arranged in the order in which she first appeared in each.

In her early days in California she appeared in *Loan of a Lover; The Dumb Belle; Our Little Treasure; Faint Heart; Our Gal; Governor's Wife; Beauty and the Beast; Melodramatic Sally; The Soldier's Bride; Ireland As It Was; Object of Interest; Andy Blake; Looking for Work; Serious Family; Family Jars.*

Until Lotta was celebrated enough to have plays written expressly for her, she was, of course, dependent on existing material. These plays included *The Mysterious Chamber; Jenny Lind* (or *Jenny Leatherlungs*); *The Seven Daughters of Satan; Mr. and Mrs. P. White; Nan, the Good for Nothing; Our Gals; Lola Montez; Uncle Tom's Cabin; Odd Trick; Po-Co-Han-Tas; Hidden Hand; Fanchon; Trapping a Tartar; Irish Assurance; Nana; Middy Ashore; Irish Boy; Old London; Pet of the Petticoats; The Little Detective.*

When John Brougham wrote *Little Nell and the Marchioness* in 1867, a new era began for Lotta. Her major productions were henceforth written to order. Lotta's repertory, however, continued to include many of the old favorites, and new plays from stock were taken over as the old ones wore out. Together, they make up an impressive list: *Captain Charlotte; The Spectre Bridegroom; Firefly; Capitola; Turn Him Out; Pepina; The Ticket of Leave Man; Hearts Ease; The Rainbow; Zip; Musette; Bella, The Charity Girl; La Cigale; Bob; Niagara; The Old Curiosity Shop; Fleurette; Mam'zelle Nitouche; Larks; Pawn Ticket 210; Spoiling the Broth;* and *Ina.* It is interesting to note that *Faint Heart,* one of Lotta's early California plays, was still being performed by her in 1890.

APPENDIX C

A Note on Sources

EVERY biography is a collaboration among the writer, his subject, and his source material. Unlike many stars of the theater, Lotta wrote nothing about herself for publication; in this respect, as a collaborator, she was no help whatever. To re-create her stage career has meant, in a sense, discovering it. In addition to the vast amount of theatrical information collected by counsel for the defense of Lotta's will, it was necessary to consult the periodical press of the time, the memoirs of contemporaneous figures who knew her, the various stage annals of the cities in which she played, scrapbooks, correspondence, and the voluminous material from the legal files in Raymond Baldwin's possession.

Material concerning the Crabtrees' family life is only somewhat more accessible, and for this we have relied chiefly on letters, legal papers, account books, and interviews with those who knew the Crabtrees, and who were still living at the time of the trials. In some cases, these persons appeared as witnesses, and their testimony is part of the court record.

The only adult biography of Lotta is Constance Rourke's *Troupers of the Gold Coast* (Harcourt, Brace & Co., 1928), a study that deals extensively with Lotta's California period, but rather fitfully with her later career, and virtually not at all with her personal life. Much new material has been unearthed since the publication of Miss Rourke's book. Helen Marie Bates's *Lotta's Last Season,* privately printed in Brattleboro, Vermont, in 1940, is rich in information concerning the final years of Lotta's career on the stage, and has been generously utilized when dealing with this period.

Among the libraries visited, we are especially indebted to the Theater Collection of the New York Public Library at Lincoln Center, and to Mr. Paul Myers, the curator, whose cheerful assistance and unfailing courtesy during a period of two years' research are models of professional behavior for librarians everywhere. Miss Helen Willard, curator of the Theater Collection at the Houghton Library,

Harvard University, aided the writers on numerous occasions when it was necessary to unearth material on Lotta from the catacombs of that institution. For his guidance through the Allen A. Brown Collection of theater scrapbooks and printed works at the Boston Public Library, we wish to thank Zoltan Haraszti, curator of manuscripts and rare books. A special debt is owed to Sam Pearce of the Museum of the City of New York for a day spent in retrieving Lotta memorabilia from the Museum's archives; to Louis Rachow, librarian of the Walter Hampden Memorial Library at the Players Club in New York City, for his hospitality to nonmembers of the club; and to Mrs. Jack Crawford, curator of the Theater Collection at the Sterling Library, Yale University.

Acknowledgment is also due the Trustees of the Estate of Lotta M. Crabtree, Boston: the late Colonel George A. Parker, John J. O'Hare, Jr., Timothy J. Driscoll, and Frank Wilson. Their interest in the book has made it possible for us to examine prompt books, playbills, photographs, and related material in the files of the Estate. Both Miss Lucy G. Perriello and Mrs. Harriett L. Rodgers, who have been employed by the Estate for many years, were especially helpful in digging out relevant information.

For material concerning Lotta's residence at Lake Hopatcong, New Jersey, we wish to thank Mrs. Alice A. Apostolik, Director of the Lake Hopatcong Historical Society. Going beyond the call of duty, Mrs. Apostolik drove us to Attol Tryst, which appears today very much as it did in the 1880s. Mr. Windsor Ridenour, of the *Tulsa Tribune,* Tulsa, Oklahoma, was extraordinarily helpful in pursuing the trail of Ida May Blankenberg and her family forty years after the "brazen adventuress" returned to Tulsa and her oil company. And for permission to examine an unpublished manuscript by the late William Parker, from which several incidents relating to Lotta's career were extracted, we are grateful to his daughter, Mrs. Jane McCosker, of Rumson, New Jersey.

All of the material dealing with the attacks on Lotta's will, and the two trials which ensued, is in the files of Raymond P. Baldwin. Without these transcripts, letters, depositions, investigators' reports, and courtroom proceedings, no accurate reconstruction of this section of the book would have been possible. Needless to say, this material has been brought to life through the personal recollections of Raymond Baldwin, who helped defend the estate against its predators, and whose encounters with both claimants and witnesses added much lively information that does not appear on the record of the trials.

Of the scores of books consulted during the writing of *The Triumphs and Trials of Lotta Crabtree,* several have been particularly helpful. In addition to Miss Rourke's, two indispensable sources of information on the California theater during the gold-rush decade were George R. MacMinn's *Theatre of the Golden Era in California* (The Caxton Press, Caldwell, Idaho, 1943) and *San Francisco Theatre Research,* the monographs prepared by the Federal Theater Project of the Works Progress Administration in 1938. John S. Kendall's *The Golden Age of the New Orleans Theatre* (Louisiana State University Press, 1952) and Robert L. Sherman's *Chicago Stage* (Robert L. Sherman, 1947) were particularly useful in providing information about Lotta's appearances in these cities. And no theater bibliography would be complete without George C. D. Odell's monumental *Annals of the New York Stage* (Columbia University Press, 1927-49).

ADDITIONAL BIBLIOGRAPHY

Binns, Archie, *Mrs. Fiske and the American Theatre.* New York, Crown, 1955.

Brown, T. Allston, *History of the New York Stage.* New York, Dodd, Mead, 1903.

Cohen, Alfred J. (Alan Dale), *Familiar Chats with Queens of the Stage.* New York, G. W. Dillingham, 1890.

Crane, William H., *Footprints and Echoes.* New York, Dutton, 1927.

Crawford, Mary C., *The Romance of the American Theatre.* Boston, Little, Brown, 1913.

De Angelis, Jefferson, and Harlow, Alvin F., *A Vagabond Trouper.* New York, Harcourt, Brace & Co., 1931.

Dickson, Samuel, *San Francisco Is Your Home.* Stanford, Calif., Stanford University Press, 1947.

Dimmick, Ruth C., *Our Theatres Today and Yesterday.* New York, The H.K. Fly Co., 1913.

Ford, George D., *These Were Actors.* New York, Library Publishers, 1955.

Fyles, Franklin, *The Theatre and Its People.* New York, Doubleday, Page & Co., 1900.

Hewitt, Bernard *Theatre U.S.A.* New York, McGraw-Hill, 1959.

Hornblow, Arthur, *History of the Theatre in America.* Philadelphia, Lippincott, 1919.

Hutton, Lawrence, *Curiosities of the American Stage.* New York, Harper & Brothers, 1891.

Jennings, John J., *Theatrical and Circus Life.* St. Louis, Hebert & Cole, 1886.

Leavitt, Michael B., *Fifty Years of Theatrical Management.* New York, Broadway Publishing Co., 1912.

Leman Walter *Memories of an Old Actor.* San Francisco, A. Roman Co., 1886.

Lockridge, Richard, *Darling of Misfortune.* New York, The Century Co., 1932.

Logan, Olive S., *The Mimic World and Public Exhibitions.* Philadelphia, New-World Publishing Co., 1871.

Modjeska, Helena, *Memories and Impressions of Helena Modjeska. An Autobiography.* New York, Macmillan, 1910.

Morris, Lloyd, *Curtain Time: The Story of the American Theatre.* New York, Random House, 1953.

Phelps, H. P., *Players of a Century.* Albany, J. McDonough, 1880.

Pitou, Augustus, *Masters of the Show.* New York, Neale Publishing Co., 1914.

Powers, James F., *Twinkle Little Star.* New York, G. P. Putnams Sons, 1939.

Pyper, George D., *The Romance of an Old Playhouse.* Salt Lake City, The Seagull Press, 1928.

Tompkins, Eugene, and Kilby, Quincy, *History of the Boston Theatre.* Boston, Houghton Mifflin, 1908.

Willard, G.O., *History of the Providence Stage.* Providence, R.I., News Co., 1891.

Wilson, Francis, *Francis Wilson's Life of Himself. An Autobiography.* Boston, Houghton Mifflin, 1924.

Wilson, Garff B., *A History of American Acting.* Bloomington, Indiana University Press, 1966.

Winslow, Catherine Mary Reignolds, *Yesterdays with Actors.* New York, Cupples & Hurd, 1887.

Winter, William, *The Life of David Belasco.* New York, Jefferson Winters, 1918.

INDEX

INDEX

A Note About the Authors

DAVID DEMPSEY is the author of *Flood* and *All That Was Mortal,* among other books, and of many articles in such magazines as *The New Yorker, The New Republic, Harper's,* and *Atlantic Monthly.* He writes "The Publishing Scene," a column in *Saturday Review.* He has been a staff member of *Reader's Digest, Time* and *The New York Times Book Review.* Mr. Dempsey was born in Pekin, Illinois, and was educated at Antioch, Yale and Columbia. During World War II he served as a Marine Corps combat correspondent in the Pacific. He now lives in Rye, New York, with his wife and three children.

RAYMOND P. BALDWIN, fresh from Harvard Law School, was admitted to the Massachusetts Bar in 1921. Three years later he found himself helping to defend Lotta Crabtree's will against more than one hundred persons who tried to have it set aside. The litigation lasted four years. His career in the law has included service on several government boards and a year as Special Assistant to the Attorney General of the United States. He was an ambulance driver in France and a flyer in Italy and England during World War I. His longtime interest in the theater resulted in *The Fun of Acting,* of which he and his wife, Joan, were co-authors. Mr. Baldwin was born in Brookline, Massachusetts, and now lives in Concord.